THE SCOLE EXPERIMENT

Scientific Evidence for
LIFE AFTER DEATH

D1513313

Also by Grant Solomon:

Stephen Turoff Psychic Surgeon (pub. Campion)

Also by Grant and Jane Solomon:

Harry Oldfield's Invisible Universe (pub. Campion)

THE SCOLE EXPERIMENT

Scientific Evidence for
LIFE AFTER DEATH

Grant & Jane Solomon
in association with
The Scole Experimental Group

CAMPION BOOKS

A catalogue record for this book
is available from the British Library.

ISBN 0-9546338-4-9

Campion Books is an imprint of Campion Publishing Limited

Printed in the UK

First published in the UK in 1999 by
Judy Piatkus (Publishers) Limited

New edition, with additional material, published in 2006 by

CAMPION BOOKS

2 Lea Valley House, Stoney Bridge Drive, Waltham Abbey, Essex EN9 3LY

www.campionpublishing.com

For all

AUTHOR UPDATE
FEBRUARY 2006

The Scole Experiment is now widely regarded as the most important scientific investigation of evidence for life after death in history. Highly-qualified and objective scientists, and a whole range of other people who attended the Scole Group's sessions, came away convinced that (mostly) invisible, discarnate intelligences were making direct contact with those present.

It is therefore understandable that the first edition of this book, which chronicled all the events that occurred during the five-year experiment, created a great deal of discussion in the national and local media when it was published in the UK in the autumn of 1999.

Numerous radio and television programmes ran the story. National newspapers devoted extensive column inches (see plate section). *The Times on Sunday* put *The Scole Experiment* on the front page of its Sunday magazine and the *Daily Mail* serialised the book in its centre pages over a number of days. *Time Out* magazine said: 'Remarkable... apparently solid scientific evidence for our continuing survival.'

If the evidence is accepted, the implication is simple: we humans do indeed survive the death event in some conscious form. Given these implications, it is not surprising that there have continued to be sceptical reactions from those who were not present at evidence-gathering sessions.

The Scole Debate

The national forum for discussion of *The Scole Experiment* was the Scole Debate, held under the auspices of the objective and respected Society for Psychical Research (SPR) at Kensington

Library, London, in December 1999. The SPR had published *The Scole Report* earlier in the year.

Before the debate, we conducted videotaped interviews with a number of the scientific investigators who attended Scole experimental sessions. They all confirmed their belief that something highly unusual and significant occurred during the Scole experiments.

One, Professor Ivor Gratton-Guinness, confirmed for the camera record that he had grabbed several pea-sized flying orbs of light in his cupped hands in an effort to prove to himself that they were not attached to fibre-optic cords or part of some other magician's device. He said to us that, to his utter amazement, the glowing orbs were not attached to anything. In fact, they proceeded to buzz about inside his cupped hands as if alive. When the professor released them, they flew off around the room again.

For our videotape record, there were many other equally mind-challenging testimonies from credible, well-qualified and scientifically-trained investigators. If these individuals conducted experiments and investigations in their own fields, their findings would be taken very seriously, noted down in learned books and so added to the store of human knowledge. It is therefore interesting to observe that these highly credible witnesses are considered by some, in this *single* instance alone, to have suddenly become devoid of all critical, experimental and analytical faculties when confronted with the challenge of investigating the physical paranormal phenomena that occurred during *The Scole Experiment*.

We should perhaps remind ourselves at this juncture that much of what is now known to be scientific fact was once placed firmly in the category of 'paranormal', that is, outside the accepted parameters of known science: this historical truth applies to both atoms and gravity!

On learning of its content, the SPR requested a copy of our videotape as an addition to the evidence for their archives.

Inter-dimensional interest

Interest in 'inter-dimensional phenomena' has grown even more quickly in the last few years. Attitudes are changing. Mainstream physics posits the existence of a number of dimensions of existence; and it is now considered at least reasonable by many to discuss the possibilities and ramifications.

Worldwide interest

Since publication of *The Scole Experiment*, worldwide English-speaking interest has grown, fuelled in no small part by the buzzing Internet discussion about the significance of the Scole Group's experiences.

The Scole Experiment has been discussed on US television chat shows. Many experimental sessions have been held in that country and around the world.

The book has thus far been published for readers in Brazil, Italy and Russia.

The Japanese media enthusiastically embraced the story (see plate section).

The Scole Experiment in the United States

Interest has been particularly high in the USA, where the Scole Experimental Group conducted numerous experiments to the wonder, delight and bemusement of many American participants in sessions.

One of the reasons that the experiments were taken to the USA was so that objective investigators could experience the phenomena at first hand. Investigators considered it important to show that the phenomena were replicable outside the confines of the Scole cellar in the UK. A review of the testimonies collected from those who attended sessions illustrates that the phenomena occurred in the US in the same way as they had in the UK. This US investigation was very important to the credibility of *The Scole Experiment*.

Physicist, Dr Ulf Israelsson, attended a session. He expressed a very positive opinion about his experience.

'Considering the fact that these new energy-based phenomena had never before been demonstrated in the United States, they were received with remarkable intelligence, understanding and enthusiasm by everyone who experienced them. It is a credit to the group that they worked so hard, and with such good humour, in order that so many Americans could experience this proof of survival and the reality of a spiritual dimension. Here they are remembered with love and awe, and everyone is asking, *When will they return?*'

One experimental session was attended by scientists from NASA, Stanford University, and the Institute of Noetic Sciences near San Francisco. This session was held in a house on a mountain. Participants reported that, during the session, a Native American materialised and performed a tribal dance and chanted. This was recognised as being a Native North American chant by some of those who attended. The Group were told by the spirit beings that the house was on a Native American sacred site.

It is interesting that some of the astrophysicists later started an experimental group of their own.

Well known medium, James Van Praagh, attended one of many experimental sessions held in the US. He went into the session quite sceptical but was amazed, not only by the phenomena produced, but also by the 'feeling of love' that was created in the room. Being impressed by his experience, Van Praagh has devoted a couple of pages to Scole in his hugely popular book, *Heaven and Earth*.

Another well known US TV personality and medium is Brian Hurst. Brian hosted numerous experimental sessions at his home in California.

The wide range of people who are interested in such phenomena is evidenced by the guest list at the Brian Hurst events. Among those who attended were Kathryn Grayson, of *Showboat* and *Desert Song* fame, and Jay North, former star of American TV's *Dennis the Menace*.

The sessions in the US saw new phenomena produced. The central table levitated then turned on its side and spun round like a cartwheel, without a single crystal falling off. More than once, participants had spirit lights enter them. People reported that they received spiritual healing in this way.

Brian Hurst commented: 'I can confirm that the light did indeed enter the bodies of several of the people present. Tricia Loar, who had been plagued by torn cartilage and other knee damage, experienced a light entering both her knee and her foot. She said that the entry of the light into her foot was "extremely ticklish" and she could feel the light moving about inside. The pain in her knee had gone by the next day.'

One American investigator, George Dalzell, who lives in Hollywood, is a licensed clinical social worker who holds a Master's degree in social work (see plate section). He is the author of *Messages*, a book which explores the authenticity of mediumship. He attended one of the experimental sessions at Brian Hurst's home. His experiences with the Scole Group 'transformed a life's worth of limited perceptions overnight'. He experienced light phenomena which responded to thought and received 'authentic communication' from a deceased friend. George travelled to the UK to take part in the Scole Debate and give evidence in the form of a first-hand account of his experiences with the Scole Group. He also brought a signed statement from a fellow US investigator to place on record in the archives of the SPR.

Tom and Lisa Butler of the American Association of Electronic Voice Phenomena (AAEVP) publish a magazine about EVP in the United States which has a good circulation (see plate section). In their magazine, they have reproduced articles taken from the Scole Group's own publication, *The Spiritual Scientist*. Interest in their research has escalated enormously since the release of the blockbuster Hollywood film, *White Noise*, on which they were advisers (see the Further Information section).

The interest in the Scole Group's work remains high in the US. There has been a great deal of demand from around the world, but especially in the US, for the Scole Group's *Basic Guide* booklet, which explains how to set up an experimental group in order to investigate physical paranormal phenomena. A number of groups have been established in the US and around the world.

However, it should perhaps be pointed out that members of the Scole Experimental Group had dedicated two decades of their lives to developing the phenomena that eventually occurred during the five years of the Scole experiments. Those embarking on this field of study might wish to first consider that similar dedication and regular commitment over a sustained period may be required for similar results to be achieved.

It remains to be seen whether another group will succeed in replicating the amazing events that took place during *The Scole Experiment*. If this happens, we look forward to letting you know.

Arthur Ellison and Montague Keen

Two of the principal Scole investigators from the SPR, Arthur Ellison and Montague Keen, have died since this book was first published. If they survived the death event in some conscious form, we, like many readers, are interested in whether they have made some attempt to communicate.

There have been a number of reports that Montague has been trying to make contact via various mediums. A number of these were reported at the Montague Keen Memorial Day, organised by the SPR in London, which we attended.

Professor Gary Schwartz travelled to attend the Memorial Day from the United States, to present the evidence he had collected concerning Montague's communication attempts. According to Professor Schwartz, Montague's communication methods seemed similar to those of the 'Cross Correspondences', which Montague was intimately familiar with.

Many have commented that perhaps the most convincing of these 'Keen Communications' are those involving Allison DuBois, whose life, at time of going to press, is being chronicled on BBC1 television. The programme, called 'Medium', was originally aired on NBC in the US.

Allison, formerly a prosecuting attorney in Phoenix, has been vigorously tested by researchers at the University of Arizona. The researchers documented her mediumistic ability, through a series of tests in which she 'scored exceptionally high on accuracy and specificity.' Her book, *Don't Kiss Them Good-Bye*, is a *New York Times* bestseller.

During research sessions, Allison brought through seemingly unrelated pieces of information (as per the Cross Correspondences), which researchers were later able to link with Montague Keen, a person she had no knowledge of.

The Scole Cessation

During *The Scole Experiment,* the data flowing from 'other dimensions' had increased in volume from a drip to a stream to a torrent. Then, with very little warning or explanation, something apparently happened that forced the communicators to turn off the tap. It is therefore somewhat understandable that many of those involved in *The Scole Experiment* were devastated by the cessation.

Robin and Sandra Foy

Since the cessation of the Scole experiments, Scole Group members, Robin and Sandra Foy, have continued to pursue their interest in physical mediumship and paranormal phenomena. Refer to the *Further Information* section for their contact details.

Alan and Diana Bennett

Meanwhile, the two Scole mediums, Alan and Diana, have been conducting other experiments. Like all the other people involved in Scole, they were keen to see if more experiments would one day be possible.

'Would a data stream ever begin to flow again?' was the question many involved in *The Scole Experiment* were asking.

The early results of their new work appear to be beyond current 'normal' scientific explanation, so we can now report that the answer to that question seems to be, 'yes'.

The first results of this further work are outlined in a new section at the back of this 2nd edition, and the new images can be seen in the expanded plate section.

FOREWORD

By Professor Emeritus Arthur J. Ellison

DSc(Eng), CEng, FIMechE, FIEE,

SenMemlEEE, Consultant Engineer

It is a pleasure to write a few introductory words to this book on the Scole phenomena by Grant and Jane Solomon.

I had the honour to be involved in the sessions at Scole from the beginning of the two-year period when three of us from the Council of the Society for Psychical Research were invited in our private capacities to attend as scientific observers. It proved an interesting two years!

I had some years earlier experienced most of the physical phenomena of Spiritualism but always involving a medium in trance and ectoplasm, the medium ending the evening in a completely exhausted state. (This agrees with the traditional view that material from the 'vehicle of vitality' or 'etheric double' was extracted from the medium and used to produce the ectoplasm.) In addition, the 'control personalities' ostensibly speaking through the medium were the traditional exotic figures such as America's Indians, Chinese and others. They spoke in a peculiar way, rather like an untrained Western actor attempting to imitate such characters. At Scole, on the contrary, the control personalities, apparently communicating through the two mediums, were normal well-educated Westerners – with the exception of one or two others who spoke as though they had been educated in the West. We all became well acquainted; indeed, the relationships developed into what might be described as close friendships, with first names being used and much leg-pulling going on. This did not seem to reduce the quality of the phenomena we experienced – indeed, it might be considered to have enhanced them.

This book describes the wide range of these phenomena, from paranormal lights to levitated objects, apports and tangible figurines and others. However, no ectoplasm was involved and the mediums seemed just as fresh at the end of the sessions as they did at the beginning. The Scole group themselves described the activities as energy rather than ectoplasmic phenomena. This certainly seemed to be a considerable step forward on tradition.

The three of us visitors were used appropriately in accordance with our background training. I was able to contribute something to the physical scientific side, David Fontana was valuable as a psychologist very experienced in altered states of consciousness and Montague Keen's literary background was especially valuable. We were often told by the communicators that we would not be able to understand explanations of what was going on. I think there were times when we all wished that they would just explain fully and let us decide whether we understood or not! But it was not to be. Also, we often explained that the scientific community would assume that, as the phenomena usually occurred in the dark, we were being deceived. The use by us of an infra-red viewer showing, from their own body heat, that everyone was in their chair during the periods when phenomena were taking place was highly desirable. However, this was not, to our regret, allowed either. We made particular efforts in our SPR report to explain how impossible faking many of the phenomena appeared to be. But the sceptic will always say that magicians can do all sorts of 'impossible' things. In this subject, sadly, the sceptic is not usually required to demonstrate how what they claim could have actually been executed without detection.

There is another important factor which is often not appreciated. Psychical researchers are well aware that investigators can be divided, for unknown reasons, into two classes: catalysts and inhibitors. In the presence of catalysts genuine paranormal phenomena more readily occur than is the case with inhibitors. This is called the Experimenter Effect. Many critics, when they have the experience qualifying them to make comments at all, happen to be inhibitors and rarely experience genuine phenomena. They are often the most virulent critics because, deep down, they perhaps consider that genuine paranormal phenomena never take place. The other class of critic is the distinguished 'normal' scientist who already knows that paranormal phenomena are impossible and therefore, *ipso facto,* they can never take place. And as they are impossible it is not necessary to study the vast scientific psychical research literature, a good deal of it produced by some of the most distinguished scientists in the UK and on the continent of Europe, before making pronouncements about the subject. However, it is perfectly possible to have a genuine open mind but still be scientific. It looks to us as though the Scole communicators were well aware of all this and selected the three of us with this in mind. We tried in our report to be objective 'good' scientists. The reader must remember also that we were invited guests. The experiments carried out were not necessarily to our choice, and the suggestions we made to tighten conditions were not usually adopted either because they were apparently in conflict with the conditions required to produce the phenomena reliably or because the communicators' timetable somehow obliged them to move on to another experiment. We did our best.

May I finally express a personal opinion? I consider that the group on 'this side' were honest and genuine. After two years we knew them extremely well. I consider that the results of the sessions were of great interest to science.

I hope that the reader enjoys this book as much as I enjoyed the Scole experimental sessions.

Arthur J. Ellison
June 1999
Written for the original 1999 edition

ACKNOWLEDGEMENTS

A large number of people have contributed to the making of this book. We cannot possibly acknowledge them all here. We would, however, like to extend our special thanks to the members of the Scole Experimental Group, Robin and Sandra Foy and Alan and Diana Bennett, for their patient and detailed explanations and the provision of a huge amount of material. We would also like to acknowledge and thank the authors of *The Scole Report* for granting us access to their findings prior to official publication. (Any minor differences between our references and the final draft version of the report are an unavoidable result of publishing deadlines.) While, of course, the authors of the report are not responsible for the opinions expressed in this book, we would also like to thank them for reviewing our manuscript and making constructive criticisms.

In addition, we would like to thank the many people who sent us personal accounts of their experiences at Scole. Special thanks are also due to Peter Williams and Lizzie Hutchins, both of whom provided invaluable help with the manuscript.

CONTENTS

INTRODUCTION

I shall not commit the fashionable stupidity of regarding everything I cannot explain as a fraud.

C. G. Jung

Four people sat in a dark cellar. Two of them went into a trance and conveyed messages from a team of spirit communicators. The other two followed the spirits' instructions. They put brand new films on the table, films which had never been in a camera. Afterwards the films were developed. Images were found on them – handwriting, hieroglyphs and other symbols and messages...

This was the work of the Scole Experimental Group. It offered thought-provoking evidence in support of the notion that there may be life after death. Similar experiments had been conducted in the past, with 'mental mediumship' being used to try to prove that conscious discarnate beings can communicate through a human instrument, the medium. Unfortunately, messages from Aunt Doris might convince her nephew, but they are not always ideal for scientific study. A sceptic can say, 'That was chance', 'coincidence', 'intuition', 'a good guess' and so on. So, in 1993, the Scole Experimental Group embarked on a five-year experiment using a revolutionary kind of 'physical mediumship' to produce tangible objects from the spirit world. The term 'tangible objects' means things recognisable to our senses or our instruments – visible manifestations, lights, sounds, touches, tastes and smells. Some of the tangible objects took the form of messages transmitted onto photographic film, audio-tape and videotape.

The idea behind physical mediumship is simple: physical evidence of survival is transmitted from the spirit world to our world. Then, once something physical is here, it can be scientifically measured and assessed. Mental mediumship is hard to prove scientifically. However, tangible phenomena are different. Experiments can be conducted, tests undertaken, scientific procedures implemented. With such experiments in the past, the aim was always to get a permanent paranormal object, a tangible 'thing' that could have only come from 'somewhere else', without any possible trickery involved. A fabled example is two interlocking rings made of two different types of wood with no join in the rings. This type of tangible object would be considered 'convincing proof' as it could not be produced by 'normal means'. The aim of the Scole Experimental Group was to produce not just one tangible object but such a huge number and variety that scientists would have to sit up and take notice.

In fact it was not long before a variety of senior scientists, including some very experienced researchers into the unknown, became interested in the phenomena being produced. The Scole group was happy to allow scientific scrutiny of their work, a fact which impressed the scrutineers. Among the investigating team were electrical engineers, astrophysicists, criminologists, psychologists and mathematicians. They were most interested in the photographic films because the time and method of production of these films could be controlled. The scrutineers asked to attend experimental sessions in order to control certain parameters. Still the images appeared on the films. Some of the scientists found this hard to explain and suggested that extra precautions be taken, including bringing their own films and putting them in a padlocked box for the duration of the session. Yet again the images appeared on the films. But now they were slightly different. Instead of being simply photos of faces and places, they were cryptic messages, clues to puzzles that the investigators were invited to solve.

Later, even more amazing images were received on videotape and messages were transmitted onto audio-tape. Objects materialised, lights danced, and solid beings appeared before previously sceptical observers.

The unique and revolutionary evidence provided by *The Scole Experiment* may suggest that solid scientific proof of survival may not be far off. If so, there are unavoidable and far-reaching implications for us all. It would be proof that we do not die ...

CHAPTER ONE

AN INVITATION TO INVESTIGATE

It is entirely possible that behind the perception of our senses, worlds are hidden of which we are unaware.
Albert Einstein

It is October 1993 in the lazy little village of Scole in Norfolk. Autumn's brown leaves rustle in the early evening breeze. Some, crinkled and spent, float down from the ancient trees around the seventeenth-century Street Farmhouse. A car rolls slowly along the gravel drive, coming to a stop in front of the building. Alan and Diana Bennett alight. They are arriving happy and relaxed for their twice-weekly meeting with Robin and Sandra Foy.

Sandra has had a bad day at the dentist. She makes her apologies and retires to bed. The remaining three are looking forward to the evening of 'work' in the Scole Hole.

They make their way along a narrow passage and down a winding staircase to a dimly lit cellar. It measures five paces by ten, and its walls, floor and ceiling are painted a deep midnight blue. The only way in and out is through a solid oak door, which creaks noisily when opened. A round table, a leg's length in diameter and an arm's length in height, sits in the middle of the room. Seven chairs surround it, one for each member of the group. On this occasion, however, four members are absent and their chairs remain empty.

Robin hands out luminous armbands, which have been activated earlier by exposure to artificial light, to ensure a strong and steady glow in the pitch-blackness of the cellar.

They will enable the movements of the group to be monitored at all times. The instruments for recording what is about to take place are also examined. Alan checks the thermometers and hangs up the flat wall microphones. Diana places the tape recorder and a lightweight aluminium cone, traditionally used in medium work, on the table. Each person puts on their armbands and sits on their respective blanketed chair – it usually gets 'as cold as the North Pole' during sessions. The lights are turned off.

Now they are sitting in total darkness. Only the luminous armbands are visible, together with the luminous tabs on the various objects used in the experiments. Robin has become expert at operating the tape recorder in the darkness of the cellar. This machine, containing a blank tape, is set to record the evening's events as evidence.

In order to establish the necessary conditions for the work and to send out the right thoughts as a signal to the spirit world that the group is assembled, Robin begins the opening prayer: 'Infinite Spirit, Creative Source of all things, be with us this evening and guide us in our work towards the highest good...'

After the prayer, a second tape recorder is switched on and rousing music bursts forth in the darkness. The group sits patiently, waiting, as they have been for many months, for something 'tangible and evidential' to occur.

Almost immediately, Diana is gently taken into a trance. In this state, her 'vibrations are raised' so that she can be used as 'an instrument of communication'. An androgynous voice begins to speak for the first time through her, although it soon becomes obvious that the communicator is a male:

> *My name is Manu. I am to be the gate-keeper between the dimensions. When last on Earth, I lived in what you now call South America. The team of beings I represent is made up of many thousands of minds from the many other realms of existence. We will be working with your group*

to provide very tangible evidence of the reality of these other realms. Our plan is to pioneer important methods of communication between the dimensions using 'energy' rather than the more traditional methods such as ectoplasm. This very evening, it is time for the new work to begin.

As Manu speaks, Alan also enters an altered state of consciousness. Now the team has a second instrument of communication, should they need it. Manu continues to impart important messages, through Diana, for some time. His words are clearly recorded on the audio-tape. He concludes with: *'What you are about to witness is a sign of greater things to come...'*

With that, there is a loud noise, like a thud, as an object lands on the table and rolls around for a few seconds before coming to a stop. What was that? wonders Robin. He cannot wait for the end of the session to see what made the noise. Manu speaks again, as if in answer to this thought: *'We have just brought you a gift from our team to your group.'*

A short while later, the experimental sitting is over. Diana and Alan have regained consciousness. The lights are switched on. There, on the table, is a coin. Robin picks it up: 'Look, it's a Churchill Crown... and it's in mint condition!' He shouts up the stairs, knowing his wife will be keen to hear the news: 'Sandra! You must come down and see this.'

Sandra joins them to see what all the commotion is about. They all examine the Churchill Crown, hardly able to believe what has just happened. The coin, their first evidential object, is carefully placed in a locked cabinet.

This was just the beginning of the extraordinary work of the Scole group.

* * *

'You are invited to attend a presentation of the work of the Scole Experimental Group...'

The invitation was addressed to our friend Harry Oldfield, the scientist and inventor who was the subject of our last book, *Harry Oldfield's Invisible Universe.* Harry smiled knowingly as he handed it to us.

'What's this?' we asked.

'It's all in there,' said Harry, nodding at the letter as he passed it over. 'Just up your street, I would think.'

'Are you going?'

'Try and stop me. This work is at the frontier of science. It's important to us all. It could change the way we collectively view the nature of life itself.'

The letter explained that a group of experimenters was actually communicating with 'dead' people, now 'in spirit', who said they had died only to awaken in another world. It was claimed that the spirit beings were manifesting in the cellar where the experiments took place. Furthermore, communication was being achieved using modern technology like cameras and tape recorders. We had been investigating such phenomena – obtained with and without instruments – for some time and were keen to examine such a story at first hand. Had these investigators really recorded contact with another dimension on modern equipment?

For both of us, our interest in the possibility of life after death had been intensified by personal loss. When Grant was still a young university student, his father died suddenly, struck down in his mid-forties by a brain haemorrhage, while Jane's dearest friend had recently died in her thirties, after a long battle with cancer.

Physical death comes to us all, and many speculate on whether it really is the 'end'. Throughout history it has been viewed by many civilisations as a transition to 'another place'. Like many others, we would like to know the answer to the survival question now, rather than having to wait until we die to find out... or not, as the case may be.

So, on Sunday 3 May 1998, we drove from our home in Essex to Lyng in Norfolk to attend a seminar given by the Scole Experimental Group (SEG). After a wet and windy journey, we arrived at the seminar and soon discovered that thirty or so others had been similarly intrigued by the invitation. We later learned that many of these people had been following the progress of the

SEG for some time. A number had even set up their own experimental groups under SEG guidance and were beginning to experience unusual phenomena themselves.

Robin Foy, one of the founders of the Scole group, introduced himself. He explained that the group had formed at the beginning of 1993 and operated completely independently of the Spiritualist movement or any other organisation. They were non-religious and non-sectarian. Their work was intended to be universal and embraced people from all walks of life, whatever their beliefs. They were involved in serious scientific research into the paranormal, using an entirely new and unique approach. They met to conduct twice-weekly experimental sessions for the development of tangible and objective physical paranormal phenomena in the cellar of a house in Scole, near Diss in Norfolk. This cellar had developed into an Experimental Science Room but they knew it, more affectionately, as the Scole Hole.

Many of the experiments ran simultaneously. The group could be performing audio, photographic and video experiments all in the same month and even during the same session.

Soon after the Scole Experiment began, a team of spirit communicators made themselves known to the group during the experimental sessions. By pioneering brand new forms of tangible paranormal phenomena they aimed to prove conclusively, once and for all, that death does not exist and that there are other dimensions of existence. These other dimensions are hidden from normal perception by the limitations of our senses and our current scientific instruments. The group was told that their spirit team alone consisted of 'thousands of minds', all working in unison towards achieving this tangible proof of the existence of other dimensions. Other teams were preparing to work with similar groups. Some had already started.

The spirit world knew that convincing proof had to include tangible evidence, which could be tested and taken away from the site of experiments for further scrutiny. The spirit team was apparently able to create 'events' in our dimension by influencing atoms and molecules 'here' using the power of their thoughts. All the work revolved around what they referred to as 'creative energy'.

This was a blend of three different types of energy, which they could then manipulate to produce the results they wanted. This technique had apparently not been possible until the current stage of the Earth's development.

Spirit scientists and technicians undertook much of the hard work behind the scenes. These were personalities who had had an interest in technology and scientific experiments while on Earth and had maintained this after they passed into the spiritual dimensions. They were able to bring the group the first real phenomenon, a teleported coin, in October 1993. Within two months the group members had witnessed dancing lights, the ringing of bells, levitation of objects, noisy crackling and loud thumps. In January 1994, water was sprinkled onto participants. Then the dancing lights started touching them. They also began to hear words spoken from mid-air. This communication technique became known as 'extended voice'. These voices came from all around the room and even from *within* the walls.

Soon after this, the spiritual photography experiments began. The Scole group placed cameras in the cellar at the request of the spirit team. These were levitated and took pictures by themselves. The developed films showed amazing images. Then the team asked the group to place flat Polaroid films on the table and 'influenced' them. This work advanced to the stage where the spirit team's 'photographic department' could put faces, glyphs, handwriting and diagrams onto rolls of unopened film, which were simply placed on the table during experiments, still in their factory-sealed packaging.

During experiments, there were considerable and inexplicable changes in the room temperature, a phenomenon which, by April 1994, included strong cold breezes.

The work progressed quickly over a period of just a few months. The team began writing on a paper pad with a pencil which was left on the floor. An electric socket was turned on and off several times, causing the group's tape recorder to malfunction. Then the group witnessed projected images of spirit beings in the cellar. There was loud clapping as the first completely solid visitors manifested. They were actually transporting themselves from their own dimension and joining the group members 'physically' in the cellar.

The spirit team often said they would welcome co-operation with men and women of science and letters, and that it would come about in the future. However, the group were never told exactly when this was going to happen. They were therefore delighted, on 2 October 1995, to welcome three leading members of the Society for Psychical Research (SPR) to an experimental session at Scole. These scientific investigators, including professors in such diverse fields as electrical engineering, psychology, mathematics, and astrophysics, were soon able to witness and evaluate some of the photographic tests and other experiments for themselves. Their investigation is now the subject of a comprehensive scientific paper, *The Scole Report*, planned for publication in 1999.

As the day went on we heard statement upon statement about the group's experiences, which would challenge anyone's credulity. We heard about tape recorders being used to convey spirit voices; direct communication; images captured on video; the construction of specialist equipment as instructed by the spirit team; teleported objects and amazing light shows. But there was something down-to-earth and honest about these people, a fact which, for us, added weight to their presentation. On the long journey back to Essex, we agreed that one thing was certain: we must find out more. As soon as we arrived home, we wrote to the group, proposing that we write a book about their work. A few days later, we received a reply. The group had consulted the spirit team, who considered the time 'indeed right' for such a book to be written.

What follows is the result of extensive interviews with the Scole group, members of the Society for Psychical Research and many others who witnessed the experiments. We were given access to the tapes used to record events and frequently we have transcribed directly what the spirit voices communicated and the interaction between the group.

It is important for a wider audience to learn about the Scole Experiment, for this story has far-reaching implications for us all. As Harry said, it could change the way we collectively view the nature of life itself. To begin with, however, we can only ask that you suspend all preconceptions for a short while.

CHAPTER TWO

THE SCOLE
EXPERIMENTAL
GROUP

**People are disturbed, not by things, but
by the views which they take of them.**
Epictetus

The story of how the SEG came together begins in August 1991.
This was the month when Robin and Sandra Foy moved to the
little village of Scole, near Diss, in Norfolk. They had often visited
the village on 'get away from it all' weekends. On these trips,
they had looked out of the rear window of the bedroom in their
favourite old coaching inn to see a picturesque house with a very
overgrown garden. Some time later they would be living in that
very house.

Many things had happened in the Foys' lives that led them to
reside at Street Farmhouse in Scole (see Plate 1). Robin is a former
RAF pilot who went on to become a manager in a paper company
and Sandra is a housewife. They have four grown-up children.
They have been interested in physical psychic phenomena for over
twenty-five years. Physical psychic phenomena, today sometimes
called 'tangible paranormal phenomena', are psychic occurrences
which can be witnessed by all people who are present at the time,
usually sitting in a so-called 'physical development circle'. The
phenomena are generally audible to the human ear and visible to
the eye, so they can often be recorded on a tape recorder or captured
on film. Fragrances generated by physical phenomena can be
detected by the normal sense of smell and spirit visitors can make

themselves apparent 'physically' by touching people, so that they are aware of their 'solid bodies' and by speaking quite separately from any human medium who may be being used as an instrument of communication by spirits.

The medium may also emit ectoplasm. The generally accepted definition of ectoplasm is that it is a physical substance, a mixture of chemicals and body fluids taken from the body of the physical medium and the bodies of the sitters. It is 'plasmic' by nature. The spirit helpers gather the ingredients together inside the body of the medium before ectoplasm is released through any or all of the medium's orifices. The ectoplasm is then moulded and manipulated by the team of spirit helpers for the purposes of producing physical psychic phenomena.

Experiments with ectoplasm are just one of the ways in which spirit teams have been able to influence events on the physical plane in the past. Of course, for this they needed a dedicated medium and the right conditions. Some mediums still work in this way with good results. One problem with ectoplasm, though, is that it can be dangerous to the medium's health, especially if the medium is disturbed or touched when in trance.

Many people have difficulty believing in such things. However, Robin has become convinced that this physical form of mediumship is genuine in many instances. As in many human activities, of course, there can be honest and dishonest people involved. Some mediums are fakes and some are genuine. Robin feels strongly that, in this particular field, it is the fakes who get the publicity and then all mediums are tarred with the same brush.

Robin and Sandra met through a physical circle in Romford, Essex, many years ago. The medium there communicated a message from a Dr Dunn, who told them that they would be working in a new way in the future, 'using energy and not ectoplasm'. This meant nothing to them at the time, but looking back now they feel it all falls into place. For them, the whole progression of their experiments has been like working on a jigsaw puzzle over a long period of time. They seemed to get a piece here and a piece there over many years and it was not until they had enough pieces that they could start to see a picture.

The Scole group now understand that they were brought together specifically to pioneer work with a new 'creative energy' rather than the traditional ectoplasm. The Scole spirit team wanted to move away from the traditional methods for various reasons. The traditional methods had not worked in convincing people of the reality of survival. In the early days of the group, however, it seemed that the team thought it important to show that they could replicate the same effects with energy that other spirit teams had achieved with ectoplasm.

The spirit team said this new energy was much safer and easier to use for a larger number of people and that there were good reasons for developing a new way of working. They also showed how so much more could be achieved using the new creative energy.

In their former home in Postwick, Norfolk, the Foys had started a small group which met for the development of physical paranormal phenomena, and they were now anxious to continue with this research as soon as possible. They were pleased that the four other people who had worked with them at Postwick were happy to travel a little further to Scole.

The end room, the library, was prepared for the work by draping very thick plastic PVC pond liner over the windows and excluding other light by various ingenious means. In the past it had been important that no light whatsoever, not even a pinprick, was allowed into the room being used for the development of the phenomena. Because it was such a problem to set up the room like this, it was left in this darkened condition permanently. Consequently, once the library had been prepared, there was no real break in the continuity of the sessions.

The Foys' ultimate intention, however, was to renovate the larger of their two cellars as soon as possible. A cellar is much easier to black out, being underground and windowless. In addition, Robin and Sandra often organised seminars where groups of up to thirty people would witness the physical phenomena. The cellar would be perfect for such demonstrations. So the renovation of the first cellar went ahead (see Plate 2).

By February 1992 it was ready. Twenty people gathered for an inaugural meeting, including the physical medium, Stewart

Alexander. Stewart and his spirit team work in the traditional way, with ectoplasm. According to those present on that occasion, there was a wealth of physical phenomena. But the main event was when White Feather, one of Stewart's main spirit guides, blessed the cellar and dedicated it to the work of the spirit world.

After the renovation of the cellar, and the inaugural meeting and blessing ceremony, the excitement and extra enthusiasm seemed to generate an increase in the phenomena. The room would go extremely cold during sessions, and then the group began to hear raps, taps and clicks from the walls and around the chairs. Occasionally, they even heard faint whistles. However, this short burst of paranormal activity soon petered out.

The Foys expanded the number in the group by three to see if this would help. There were now nine of them meeting on a regular basis. Unfortunately, this did not work. The weeks and months rolled on but, instead of the phenomena progressing, quite the reverse happened. Before long, boredom set in for some members of the group and they left. Harmony amongst the group members, an essential component of successful phenomena, suffered as a consequence. The group plodded on through the summer of 1992, but it became clear that changes would need to be made.

There were, however, a number of bright spots during this dull period. On some occasions, when physical mediums like Stewart Alexander were invited for special sessions, the cellar would be packed, with as many as twenty-eight people filling the room. At each of these sessions there was an amazing variety of physical paranormal phenomena. One particular demonstration of traditional physical mediumship, held on Sunday 30 August 1992, stands out among all the others in Robin's memory, for it gave him his ultimate proof of life after death. He remembers:

> During the course of the séance, my father, who had passed into spirit in 1987, materialised quite solidly. I was able to embrace him, and I recognised his voice beyond a shadow of a doubt. Let's face it, who among us would not know their own father? We had been extremely close in life and were able to carry on a

personal conversation during which my father spoke of things that only he and I in the world would know about. He gave me some very valuable advice about my health, which I immediately and wisely acted upon, as it proved to be extremely accurate when I called on my GP for confirmation the following day.

The Foys were then given a message from the spirit world, via a friend who was a medium, which indicated that the energies of the various people in their group did not mix, hence the lack of progress. It is very important that the energies are right in any group experimenting with physical phenomena. Once they had received the message, the Foys were concerned about what they would say to the other group members. To their complete surprise, the remaining members said they were thinking of leaving anyway, because of travelling difficulties. So, thirteen months after the start of the Scole home group, the Foys were back at square one, with just the two of them sitting together in the cold dark cellar. They stuck to a rigid regime of regular sessions, to ensure the continuity of the energies, while contemplating the daunting task of rebuilding the group once again.

It came to their attention that a French businesswoman called Mimi, who lived in the nearby town of Diss, was interested in sitting regularly as part of a group. The first session with Mimi took place on Monday 21 September 1992. The atmosphere felt good and the group was very optimistic. Robin started the tape recorder. As usual, they played sing-a-long music, which spirit people say helps to raise the vibrations. The session seemed to be progressing without much happening when, suddenly, just as the Morecambe and Wise song 'Bring Me Sunshine' started playing, they heard the clicking sound of clockwork false teeth in mid-air. On one level, they thought it might be the spirit people having a joke, because everybody knows about Eric Morecambe's antics with those chattering teeth. But on another level it was much more important. It was the Scole group's first significant phenomenon.

Following this 'Bring Me Sunshine' sitting, strange paranormal activity began to build up in the house between the Monday night sessions. 'This mostly happened in our bedroom,' said Sandra. 'There were constant raps and taps on the walls, doors, ceilings and light bulbs. Then they started tapping on the headboard of the bed!'

'From our knowledge and experience of such matters,' continued Robin, 'we thought that the psychic energies were being gathered together in preparation for the work that might one day be done in the cellar. In the light of what's happened since, perhaps that was a fair assumption.'

Soon after this, Sandra and Robin officiated at a residential weekend for people interested in physical mediumship and met Ken and his friend, Bernette. It was agreed that they should join the Scole group.

On Monday 23 November 1992, all five members sat together for the first time. But the mix of energies still did not seem strong enough to produce the significant physical paranormal phenomena that the Foys were aiming for. They needed to find still more people.

A sequence of events then took place that would change their lives. Robin and Sandra placed an advertisement in a regional newspaper for new members. It was answered in December by Alan and Diana Bennett. The couple had lived in Norfolk for twenty-two years and also had four grown-up children. Alan is a carpenter and Diana runs a healing practice. They had been meditating together in an attempt to sense energies. While they were doing this, light bulbs would pop out and other unusual things would happen. Strange things occurred when they were apart as well, but when they were together it seemed as if their energies were much stronger. Once they went to a house and the lights kept going on and off. One light bulb even shot across the room. They clearly brought powerful energies to the Scole group.

And so there were seven in the group: Robin, Sandra, Mimi, Ken, Bernette, Alan and Diana. The Bennetts participated for the first time on 4 January 1993. In those early days, none of them could have any idea that with the introduction of the energies of Alan and Diana, it was time for the real work of the Scole home group to begin. Yet, as Robin recalls, the home circle at Scole 'certainly felt different. To describe it as "alive" and "vibrant" would certainly be no exaggeration... There was a mood of optimism and excitement.'

At this stage, the group was still operating along the traditional lines of development for any circle seeking to develop physical paranormal phenomena. They had, as part of their equipment, an aluminium 'trumpet', which stood upright on the circular central table during sittings. This piece of traditional séance apparatus is a conical, megaphone-like object through which spirit communicators speak. At Scole, it had never shown the slightest sign of moving, let alone being used for spirit speech. Not, that is, until Monday 26 April 1993. Then it was knocked off the table for the first time, falling onto the leg of one of the sitters and then noisily onto the floor. At last they had a tangible result on which to build.

The following week, all seven members were present. They experienced clicks and whispers, as well as an incredible coldness. The trumpet fell over again, into the lap of one of the sitters, but this time its descent was more controlled, as if in slow-motion. When the audio-tape recording of the sitting was played back, the group realised that there was constant interference, rather like static, on the tape until the very moment that the trumpet moved. Immediately afterwards, the static ceased and the proceedings on the rest of the tape were as clear as a bell, making the group think that some sort of 'energy' had been built up by the spirit people in order to move the trumpet.

Throughout the summer of 1993, the phenomena continued to develop. The faint spirit lights which had sometimes been seen became brighter and more regular. Patches of mist began to appear. Sitters were even splashed with water. A profusion of audible sounds developed and those present felt their trousers, shirt-sleeves or cardigans being tugged and pulled. In the early days, Sandra and Robin were used for trance communication. A large number of communicators spoke through them, all promising that they were now extremely close to getting very good phenomena in the group. Sandra, however, was not happy at the prospect of developing her trance mediumship further. She felt under psychological pressure to 'perform' during the sittings. It was at this stage that the group members agreed to throw the whole thing open to the spirit world and let them decide which was the best way forward and who was to be used for what purpose. From that moment on, the phenomena began to take off at an incredible rate.

First, the spirit people took Alan into trance. He had never been used in this way before, however, and his first attempts at communication were fraught with difficulty as the spirit people familiarised themselves with using him as an instrument. Extra sittings were planned for practice and Alan's level of trance quickly became much deeper. Very soon, he was totally unconscious during group sessions while the spirit people made use of his body. At the same time, Diana also began to be used in the same way. Having received instruction in trance mediumship in the past she was much more familiar with the trance state and soon the spirit people had complete control of her during sessions. So the spirit people now had two effective 'instruments' and the Scole home circle had seven harmonious and enthusiastic members. Everything was set to begin.

Right from the start, the group was amazed at what happened during the sessions. Even some of the early phenomena were quite spectacular. The sessions in the cellar were like stepping into another world, a place where different rules apply.

The Scole group learnt that these new ways of working with energy had been tried before the Scole Experiment began but the spirit teams had failed because the time was evidently not right. It had only been in recent years, since certain energies had been coming to Earth, that the spirit world had been able to reproduce the phenomena on a regular basis. Additionally, the mix of energies of the members of the Scole group were a major factor in what was achieved during their time together. With the energies of Sandra, Robin, Alan and Diana an extraordinary new phase in medium work had begun.

One of the spirit team, John Paxton, explained to the group the four main differences between the more traditional way of working and the new energy-based technology now available to the spirit world. First, this energy was a creative energy made up of a blend of Earth, human and spiritual energies. As such it was much safer for the medium, although trance was still necessary. Second, using the new energy, phenomena could be developed much faster, in months rather than years. Third, the variety of different phenomena that teams of spirit helpers could produce through any experimental group was far greater. Fourth, the new energy-based methods were a blended product of the energies of each and every one of the people within a group and the energies brought by the spirit team. In this sense, the blended energy product did not rely solely on the physical attributes of the medium or mediums, which was generally the case with more traditional forms of physical mediumship. Because of this, the development of energy-based phenomena was more of a shared experience, a group effort.

During experimental sessions at Scole, both Alan and Diana went into an altered state of consciousness or trance, allowing their bodies to be used by a few members of the spirit team for verbal communication so that the whole team could talk to the group. Diana said that as she went into trance during the experiments, 'a sort of detachment' took place. Robin, Sandra, and others present remained conscious so that they could observe and interact with the communicators.

Many people have asked why both Alan and Diana needed to be in trance at the same time. The team answered that it was easier for them to operate effectively when two separate mediums were in a parallel trance state. The one could balance out the other to a certain extent. Also, there were so many communicators that it was often useful for, say, a spirit scientist to be giving one type of instruction while other team members relayed other information simultaneously.

Once the team arranged a special session where Alan and Diana were not required to be in trance and so they were able to witness the spirit lights and experience the movement and activity in the room. On this occasion the lights were awe-inspiring. Alan had taken part in quite a few physical circles, but he had never been particularly impressed with the phenomena. Now he understood what spectacular phenomena were being produced at Scole. He explained:

> In one way it was good not to have had that experience before as I then understood how everyone else who was new to the phenomena felt. People came to our seminars and they had to listen to us telling them about all these things, but they had not been there at experimental sessions and so hadn't had the benefit of the personal proof. For the people who actually came to the experimental sessions, that was a very different thing, of course: they were truly moved by what they saw.
>
> And it wasn't just about seeing. I can think of one woman who had a very moving experience at a session. There were lights actually going into her body and giving her healing. She was reduced to tears. It must be a fantastic thing to happen to you.
>
> So we're not just talking about witnessing something for the sake of simply seeing unexplainable phenomena at first hand. We're talking about things which are thought-provoking and which really do change people's lives.

CHAPTER THREE

THE SCOLE SPIRIT TEAM AND EARLY EXPERIENCES

This sort of thing is more difficult to do than it looked.

Professor A. W. Verrall (posthumously)

It is hard enough to contemplate the implications of personal survival in another realm of existence. The idea that once we have acclimatised to our new environment, we might each become a member of a team doing spiritual work is even more thought-provoking. Nevertheless, according to the spirit beings who came through at Scole, there are many such teams working towards communication with our dimension. Each individual member brings their own talents and attributes to the team, thus making each team unique in its approach and abilities.

In order to understand what happened at Scole it is essential to understand more about the spirit team.

When one researcher asked a member of the spirit team how he knew it was time to come to a session, the reply was: *I know when it is time to come, I sense it. It is like a pulling, a signal that I recognise. It is a slowing down of the mind's senses where I can actually come and speak with you. I put my thoughts into words and use the medium in this way, like an instrument of communication.'*

According to all those who witnessed the events, the Scole spirit team made the sessions interesting and, strange though it may seem, fun. They each had very individual personalities and characters (see Appendix 1). While there were thousands of minds in the spirit team, there were only a small number of personalities who were able to communicate. During the five years and 500 sessions of the Scole Experiment the group was introduced to a number of communicators, some of them for a very brief period only. As the experiments progressed, different regular communicators were employed by the team. Four of the main spirit scientists who came through were introduced as William, Albert, Joseph and Edwin. Each new communicator would come through and give advice and guidance as necessary. The team had conversations with the group on a huge range of subjects via these regular communicators.

These individuals often functioned as a kind of 'go-between'. For example, Mrs Bradshaw, one regular communicator, had had little scientific knowledge during her lifetime on Earth. She could not therefore be expected to know all about the science of space, time, matter and energy – subjects which often arose when there were visiting scientists present – just because she was now in spirit. When asked a question, for a brief moment, she appeared to be listening to a scientific expert on her side. She then proceeded to pass on the information to the questioners on our side. She often began with, *'They are telling me that...'* before going on to give the answer. An interesting feature of this communication was that she would listen for, perhaps, one second and then talk on the subject for five minutes.

HOW THE SPIRIT TEAM WORKED

In a typical session, Manu – a powerful guide who was the 'gatekeeper' from the spirit world – would come through first, welcome everybody, and then 'go behind the scenes' and blend the energies so the work could begin. There was usually a little jocular banter from Patrick McKenna – who had been a priest while in the physical world – maybe pretending that he would not allow the Indian guide Raji through. He would eventually concede that some marching music (Raji's cue) should be played. Raji generally exchanged pleasantries with the assembled company before discussing seriously with them the photographic or other experiments which were planned for the session or future sessions. Raji's assistant, Charlie No. 1, often accompanied him, and would move about the group touching people with his small fingers, or patting them on the head.

Somewhere in the midst of all this, Edward Matthews, apparently a scientist in a previous existence, might address the group, usually speaking of his plans for scientific experiments and outlining some of the wonders yet to come. It seemed clear that Edward had taken this function upon himself. He was usually the most enthusiastic about the experiments, carefully outlining his instructions for, say, the making of specialist pieces of equipment. For the group, it was as much a joy to listen to this emotional and gentle soul as it was to listen to the very evolved spirit being, John Paxton.

Paxton was only able to speak to the group in 'closed session', when there were no visitors present. This was mainly due to the practical difficulties of communication from one of the higher spiritual planes, but Paxton delighted in bringing through specialised teaching and instructions from the more evolved souls in the spirit world.

Throughout most sessions, Mrs Emily Bradshaw would pass occasional comments through her entranced medium, sometimes helping Patrick or Raji to put over a particularly pertinent point. It was also her function to help personal communicators in the spirit world pass on messages to any friends and loved ones present, thus providing evidence of survival to visitors and group members alike. Mrs Bradshaw was very precise and accurate with this information.

Finally, after what was normally an interesting and uplifting evening, Patrick would announce that it was time to close. He and Mrs Bradshaw would then take the lead, with Patrick sometimes demonstrating the 'extended voice phenomenon', speaking from any part of the room he chose. He sometimes spoke from all over the cellar at once and the group even heard him speaking from a point that was deep *within* the cellar walls.

EARLY EXPERIENCES

After the first apport, the Churchill Crown, events at Scole continued to develop rapidly. The group went on to receive seventy or so physical apports (from the French *apporter,* 'to bring'), during the course of the Scole Experiment (see Appendix 6). On 1 November 1993, again with all seven members present, Manu said: *'We are going to bring you a collection of gifts which have been carefully chosen by the team to be relevant to those present, and are brought with a tremendous amount of love and goodwill.'*

Tantalisingly, this did not happen immediately, as the group expected. Nevertheless, the sitters heard a series of intermittent thuds throughout the evening. At the end of the sitting, when the lights were turned on, there were seven objects lying on the table, just as promised. An interesting feature of these gifts was that there were seven people present, four women and three men, and four of the objects were for women and three for men. The objects were: a silver thimble; two small silver lockets; a silver chain bracelet; a St Christopher medallion; an ornate miniature spoon with spiral metal handle, decorated bowl and inscription in French on the reverse; and a tiny gold medallion with hieroglyphics (see Plate 3).

At this stage the group was unaware that the team was not using the traditionally understood methods of achieving the apportation of objects and the other phenomena that were occurring with such regularity. Consequently, they were continuing to observe the traditional convention of placing a séance trumpet, the aluminium cone, on the central table during sittings. Although the group had been achieving major phenomena such as the apports, very little had been happening with the trumpet for many months. This situation changed dramatically, however, on 13 December 1993.

During that sitting, with all members present, Manu, speaking through Diana, opened the proceedings as usual: *'Good evening my friends... I would like to tell you more about what we would like to do. A number of us on this side of life are going to be helping with the work. Each is very different in personality and skills.'*

Then a string of cowbells hanging from the ceiling began to ring merrily. With that, another communicator introduced himself through Alan: *'Good evening to you, one and all. My name's Patrick, and in case you hadn't guessed already, I'm an Irishman.'* It was soon obvious that Patrick had a well-developed sense of humour. *'I was a priest in my lifetime, but not a very good one! Kept getting into trouble I did, to be sure.'* He explained that the year of his passing was 1942 but, at the time, he had been well away from the war that was raging around the world.

After more from Patrick about the team's plans, the group members talked excitedly amongst themselves. They speculated enthusiastically on what might happen next. They would not be disappointed.

LIGHTS AND LEVITATIONS

Soon after Patrick had finished speaking, the group began to see small bright lights which appeared from nowhere and darted about the room. These lights were spectacular, resembling shooting stars and curving downwards from the ceiling at high speed before disappearing into thin air. Sparks and a distinctive crackling noise accompanied them.

It was now that the trumpet gracefully moved off the table, its movements made visible in the darkness by the luminous bands around both its narrow and wide ends. The metal cone floated gently up to the ceiling before 'circumnavigating the whole room in a smooth orbit'.

Patrick explained the phenomenon:

> *Clever stuff, isn't it? The object is being manipulated by two young personalities, children from our world. They are standing on the central table. Our team is pioneering completely new methods of inter-dimensional interaction. We are demonstrating a form of spiritual science technology, which utilises a special kind of energy.*

CREATIVE ENERGY, THE DOORWAY, AND ENERGY FORMS

The group asked the team to explain what they meant by 'energy'.

Manu replied:

> *The energy of which we speak is a blend of 'creative energy' from three specific sources. The first we will call 'spiritual energy', which we bring with us from our world. The second is human energy, which we take from your bodies during the experiments. And the third is Earth energy, which is drawn from 'columns' or 'reservoirs' of natural energy that exist in certain geographical locations of your world. These energies were understood and used by the ancients, but this is now forgotten knowledge. We are trying to help humanity to remember.*

The effect created by the energy was explained to the group as being akin to an electromagnetic field.

While the conscious members of the group talked to Patrick, the aluminium cone continued to move gracefully around the room. Then it began to weave through the legs of the chairs before finally coming in to land gently in an upright position on the table. There, much to the amusement of the group, it began to rapidly rotate and rattle.

Now it was the turn of another communicator to introduce himself, through Alan: *'I am Raji.'* This commanding gentleman said it was his pleasant duty to explain something of what was to come. The spirit communicators were experimenting with the energy. One of their ultimate aims was to make various 'visitors' from the other realms of existence actually visible to the group's eyes during sessions in the near future.

In order to carry out the planned experiments, Raji explained, it would be necessary for the spirit team to construct a canopy of energy over the group as they sat around the table. Such a canopy had by then been perfected and could be erected in seconds. The team was going to do this henceforth at the start of each session and all the work would take place under this umbrella of energy.

Raji also explained that a 'spiritual doorway' had been constructed in the area of the central table. Through this doorway fully manifested spirit personalities would pass in the near future.

The information about the new 'creative energy' and the 'spiritual doorway' was a turning-point in the work of the group. After that, the phenomena in the Scole Hole became more and more spectacular by the week. There were constant loud raps and thumps on the chairs, the table and the cellar walls. The supernormal lights, having first behaved like shooting stars, settled into a gentler movement and seemed to be methodically exploring the whole area of the cellar every time the group met.

'We thought they might be getting their bearings, feeling their way around,' explained Robin. 'These phenomena were spectacular enough. But nothing could have prepared us for what was to come.'

From now on the progress of the Scole group was meteoric. The phenomena went from strength to strength. The cellar began to feel 'alive' with energy. By this stage the group had placed four luminous tabs on the table so that they could monitor its movements. Dense energy forms began to move around the room and would occasionally obscure the luminous tabs as they did so.

MUSIC, MEDITATION AND HEALING

At the end of December 1993, Manu also asked the group to be more careful in choosing the music played throughout the sessions as any tunes that were too mournful hindered the work. Apparently, progress depended on creating the right environment, which included the 'vibrations' caused by the music. Mournful music lowered the vibrations while jolly music raised them.

All seven members were asked to meditate for a short period each day from now on. Meditation was important to prepare them for the work that was ahead, as it allowed each individual to 'touch the spiritual realms' on a regular basis and this helped to raise the vibrational rate of their bodies so that they could be used as instruments more easily and effectively.

Manu explained that the meditation and the harmony and love present during the sittings would all help to generate powerful healing energies within the group. The group members would thus become instruments by which the team could transmit healing energies on the Earth plane and they were asked to mentally send out these healing energies just before each closing prayer to those people whom they knew were in need of it. It wasn't long before the group started to get regular feedback from people who said they were benefiting from this 'absent' or 'distant' healing.

VOICES AND OTHER NOISES

Following the revelation that the new way of working was to be with energy, rather than ectoplasm, the team also explained that the new energy would be used to generate 'energy voices', which could address the group from mid-air.

During one early sitting, Raji came through his medium, Alan, for most of the evening but, for a few brief moments, the group was highly amused as Edward Matthews – a sensitive spirit who had been killed during the First World War – strained to make himself heard. Afterwards, Raji explained Edward's difficulty: this had not been an attempt at an 'energy voice' but an experiment in using the medium in an entirely new way. The team said they were using the medium's own vocal cords for the communication but they had 'stretched' them to a point well outside his body, hence the voice appeared to be emanating from elsewhere in the room. Thereafter, the group called this the 'extended voice' phenomenon.

Critical reviewers have queried whether 'stretched' is quite the right word in this context. Obviously the vocal cords were not *physically* manipulated in this way, as this would be injurious to the medium's health, to say the least. The group's answer was simple: 'The team tried to use words that described the phenomena graphically and adequately, but sometimes this got them into trouble. The vocabulary simply is not available yet to explain some of the things that happened.' The point was that the spirit team had used the physical, energetic, and spiritual attributes of the medium to achieve the phenomenon. It will take time to establish a common vocabulary to describe such things and the group asked us to bear this in mind when presenting the material.

Other communicators soon learned to speak via the extended voice. Arnold was the first of them, but he had great difficulty at first in making himself heard using the new technique. The second communicator had no such problems. White Cloud was obviously a very powerful guide. His voice quickly became audible to all. However, he told the group that he had tried to speak to them many times before in the circle but none of them had heard him because the frequency of the vibrations had always been wrong for this type of communication. He had nevertheless persisted until the conditions were perfect.

As well as the raps on the table, which sounded as if they had been produced by a pair of wooden drumsticks, the Scole group had by now experienced many noises, including several very loud thumps on the table and thwacks on the cellar walls and chairs. These other noises were destined to become a major feature of their experience during the Scole Experiment.

MORE PHENOMENA

Everything seemed to be going according to a plan. It was explained that all of the people in the group would be used in a combined effort to develop phenomena, with each having strengths in a different area. The team certainly seemed to know what they wanted to do.

However, it is interesting to note that the spirit personalities were not all-knowing and did not get everything right first time. Much of what was achieved was apparently the result of trial and error. Manu explained, for example, that the lights the group had been witnessing were the by-product of other experiments being carried out by the team. However, since the group members had enjoyed the 'artefact lights' so much and found them so evidential, the team decided to develop them for demonstration to wider audiences in the future.

Some of the conversations were very simple explaining what was needed for sessions and the purpose behind the experiments. There is an irrational expectation held by some that spirits should only reveal profound or arresting insights. It simply does not matter what is being transmitted: the important thing to remember is that the receipt of simple words or wise pronouncements would both support the survival hypothesis.

The spirit team could also display a sense of humour. Once, when the room lights were restored after a sitting, the group discovered that Alan's chair had been silently turned round by 180°, with him on it!

New Year 1994 found the members of the Scole home circle very optimistic about the future development of the phenomena. On 3 January, this being the first time for three weeks that the circle had been at full strength, the team took the opportunity to really show what they could do with the new energy.

This sitting began with a loud ping on the ceiling light bulb, announcing the arrival of Manu. A little while later, the cowbells rang: Patrick's cue. The now familiar light show followed, but the illuminations were more sustained than they had ever been. The shooting star effect was improved on and some lights even danced on the table and ceiling.

The team asked the group to sit in silence for a while and concentrate their thoughts on the 'golden gateway' that had been constructed on the table. The table then began to stretch between the luminous tabs on its surface. Patrick confirmed that this was what the team had done. This would obviously have been impossible under normal circumstances, as the table was made of wood. But the group are adamant that it happened and they all saw it clearly.

Then the table levitated to about one foot off the ground, tilted and moved right round the circle before coming to rest. The 'drummer' again used 'drumsticks' to beat on the table – although there were no drumsticks in the cellar. Drops of water were sprinkled onto three of the group. Then the trumpet raised itself again and moved gracefully around the cellar, visiting every part of the room on its travels. The group asked the team whether the trumpet could be made to hit the cowbells, which were suspended from the ceiling. Immediately, the aluminium object headed straight for the bells and collided with them noisily. Then kisses were blown through the trumpet before it finally came to rest. This seemed to be the finale for the trumpet work.

At the end of the evening the group was given specific instructions by the spirit team regarding the objects that should be placed in the room from then on. The team said they wanted to differentiate the SEG from other physical paranormal phenomena groups who were working in the more traditional way. They explained that any object could be used for experiments with levitation, and particularly asked the group to provide two balsa-wood cubes and a cardboard cylinder for this specific purpose. The group decided to mark these objects with small luminous tabs so that their movements could be seen in the darkness.

Throughout the evening there had been a series of seven loud thuds at intervals, just like those heard when the apports had been brought before. The whole group was keen to see if they had been brought more gifts. When the lights were turned on, this proved to be the case. Seven objects were on the table: an ancient whalebone spoon; a mother-of-pearl necklace; a carved ivory cocktail stick; a pearl and leaf brooch; a marcasite necklace; a silver anchor, cross and heart charm inscribed 'Faith, Hope and Charity'; and a silver St Bernadette medallion, inscribed 'Kara' (see Plate 3).

As instructed, throughout the following week, the group collected together various objects for the forthcoming levitation experiments. During the next session, on 10 January, six members of the group were present. The fourth tune played was 'Sleepy Shores'. At the end of this tune, Manu came through. 'Sleepy Shores' then became his signature tune. The group noticed that the phenomena began earlier on in this session. When Manu had spoken for some time, the cowbells rang and Patrick came through, shortly followed by Raji. Each explained a little of what was happening as the balsa-wood cube, a small box covered with silver foil and two cardboard tubes were levitated and moved around the cellar at different times during the evening. The group was then asked to remove the bowls of water that had been placed around the room in line with the traditional methods of producing phenomena. Apparently, this water was increasing the relative humidity in the room and affecting the team's ability to produce what they were now calling 'energy voices'.

It was explained to the group that they were the first people to be successfully used by the spirit world to pioneer this new form of energy work. They were asked to keep the results as secret as possible, until the phenomena were more advanced. The group was given the impression that the spirit team was building up to the time when physical mediums would no longer be such an essential part of communication. Apparently the combined energies of each group would one day be enough for the energy voices to come from mid-air, rather than through an entranced medium.

The spirit team also wished to work towards bringing their own form of visible light, with which the group would be able to view the phenomena properly. The group was not to use artificial light as this presented the team with great difficulties. The team also said there would be a time when the group could take their own pictures of the phenomena with standard cameras, so long as these were not fitted with a flash. There were no spirit lights or apports during this 2 ¼ hour session but it ended on a high note: the team told the group that they would shortly be bringing some more 'tokens'.

The phenomena continued. On 17 January, the group said the spirit lights were 'amazing'. They danced about in mid-air during the whole session, often at breakneck speed. At one stage the group counted nineteen of them as they fell from the ceiling, one after the other, as if in formation, to disappear into the table. Shortly after this dive-bombing display, the same number shot out of the table again, rising one after another into the air. One light described a perfect circle in front of their eyes, revolving so fast that it appeared to be a continuous ring of light above the group, rather like a Catherine wheel.

There were also more experiments in levitation. First, one of the cardboard tubes moved right up to the ceiling before gracefully floating around the room. It behaved in a very similar fashion to the now-removed trumpet. Both balsa-wood cubes performed similar gyrations in mid-air, at one time hovering no more than a few inches from the faces of the sitters. An amusing moment was provided when the cubes 'nodded' in response to questions. A second cardboard tube and the foil-covered box were also used in a controlled way, climbing into the air for all to see. The table was once again partially levitated as 'staccato raps, which sounded like a machine-gun', were made upon it.

The question of light during experimental sessions was discussed with the spirit team, who explained:

> *The reason we need to provide our own lighting in the future, rather than the electric lighting which you could provide, is not due to the artificial light itself. The problem is essentially with the electric current used to produce the artificial light. Regrettably, this serves to dissipate the very special energy we employ, without which there can be no phenomena.*

On 24 January, Manu and Patrick arrived on cue as usual and there was a further development with the spirit lights. This time they were so prolific and so bright it was like a firework display. They danced all over, moving at lightning speed from one location to another, circling the table and 'skating' across its surface. Then the lights seemed to merge with the levitating objects. For the first time, they touched two of the sitters. One, Ken, was touched on the head, a feeling he described as akin to 'the fluttering of a butterfly'. Sandra was touched on the hand by another light. The sensation was like a twig being scraped over her skin.

The staccato raps were repeated at this sitting but there were also new audible phenomena. A tambourine, introduced that very evening, was tapped loudly, while chairs in the outer part of the room moved and creaked as though a number of solid spirit people were sitting on them.

Then Hoo, a Chinese guide, spoke through Diana. He was very wise and his words were extremely encouraging, as he spoke of *'the wonders yet to come'*.

Then Patrick piped up to tell them more:

> *Four sittings from now, I will be allowed to preside*

over what we might call 'Patrick Night'. Please
provide a partially enclosed area, two feet deep with
an open front and curtains at both sides and above.
The cellar wall will provide the back of the enclosure.
I will not tell you exactly what is planned, but I think
you will certainly see something special.

While awaiting Patrick Night, Robin and Sandra organised another demonstration of physical mediumship by Stewart Alexander on Sunday 30 January. Thirty-five people were present. As we know, Stewart is a traditional physical medium and his spirit guides employ ectoplasmic methods. During this session, witnesses reported 'a very impressive football-size cloud of ectoplasm gathering in front of the medium's face'. This was seen in red light, which was shining on the medium.

The Scole group had not even thought about whether the traditional ectoplasm séance and their new energy experiments would be incompatible. It had simply never crossed their minds. But on Monday 31 January 1994, their sitting was much quieter, with very few phenomena. Manu explained, in detail, that the Scole spirit team was having a great deal of difficulty in getting the energy vibrations right at this sitting. He said this was due to the fact that a demonstration of physical phenomena using ectoplasm had taken place recently and the other medium's guides worked in a different way. While neither the other spirit team's methods nor the Scole spirit team's methods were wrong, the two were incompatible.

Fortunately this minor setback was soon overcome and the hanging cowbells started to ring at intervals, often in time to the background music, and much work was undertaken during this session to improve the light phenomena. By the end of the evening the lights had become larger and more sustained than ever before.

Patrick said that the team was giving much thought to which of the phenomena to keep 'in the programme' when the group went public with the work. The team's first priority was to duplicate existing ectoplasmic phenomena using the new energy methods. Then they could move on to new and very different forms of phenomena that had never been tried before. It was made clear to the group that the pioneering work done during the Scole Experiment was aimed at producing physical paranormal phenomena suitable for public demonstration to audiences around the world in order to prove, once and for all, to the whole of humanity, the reality of life after death.

The phenomena continued. The group had introduced a new set of wind chimes into the cellar, which hung from the ceiling in addition to the cowbells. The spirit team rang these new chimes on request. The lights became much larger and brighter than any seen before. The group learned that, like earlier lights, these larger lights had substance. Two of those present reported that they had the sensation of a marble hitting them when the lights collided with their feet. But again, like the earlier lights, these larger lights were also able to pass straight through solid matter. As before, they entered the table a number of times and shot back out again with equal ease.

Towards the end of 'a very entertaining session', White Cloud joined the group. He said he was there to gain knowledge of the new way of working with energy, with the intention of helping other groups throughout the world to achieve results in the same way.

In an exchange that gives some idea of the mix of happenings in the cellar during these early sittings, two members of the spirit team gave clues to their identities. One simply gave the initials 'ACD'; the other offered an address, '91 Circle Gardens, Merton'. On investigation, this address was found to exist but it was not possible to verify whether the communicator had ever lived there.

This raises a number of questions about the Scole Experiment. It certainly appeared that some of the events which occurred in the Scole Hole had both important scientific implications and an experimental basis, allowing them to be checked, tested and verified. Other events seemed to be of a more personal nature and were harder to verify.

This has led some commentators to value the scientific experiments more highly than the personal communications. We are all, of course, somewhat constrained by our individual perspectives. Some people may consider it very important to know how their relatives are coping in the next life whereas others place more value on whether the spirit personalities can tell us whether or how we might use water to power our cars and light to propel our spaceships.

However, whether verbal communications have scientific or personal implications, they could all be of value as evidence in showing that we survive, as long as it can be demonstrated that the information comes from outside the medium. But, in the case of mental mediumship, this has always been somewhat difficult to demonstrate to the satisfaction of everyone, as critics can convincingly argue for the alternative explanations such as the fraud, alter-ego or super-PSI hypotheses which we discuss later (see Chapters 5 and 9). Hence the need for physical mediumship to create phenomena which can be tested and verified more easily and so satisfy more of the demands of more of the critics.

On 14 February, St Valentine's Day, all seven group members were present. The team said they would bring seven gifts 'in the spirit of love' and at the end of the evening, seven objects were found on the table: a lady's handkerchief with the initial 'H'; a 1923 French franc token, bearing the legend, *'Chambre de Commerce de France';* a penknife with a mother-of-pearl handle; a silver charm of the Grim Reaper; a silver sports medallion; a pearl tie-pin and a marcasite necklace (see Plate 3). As usual it was Manu who appeared to be most involved in bringing the gifts. He said he was assisted in this happy task that evening by two spirit children from the Victorian era. They had also helped him to choose the gifts.

During the sitting, two spirit lights moved in tandem, exploring the cellar at a constant separation of about 4 inches. They behaved like a single light as if directed by a single intelligence and, when requested to do so, touched the hands of two of the group. Luminous patches then began to appear all around the room.

Since the next sitting was the eagerly awaited Patrick Night, the latter part of the 14 February sitting was spent receiving last-minute instructions in preparation for that event.

We would like you to sit in an arc in front of the curtained enclosure in which Alan will be sitting,' said Patrick. *'Please put the table in the space between you and the medium.'* Patrick's comments were made using the newly-developed extended voice, with his final 'Goodbye' emanating from a position two feet behind Alan's entranced body.

Patrick Night finally arrived. Little did the group know that it would last a full three hours. Robin smiled as he told us about some of the preparations. 'As a bit of a joke, we placed an ashtray, a cigar, a large can of Guinness and a pint glass on a wooden chair at the back of the cellar while we sat. We knew Patrick had enjoyed his cigars and his "pint of the black stuff" when he was alive.'

Alan, Patrick's medium, wore luminous tabs on his knees so that the others could see where he was at all times. Since there had been such a build-up to this sitting, there was intense excitement at the thought of what might happen.

First Manu came through. Then the bells rang and Patrick introduced himself in his familiar Irish brogue before explaining something of what was to happen. *'All the energy during this session will be conserved for one main purpose the team has in mind. Don't miss it!'*

The small lights began to fly around the room. They were much brighter than ever before. The luminous patches appeared and lit up the table for the first time as they passed over it. Then the smaller lights started to emit beams of light, similar to torchlight, as they moved about the cellar. Bright pillars of light formed beside and above the curtained off area where Alan was sitting. These luminous pillars were five feet long and eight inches wide. 'Sheets' of light appeared sporadically. These were three feet square and brilliantly illuminated the area within them. The whole light show seemed to be building towards a climax. Suddenly, Patrick told them to pay attention: *'Look towards the curtains!'*

All eyes focused on the draped material, where one of the beams of light was illuminating the materialised figure of Patrick himself. The group members report that they were able to able to see his head and shoulders. One of them even saw him clearly right down to his waist. Patrick was able to repeat this materialisation five times before it faded, so that all had a good opportunity to observe him in the specially projected spirit light. Then he explained:

The complicated mechanics of these new type of energy-based phenomena involves the use of quantum physics, with the manipulation of atoms and molecules being important... These are early beginnings but we expect to be able to repeat these phenomena all around the world in other groups.

He then went on to describe the team's plans for experiments with paranormal photography based on the hitherto unknown principles of spiritual science.

When the sitting finished and the lights were turned on, the group noticed something different about the chair on which Patrick's drink and cigar had been left. The ashtray had been turned upside-down, with the can of Guinness placed on top of it. Not only that, but the cigar sat on top of the can.

So it was that the group's strange experiences developed in intensity between the autumn of 1993 and the early part of 1994. As we have learned, the main phenomenon during this period of intense change was the apports. 'The spirit team certainly came bearing gifts with love,' said Sandra. 'We and our guests have now received over seventy of them in all.'

The apports continued to arrive at sittings for many months. On Monday 11 July 1994, after Manu's initial greeting, the 'plop' as an object dropped on to the table sounded different from normal. Manu explained to Robin that the apport was *'from one of your spirit helpers and you will understand why this particular item has been chosen when you see it'.*

Once again, the group was left wondering what the team had brought them. With the restoration of light, they saw that it was a newspaper, apparently an original copy of the *Daily Express,* dated Monday 28 May 1945.

Robin knows a great deal about newspapers as he has been in the paper industry for many years. He comments:

The obvious charge of those sceptical of the supernatural origin of apported newspapers is that anyone could send off for a modern copy of an old newspaper, as they are readily available as birthday presents. However, although identical in every way to the originals, these modern copies of old news-papers are obviously printed on modern paper.

The apported *Daily Express* was printed on paper of the type used in the early- and mid-1940s, but it was in almost mint condition. This in spite of the fact that it was apparently forty-nine years old! There was no sign of the usual yellowing which would have occurred if it was an original from the end of wartime Britain. This yellowing happens because the paper used for everyday copies of national and provincial newspapers during the war was made from mechanical wood pulp. The pulp contains the chemical impurity, lignin, which causes the paper to rapidly turn yellow when it comes into contact with sunlight and air. If one of our number had introduced an original wartime newspaper, trying to pass it off as an apport, why did it not show the usual signs of ageing?

Interestingly, just a few weeks later, the apported newspaper, although carefully stored away from light and air, *had* turned yellow.

Robin said that the content of the newspaper was very relevant too. On the front page was a photograph of Sir Winston Churchill, whose presence as a spirit helper Robin certainly understood, having in the past received many communications from him. The earlier apport of the Churchill Crown had the same relevance. (How Robin's relationship with Churchill came about is described in his book *In Pursuit of Physical Mediumship* (Janus, 1996).)

A criticism of the apport phenomena would be that one (or more) people in the group was tricking the others. Yet this would be a very elaborate and expensive trick given the sheer number of objects, their geographical origin, their rarity, their value, and the materials they were composed of. This diversity was an important aspect of the evidence that the team was trying to provide.

CHAPTER FOUR

PROGRESS

They delivered messages from no-where
into now-here.
Dr Ernst Senkowski

Patrick Night had ended with an interesting revelation by the spirit team. Just before leaving, having already said that the team was using the science of atoms and molecules to achieve their results, Patrick explained that in the very near future the group would be able to experiment with a camera during the sessions. He also said that the team might ask the group to leave a photographic film on the table to see whether the team could impress images on to it. This signalled an amazing new phase within the Scole group: spiritual science photography.

'I suppose this is the point when our "Scole group" became the "Scole Experimental Group", our "Scole Hole" became the "experimental science room" and our "sittings" became "experimental sessions",' comments Robin.

EARLY PHOTOGRAPHIC EXPERIMENTS

After Patrick Night the group held a couple of sessions in which they were told more about the cameras and other equipment they would need for a spiritual science photography experiment. Not surprisingly, this experimental session of 28 February 1994 was eagerly awaited. Following instructions from the team, the group had selected a 35mm camera without flash facility, and loaded it with conventional 24-frame, 35mm colour film.

During the session, this camera was placed on a wooden chair beside Sandra, who had been briefed by the spirit team to take photographs in the total darkness whenever she was specifically asked to do so. It is important to bear in mind that there was no normal source of light in the room; hence it would not be expected that the film could be 'exposed'.

As the team created 'supernormal lights', which started to fly and dance about the cellar, they explained that they would try to communicate messages by projecting images into the camera and onto the film. Sandra was instructed to pick up the camera and wait for the team to give the word before taking a picture. For a brief moment, one of the small bright lights stopped its rapid rotation around the room, hovered and 'posed' in front of the camera. On the command, 'Now!', Sandra pressed the button.

A little later, she was told that she could take pictures as she wished, at her own pace. She obliged by taking snaps, trying to aim the camera towards the lights. After taking a few snaps, she put the camera down on its own seat next to her, where it continued taking its own snapshots without her pressing the button. Much to the group's delight and amusement, the camera wound itself on after each click. The last five frames on the film were used in this way.

At the same time lots of other things were happening. The bells and chimes rang constantly. The lights performed all sorts of aerial displays. The cowbells were untied from their ceiling anchorage and floated gently down to the floor. A number of the objects left scattered about the cellar for levitation experiments were moved, as was the table. Raji then requested that the group only put a couple of these objects out in future. He explained that the light from the luminous tabs on so many objects was too great and was causing some technical problems for the team. Despite this, towards the end of the session, the lights began emitting 'scanner beams' which lit up the legs and feet of all those present.

The next day, the film was developed and the results were startling. The group's first reaction was that they must have been given the wrong film by mistake. But it *was* their film because the first shot was the view from one of the Street Farmhouse windows, taken when the film was first loaded. The rest of the film was incredible. There had been no fewer than eleven definite attempts by the spirit team to put images on it. The group decided that this was a minor miracle in itself.

The subjects of the photographs varied greatly and appeared totally unconnected. To the group's utter amazement, on the first photograph was what appeared to be an image of St Paul's cathedral in the 1940s' Blitz, with smoke all around it (see Plate 4). A second frame was of the same image, but sideways on. Another appeared to show a wrecked bus after a night of wartime bombing in Coventry or London. There was a further shot of this, also sideways on. The fifth image showed the front page of the *Daily Mirror,* dated 16 December 1936 (see Plate 5). The sixth image showed a group of soldiers from the First World War, two officers and seven men. The seventh showed a brilliant light, presumably the one which had 'posed' for the camera. Pictures 8, 9, 10, and 11 were much fainter, but represented various groups of people. One appeared to be a wedding photograph with the bride holding a bouquet.

Not surprisingly, the group began to investigate the origins of the photographs. They could find out little about the pictures initially, but they did send off to the *Daily Mirror* for a copy of the newspaper dated 16 December 1936. When it arrived, the front page was almost identical to the photograph, but with a few differences, which indicated it might have been from another edition on the same day.

With another of the photos, Edward said he had actually taken the original of another of the shots when he was alive and he confirmed it showed his comrades during the First World War. Later, Patrick would tell the group that one of the other pictures was of his own uniformed brother.

Most groups seeking physical psychic phenomena in the past would be extremely pleased with the odd voice or slight movement of objects by paranormal means. This photographic phenomenon was a completely different matter, however. It represented a tangible means of communication between the dimensions, which lasted beyond the couple of hours spent in the experimental science room. If it could be repeated regularly, it might offer conclusive proof of the reality of survival. This potential was not lost on the group. They were elated.

It was in this frame of mind that they looked forward to the next session. The following week, the 35mm camera was again placed in the cellar. The group had also decided to put out pencil and paper in case the spirit team wanted to write a message. Very early on in the session, the bells jingled, the chimes jangled and Patrick was soon communicating. To the group's initial disappointment, he said that the team would not be conducting photographic experiments that evening. Rather, the team wanted the group to join in an experiment to show that the 'balls of living energy', which the group called 'spirit lights', could be jointly controlled by the group and team together, with thought.

The spirit lights had now increased to saucer-size and the group all had great fun in trying to direct their movement around the room. Twice they successfully managed to get a light to fall gently from the ceiling. Both times they were able to make it come to rest exactly in the centre of the table.

The group also experienced two instances of what they called 'visual projected images'. These were a new phenomenon in which a three-dimensional image was projected into the room by the team so that the group could see it in its own illumination, something like a hologram. The first appeared to be a piece of material about the size of a man's handkerchief. The second, a much more exciting example, seemed to show an indistinct head hovering at what would be normal height for a man, but without the body. It had what looked like draped material over it, hanging down both sides.

Midway through the session, Raji spoke, saying that the team was building up to something special that evening. In order to achieve it, there would be a considerable lowering of the temperature. With that, the cellar temperature began to drop. It got colder and colder. Then a commanding voice penetrated the darkness:

> *I am Paxton. It is not normally possible for me to communicate directly with those on Earth. Usually guides such as Patrick and Raji would pass on my communications. However, there has been an*

important decision by the Council of Communion, of
which I am a member. We have decided that I will
communicate directly with your group from time to
time. The work that you are doing now and will be
doing in the future is considered very important.

This was the first time that the group had heard of the Council of
Communion, with its membership of thirteen evolved souls. There
are apparently many such councils. They deal with all sorts of
matters, including healing, communication and physical
phenomena. Their role is to oversee and plan, down to the finest
detail, the experimental communication between the spirit world
and groups on the Earth plane. All the work of the Scole group
was overseen by the Council.

After this inspirational communication, things returned to
'normal' (if that's the right word!) in the cellar. Raji asked for
some livelier music. An array of shining lights performed acrobatic
manoeuvres, with others illuminating the knees, legs, and feet of
the sitters. There was a levitation display with the cardboard tube
and balsa-wood cube. The central table was also levitated. The
tambourine was lifted and beaten in time to music, and there were
loud raps, taps and thuds, and plodding sounds, 'as if spirit people
were walking around the room freely'.

Then, at the end of a very enjoyable session, Patrick amazed
the whole group by speaking from many different parts of the
room within a split second. 'He was everywhere at once!' When
the room lights were restored, one of the group saw something on
the paper lying next to the pencil. It looked like the letter 'P'.

At the next session, on 21 March, Manu spoke first as usual.
While he was talking, two now familiar thuds signified the arrival
of a couple of apports. A profusion of spirit lights was witnessed
once again, as were many levitation experiments. This time the
central table levitated to a height of about four feet and hovered
steadily for some time before rising a further two feet, a position
it maintained for over five minutes before gracefully floating to
earth. Cowbells, wind chimes, drumsticks, raps and taps all made
their contribution to another successful evening. The tambourine

was hit so hard by the spirit team's energy that its surface was punctured. The group explained:

> We also repeated the exercise to jointly control a spirit light mentally. All working together, we were able to move it gradually downwards from the ceiling until it rested on the table top. The lights also touched us on the hands and faces. And this time, the paper and pencil experiment produced a square drawn on the paper, together with several attempts at what seemed to be the letters 'C' and 'G'. This was a great improvement on the single attempt we had received the previous week.

Significantly, this experimental session also featured another attempt by the team to produce paranormal photographs using their spiritual science techniques. This time, two 35mm SLR cameras, both loaded with completely new film, were placed on the table before the session started. Both cameras were heard to click as they took a few pictures in the darkness, winding themselves on each time.

After the session, the apports proved to be old pennies, dated 1936 and 1940 respectively. The dates on these coins were possibly significant, as they seemed to tie in with two of the photographs the group had received a couple of sessions before. This might not have been the connection but you will remember that the *Daily Mirror* was dated 1936 and the St Paul's photograph had meantime been traced to an almost identical picture taken in 1940. One of the scientific investigators later pointed out that the group's image was slightly different from the original. They had no idea why this should be so. They often had to guess at the relevance of things because the team's communicators said they would tell them things and provide information on a 'need to know basis'. Sometimes this was exasperating!

When the films were developed the next day, one had a single image on it while the other had two. All three images were of the sepia type. Virtually identical, they showed a central circle of light surrounded by a 'spider's web' or net. Lacking information from the team at that point, the group surmised that the web might portray the canopy of energy that the spirit team had erected over them at the beginning of each session.

Very occasionally, one of the group's sessions developed into 'a classic'. They never knew when this was going to happen but the session of 28 March 1994 proved to be one of them. The session was different almost from the start. First Manu gave words of encouragement and told the group something of the future plans. Then the cowbells rang and Patrick said, *'Hello'*, in an extended voice from one corner of the room. But overall there was a general lack of lights and other phenomena. Robin made a joke about being 'de-lighted'. The team immediately sent about half-a-dozen token lights to show they were listening, but these were not sustained for long. The group learned the reason for the strange atmosphere when Patrick explained that the team was trying to achieve 'solid projections' during this session.

Shortly afterwards, two of the group felt solid hands resting on their shoulders. The fingers were animated 'in normal human fashion'. Others felt regular touches by various objects 'rather like gnarled twigs'.

'These are "solid energy structures",' said Patrick. This was confirmed by Raji and Edward, who also now spoke with extended voice, illustrating how the team members were all learning to use this particular technique.

The group had brought the two 35mm SLR cameras into the cellar prior to the session and Raji asked Sandra to pick up one of the cameras and aim it at the table. As before, she was then instructed to take a photograph whenever she heard, 'Now!' While this was happening, the team levitated the second camera. The group could hear it moving around the room, clicking to take photos and then winding itself on. Both cameras had brand new films in when they started and neither was equipped with a flash. Since the films were at no time exposed to light of any kind, there was no way, in the conventional photographic sense, that they could have contained images when they were developed. But this, of course, was not conventional photography.

When the films were used up, the team went silent again, as if regrouping for the next experiment. 'Then we saw the big and little heads,' said Sandra. 'The team told us they were "projecting" these images. They were self-illuminated and contained recognisable faces which appeared in mid-air. The clearest image was life-size and belonged to a man whose head was bowing down. A second head appeared in miniature on the table. There was also a projected image which resembled a crumpled handkerchief; but others were less clear.'

The group knew something special was happening that night but were not sure quite what it was. The phenomena continued with the levitation of the table. One moment it was in its normal position, then, in a split-second, as if propelled by silent rockets, it was rising to the ceiling. It stayed there for more than ten minutes before gently descending.

The wooden table is very heavy. It is unlikely that one individual could hold it up on the ceiling with outstretched arms for five minutes, let alone ten. For a person to physically achieve this feat, it would also be necessary to stand up. This would mean a high likelihood of detection by others in the room who would notice, for example, the sounds associated with such an act. The whole feat would, in addition, have to be achieved while appearing to remain seated in a chair wearing luminous armbands.

After this session the group could hardly wait to get the photographs developed. Each of the two films contained eleven specific images, making a total of twenty-two photographs. Every image was different. The subjects were quite varied, including people, places, objects, statues, and architectural features from all over the world. Some of the pictures seemed to be grouped in themes: the First World War, Second World War, European architecture, the Far East, religious ceremonies and portraits. There was a photograph of a religious procession, probably Catholic. An image of the River Seine was obviously taken from the top of Notre Dame Cathedral in Paris as it showed one of the cathedral's steeples (see Plate 6). There was also a very clear full-face image of an Indian gentleman, complete with a turban and friendly grin (see Plate 7). Was this Raji? Later the group was told that it was not.

Further scenes were from India and the East. One comparatively clear image showed Asian men on a railway platform. Another was of an Indian mounted soldier on a horse. A street scene of Amsterdam in the 1920s or 1930s was featured, together with a statue in Belgium of Charles de Lorraine. Two of the photographs showed parts of a map and the group later learned that these depicted the very first map of French Canada.

What is particularly interesting is that some of those early images were black and white, although taken on a colour film, while others resembled the old-style sepia prints. Between them, they constituted a diverse collection of images from all parts of the globe. Despite the fact that the images were basically black and white, some did show backgrounds containing areas of colour, almost rainbow-like in places. There seems to be no normal explanation for this.

Notions of normality should, however, perhaps be put aside while we assess the merits of the subjects covered by spiritual science. What is normal to personalities in another dimension may be totally inexplicable to us in our physical world. For example, some of the team's communicators had great difficulty in explaining how their world appeared to them.

On one occasion however, a team member tried hard to explain to the group how this type of photographic phenomenon was made possible. There was much similarity with the form of communication in which a human experimenter, in an altered state of consciousness, is used as an instrument with which the team communicator can 'merge' his own psyche. But, in the case of these photographs, the images, which were actually thought patterns in energy form, were merged with the energy in the room. The communicating members of the team often had prior knowledge of what images their colleagues in spirit intended to transmit onto the films. From what was said, the group believe that members of the team were influencing the process with their thoughts in some way.

The pictures referred to here are those that were received during the series of early experiments. The three sessions that produced them gave the group first eleven photographs, then three, then twenty-two. These images on photographic films constituted tangible evidence that could be taken away from the cellar and examined. One shows a street scene, perhaps in some European city. When the group studied this picture for a while, they noticed a Singer sewing machine just visible above a shop doorway sign. They felt there was a strange familiarity about this busy street, wherever it was. The sun is shining in the picture. Perhaps it represents a happy personal memory of the team communicator who was projecting it. If this is the case, it may be that some of those pictures were more than just attempts to demonstrate that this form of communication between the dimensions is possible. The communication is a wonderful thing in itself, but the images could also offer glimpses into the surviving personalities' thoughts, thus enabling them to share with us some of their own personal recollections.

As already mentioned, the group's research had uncovered the fact that the image of St Paul's was from a famous picture taken one night during the Blitz. This picture appeared on their film twice, the other shot being a closer view, but unfortunately not so clear as the first. The group tried to come up with explanations for the pictures. It could be that St Paul's during the Blitz is either a memory of St Paul's cathedral or a memory of the City of London during this period. It could even represent a memory of seeing that actual photograph when it was first published all those years ago. The group is not suggesting that all of these photographs represent the memories of surviving personalities, but they feel that some of them might be.

The picture of Notre Dame is not very clear, but the River Seine can be seen winding through Paris below. This image is one of the black-and-white pictures that have rainbow colours in the background. In this case, the colours appear in the sky behind the cathedral, giving a striking contrast between the detail and the background. As yet, the group and the specialists they consulted are unable to explain how, or why, this occurred.

The spirit team explained that, in these early experiments, the great majority of the images received were actually copies of photographs or printed material that already existed somewhere in the world. Later pictures would not be the same at all.

From April 1994, the sessions were notably devoid of photographic phenomena. When questioned about this, the team said that they were now concentrating on developing other phenomena, adding that they would come back to the photographs later. The group felt somewhat disappointed about this, but have since had time to reflect however and believe that it was 'probably a good thing':

> When we asked the team questions they often said we would be told things on a need-to-know basis. We came to the conclusion that this was probably a good thing. If we had been told what was planned for a year's time, we might have got ahead of ourselves and set the work back. Our thought processes were very important to the work apparently. The same was true of visitors. We came to trust the team completely and were guided by them every step of the way.
>
> One of the really interesting things about the photographic and other messages, of course, was that many of them were puzzles. Through means such as this book, the scientific report which has been compiled, the national media and our lectures and slide-show presentations around the world, we are hoping to invite members of the public, historians and other academics to have a go at solving some of these riddles that the spirit world has posed. While the work was always very serious, the spirit team seemed to be playing with us on one level, albeit very gently and in a spirit of love. And, since the communications were increasing rapidly in number and complexity towards the end of our five-year experiment at Scole, we began to think that these puzzles might keep even the brightest investigators occupied for years to come. The spirit world really did seem to be well on the way to fulfilling its promise of supplying convincing proof that we all survive physical death and live on in another dimension.

A PERIOD OF PROGRESS

In order to provide incontrovertible evidence of survival for the whole world, the spirit team planned a 'period of progress' between the beginning of April 1994 and the end of September 1995. The progress would be achieved in various ways. One part of the plan was that first a single visitor and then many visitors would be invited to sessions. A second was that the work would be taken out of the cellar, for demonstration to a variety of audiences, initially at home, but later abroad. A third was that a bulletin would be published to collate and disseminate information to a world-wide audience. The fourth was that men and women of science and letters would be invited to investigate the phenomena and report on their experiences to the world. This would give the work greater credibility. All this indicated to the group that the team was going to follow its own agenda, irrespective of what the human participants might have wished to happen. As it turned out, most of what the team said was planned came to fruition.

This, then, was what was to come. Returning to 4 April 1994, Manu came through to state that there was a 'plentiful reservoir of energy' available that evening. He suggested that there would be good work done that night. As he finished speaking, all of the objects normally used for levitation were thrown to the corners of the room by the spirit people. It seemed that the team was making more room for the activity that was planned.

Patrick then spoke, saying that the spirit team had made great strides forward in the development of the phenomena thus far. What the team had originally believed would take months, or even years, had actually happened in just a few weeks. Then the temperature plummeted, signalling the arrival of an impressive personality called Abraham, who said:

> *Like Paxton, I am a member of the Council of Communion. As you have been told, we are very pleased with the development to date. We have achieved almost all of our original objectives. There are a few more things to do, then it will be time to invite our first visitor.*

This was the major revelation of the evening. Over tea upstairs in the lounge, the debriefing session was about little else. At last, they were going to be able to show these important happenings to others. Who would be the first visitor?

On 11 April 1994, however, Patrick said there had been a few problems stabilising the energies for the next period of progress. He went on to request that, from the next meeting onwards, four of the seven sitters should exchange places diagonally across the group 'to give a better balance of the available energies'.

The following week the group changed places across the table as they had been asked. It soon became apparent that this session was very different from those that had gone before. This was confirmed when the group was told that the new positions created an extra 'wave' of energy, which would considerably help the development of the phenomena. There were lots of touches by 'hands' as before, but then there were also touches by what felt like solid 'tassels' being dragged across hands, legs, faces and heads. These 'felt initially like strands of rubber or PVC but, as the evening progressed, the substance seemed to become more refined, so that it finally resembled a softer, silky material.'

The various lights landed on the luminous tabs on top of the table, as if attracted to them 'like moths to a light bulb'. The whole cellar was lit up by this light show: ceiling, walls, floor... and sitters too. Alan's knees were continuously lit for several minutes, while other phenomena occurred simultaneously all around the room.

For a short while, the lights illuminated the surface of the table. The spirit team then said they were going to demonstrate their control over physical apparatus. With that, the tape recorder, running on mains electricity, was turned on and off several times at the wall socket. The group was highly amused as the red light on the extension lead flashed on and off. They could all hear the switch at the wall-socket being flicked.

Sessions were now extended to an average of two and a half hours. The energies seemed to be changing considerably. The next meeting, on Monday 25 April 1994, proved to be a real milestone because it was on this occasion that the group had their first contact with Mrs Bradshaw. At the beginning of the relationship, Mrs Bradshaw struck them as a very refined, but slightly severe lady from the upper classes. Her diction, in the best 'Oxford English', was clear and precise, and she showed very little humour. Her manner was exact and respectful at all times, albeit initially rather cold. The group later learned that, in her lifetime, she had mainly been involved in charity work with poverty-stricken people. Since she still had relatives living, Mrs Bradshaw was reluctant to give too much personal information about herself. The group did not know at first that she was called Emily – but would not have dared to call her by her first name anyway in those early days. Mrs Bradshaw it was – and so it remained for almost two years more.

It was obvious from the beginning that one of Mrs Bradshaw's main tasks was to bring accurate personal evidence of survival to the group. She began to do this straight away on 25 April, providing personal facts regarding Robin and Sandra's relatives that were at that time unknown to either of the two mediums. Robin was told that his mother was present but too emotional to speak for herself. Mrs Bradshaw correctly gave her name as Constance, and correctly stated that she had passed to spirit eight years previously. Through Mrs Bradshaw, Robin's mother also communicated the fact that she had been somewhat of a burden on his father towards the end of her life. This was true, but Robin was pleased to learn that his mother was now looking after his father in the spirit world. His father was also present. Mrs Bradshaw accurately relayed his Christian names – Hubert Stevenson – and that he had passed to spirit not long after his wife, in 1987.

DOMES AND OTHER EXPERIMENTS

A few weeks later, at the session of 16 May 1994, the team asked the group to remove all the experimental objects from the room, including any cameras, the pad and pencil, and all the levitation objects. Only the table itself was required from now on. Its four luminous tabs would give the group a visual reference point during their meetings. Patrick also explained that, *'Ideally, there should be no recording equipment in the cellar, as all electrical equipment gives the team problems. But we do understand that you need to record the sessions. So could we ask you to use only one recording machine and ensure that it is one which emits no light whatsoever?'*

It was obvious to the group that the team was embarking on a very different path. As if to confirm this, Patrick made a somewhat unusual request: *'Please provide a glass dome for future experiments, with a wooden base. This dome will be used to store energy. It should be of a size that would hold a stuffed parrot!'* The team explained that the dome would enable special energies to be built up and maintained for more complicated experiments.

The first dome the group acquired was considered *'a little too small'* by the team. A larger dome with a wooden base was then found. The team approved. They asked the group to make a small hole in the centre of the base to allow surplus energy to be released. The dome was placed on the central table and experiments using the energy stored in it got underway.

At the time of the early dome experiments, others were taking place simultaneously and still others being planned. The group and team regularly discussed their ideas. One team member wanted the group to provide a sheet of plate glass about six inches square. He intended to imprint his image permanently on to it.

The group was also told that the team wanted to conduct an experiment to provide lighting in the cellar. They needed two separate free-standing blocks of wood, each with a slot along the top, into which a metal plate, six inches square, was to be inserted. To each metal plate, a wire was to be attached, leading to one of the two terminals on a bayonet-style bulb holder. A light bulb with normal filament was to be placed in the bulb holder, and covered by a series of light filters, which the team would specify. The blocks of wood, holding the metal plates, were to be placed some distance apart. It was the team's intention to light the bulb using the special creative energy formed at the start of each session.

The session of 23 May 1994 was a lively one. Bang! A loud noise on the central table made the group all jump out of their skins. It was clear that something had just arrived in style.

'The object then fell on to my foot,' recounts Robin. 'Whatever it was, it was heavy!' Manu came through, slightly amused, to say that the gift came from a long way away. He instructed Robin to pick it up and feel the heat within it. Robin did this and from the feel of it got the impression that it was a large crystal cluster. It was still very warm to the touch, although he could not describe it as hot. When the group examined the object later, it proved to be a large and beautiful cluster of amethyst crystals, bigger than a man's fist. They speculated that if it came from a place on Earth, the likelihood was that it originated in Brazil or another area of South America. Robin says that the warmth of the crystal cluster confirmed something he had always wondered: that a large amount of heat is involved in the process of apportation.

On 20 June 1994, the temperature plummeted soon after the start of the session, heralding the arrival of Paxton. He said that the instructions necessary for the group to forge ahead would be starting soon. The group would also receive guidance about helping others to achieve similar results. The work would be split into several sections, with each being further sub-divided. Later the spirit team dictated a detailed set of instructions, which were incorporated by the group into *A Basic Guide* booklet for other groups to use.

At this time, the group did not think that it would be possible to demonstrate the phenomena to audiences, as it seemed too soon. However, the team reassured them that there would shortly be demonstrations of the new energy-based physical paranormal phenomena around the world. Practice sessions would be necessary, however, to get used to working outside the cellar.

In preparation for the first public demonstration, planned for Felixstowe, in Suffolk, the group held a session in the ground-floor library at Scole, at the team's request, on Friday 23 September 1994.

The group did not know what to expect, or indeed whether any phenomena could be achieved away from the cellar. But they were not disappointed. Again, Manu came through his medium, Diana, at the start of the fourth tune, 'Sleepy Shores'. He said that, from the next session onwards, it would be possible to omit one of the first three tunes, so that 'Sleepy Shores' would become the third. This would allow him to manifest earlier, and save time. The intention was that when visitors came to the group, Manu's communications would be briefer than those the group had become accustomed to. He would, however, continue to be the first communicator at each session.

Raji addressed the group briefly on how the team would soon be returning to their experiments with spirit photography. He said that now, instead of copies of existing photographs, the group would be receiving original images. Many of these images would be of the spiritual dimensions themselves. The team would be attempting to impress images onto films simply left on the central table during sessions. Therefore, they would not require a camera.

Patrick then broke into the conversation to inform the group that initially, for the best results, the spirit team needed the films to be flat. He asked whether the group could try different ways of providing flat films, for the team to experiment with. It is worth noting that the team and the group were both often unsure as to how to approach each experiment. As we have said, the team certainly did not display any sort of 'all-knowing' capabilities. While the film discussions were going on, Mrs Bradshaw asked for the proceedings to be halted for a moment and suggested that the group concentrate on the centre of the table. They did as asked. Immediately, a number of spirit lights started to manifest, continuing for the rest of the session and performing wonderful aerobatics. A new pendulum movement was displayed, with lights swinging across the group. Group members were repeatedly touched by the lights, as well as by solid energy structures and unseen fingers. Ken was almost pushed off his chair. Raps, taps and noises came from all parts of the room, including the bookshelves and lampshades. This 'dry run' in the library had proved to be a success.

Back in the cellar for the next session, the group experienced a similar display of spirit lights and raps, as well as the familiar ringing of bells to herald the arrival of Patrick. One spectacular light literally hovered at ceiling level until hornpipe and jig music began playing on the audio-tape. Then it gave a visual display, at one stage splitting into two before performing an audible and visible tap dance on the table and following this with 'flea hops' across the floor, all in perfect time with the music.

The group stretched a 35mm film roll out along a board in the darkness. They also put out a couple of the square instant-type flat Polaroid films. Most people are familiar with these. There are ten of them in a cassette and each individual film has a sachet of developing chemicals inside which is squashed, releasing the chemicals, when the film goes through the Polaroid camera's rollers. Obviously, since the films had merely been removed from the cassette and placed on the table, a way had to be found to develop them after the session.

'We tried – quite unsuccessfully – to develop them by bashing them with a rolling pin,' explained Alan. 'It was very early days with the film work, and we were not able to achieve any positive results with either the rolls or the square Polaroids at this time.'

However, progress was made in other directions. During the next session, there was a soft plop on the central table as Manu was speaking to the group. Mrs Bradshaw explained that the famous physical medium, Helen Duncan, was there that evening, and wanted to wish the group luck with their public launch. She was, however, unable to speak to them directly because she was used to the more traditional type of mediumship, but in order to prove her identity, she had brought them something 'from an unhappy time in her life'.

After the session, the group discovered that this was, in fact, an apport: a copy of the *Daily Mail,* dated Saturday 1 April 1944. Like the earlier newspaper apport, this was an authentic newspaper from wartime Britain in almost mint condition (apart from folds), with no sign of the yellowing that would have been expected from the impurities in the fifty-year-old newsprint. (Much later a piece of this newspaper was sent off by investigators to be analysed by the Paper Industry Research Association. It was tested and found to be genuine wartime paper.) The newspaper's lead story was an account of the guilty verdict that had been pronounced at Helen Duncan's trial, under the Witchcraft Act, in 1944. She had been sent to prison. It is now widely believed that this was orchestrated by the intelligence services to prevent any official secrets from being revealed by materialised spirit beings at her séances. It was, after all, just prior to the D-Day landings.

Despite these developments in other phenomena, there was still considerable emphasis on the photographic films at this time. At a subsequent session, the group put out a 35mm film roll that was still in its factory-sealed tub. After a while, Raji said that the team had been able to get 'inside' the tub, and it would therefore no longer be necessary for the group to stretch films out and secure them on a board. Two instant Polaroid films had also been placed on the table, face down, during the session. The group were able to develop them afterwards, having now thought of placing the films back in the cassette and running them through the rollers of a Polaroid camera with its lens blacked out. Though no clear images were produced, the group felt that there was definite evidence that the spirit team had influenced the films, for shapes appeared on them that should not, logically, have been there, as they had not been exposed to any form of light. Also, this type of spiritual photography was very evidential because there were no negatives with which the group could have been accused of tampering.

FIRST VISITORS

It was now time to invite visitors. The first visitor was Bill Lyons, known to the Foys because of his interest in mediumship. He attended a session on 4 October 1994.

During the evening with the first visitor present, Raji said that the team thought they had had some success with the photography and that the group should develop the film. Usually, the group did not develop the films unless they were told to, as this was an expensive and futile exercise. The faces of the staff at the processing firm were apparently a real picture when they were handed 35mm films, still factory-sealed in their original containers, and asked to process them. When the films showed positive results, the technicians were even more baffled.

Once developed, the latest sealed 35mm film roll appeared to be mainly green along its entire length, apart from one image, which was a shape consisting of three different shades of red. The group thought this was an interesting result because the film had not been exposed to light, so should have simply been black all over when developed.

The group had also put out two instant Polaroid films on the table, which they then ran through their 'blacked-out' Polaroid camera to develop them. Like the 35mm film, the instant Polaroids had not had any interaction with light, but, nevertheless, one showed a yellow expanse of colour all over it. The second also had a yellow background, but contained a green rectangular image in its centre. The group concluded that there was no doubt that the spirit team had been able to affect all three films used in that session in a paranormal way.

Soon after this first visitor session, two people were invited, then six, then many more. The number of visitors was increased on the instructions of the spirit team. This was so that the team could prepare for their public debut, the seminar organised by Bill Lyons for forty or so people in Felixstowe. The team needed to work up gradually to creating the phenomena with the energies of such a large number of people. Each of the visitor sessions was successful and this gave the team and the group confidence for the forthcoming public demonstration.

PERSPECTIVES

JENNIFER JONES

A group of fifteen people gathered at Scole. Nine of us had been invited as an experiment to see if it were possible to re-create the phenomena which the Scole group had been able to establish in its closed circle over the previous two years. Would the spirit world be able to blend the energies of the whole group sufficiently well to allow some physical phenomena to take place?

We were shown our places in the cellar before the lights were switched off and we were plunged into pitch blackness.

On the table were a lump of quartz crystal and a Pyrex glass dish in which a ping-pong ball, with fluorescent tab, had been placed.

In what seemed like a very short time, Manu came through and spoke to us, followed shortly afterwards by Mrs Bradshaw and Patrick. They kept things very light-hearted and explained a little bit of what they would try to do. Joseph also came through and introduced himself briefly.

Then a streak of light flashed across the room. This was followed by another shaft and then another. A little light, which was smaller in diameter than a 5p piece and which appeared to have a mind and almost a personality of its own, whizzed around the room, making patterns and beaming a ray like a torch. It appeared, at close quarters, to resemble the shape of a cat's eye. It moved inside the glass dish, moving round it slowly and lighting it up. There was also a strange voice from the middle of the room. This voice was not coming from either of the mediums. Robin said that this was an 'energy voice'.

Several of us mentioned that we felt something touch us and I said that mentally I had been asking for the little light to come into my hands, which were resting, palms up, on my lap. Within seconds I let out an involuntary scream, as something resembling a tiny bumble bee leapt into my hand... and leapt out again. I felt as if I had been pinched.

The energy voice was heard again, quickly followed by another scream from me. 'It's rather like an electric shock,' I laughed.

The energy voice spoke then. *'Static. It's static.'*

'It doesn't hurt,' I said. 'It's just very strange.'

At this point we could all see the light move into the crystal on the table and, as it lit up, we distinctly saw it lifted into the air, apparently carried by some fingers which were clearly visible. The ping-pong ball in the glass dish also levitated right up to the ceiling before being dropped. It bounced on to the floor by my feet.

There was a sound of something falling onto the table

and there was some discussion about whether it might be an apport. There was quite a lot of activity now and those in the room could feel people moving around or breezes on their faces. Mrs Bradshaw asked: *'You don't mind if we pass among you, do you?'*

Mrs Bradshaw and Joseph then started chatting, beginning to draw things to a close. They thanked us for allowing them to experiment and talked about life in the spirit world. Joseph said it was silly to think death was the end of life; it was really just going home. He said:

It's much more 'real', more 'home', than where you are now. Our spirit selves are really travellers and the point at which you are now is the place to which you have decided to travel.

What you have experienced this evening is very new, very different. In time there will be a wealth of phenomena and it will continue to grow. We want to awaken in all mankind the truth and help people find it in their own way; to awaken the desire to question; to look deep within themselves. There they will find something wonderful: the spiritual self. No one else can do it for you. These energies will help you to find the truth. Not just the energies here, but the energies coming to the Earth at this time.

There is a tremendous amount of new energy, not only in the physical way, but also in a truly spiritual sense. Love is the key word. Love makes things happen. Love is a very creative thing. True spirit energy is a creative force.

When the lights came on at the end of the session, there was a postcard of the saucy seaside variety lying on the table, which had obviously been apported, and this bore the legend: 'If living, please write – if dead, don't bother!'

There were no fewer than thirty-nine participants at the first public demonstration, on Friday 4 November 1995, including the seven people in the Scole group. The visitors were generally enthusiastic and responded positively to the 'double-act' performed by Mrs Bradshaw and Patrick. Visitors reported seeing many dancing lights and Mrs Bradshaw delivered several evidential messages. One light repeatedly passed *through* a Pyrex bowl which was standing on the table. It then passed down through the table before emerging up through it. Those attending were certainly not disappointed and this gave both the group and the team even more confidence that they could travel further afield with demonstrations. There was another interesting development, as Robin recalls:

> We also received more 'coloured energy' images on the flat instant Polaroid films we used at Felixstowe. For some time we had wondered if Polaroid themselves could give us any normal and rational explanations for the results we had been obtaining on their films. We also thought they might be interested in the images, as these had occurred under what might seem like impossible circumstances. It turned out that they were interested. They told us that, as well as instant films in the cassettes, they also manufactured 35mm film rolls which could be developed at home using a special machine and developing chemicals.

The group quickly acquired such a processor, so that, if the team felt they had influenced a film, it could be developed at Scole immediately.

Another visitor to Scole during the early period of progress was Dr Kurt Hoffman, who studied philosophy and psychology at Basle and Munich universities before gaining a PhD at Harvard. He is a member of the Society for Psychical Research and the Scientific and Medical Network – an informal international group consisting mainly of qualified doctors, scientists, engineers, philosophers, therapists and psychologists. The aim of the Network is to deepen understanding in science, medicine and education by fostering both rational and intuitive insights.

Dr Hoffman was an executive with Bavarian radio and TV for

twenty years and has been an independent TV producer since 1982. He has produced thirty-two documentaries in the fields of science and religion for British (Channel 4), German, and Austrian television companies.

PERSPECTIVES

DR KURT HOFFMAN

After the preliminaries – Robin's introductory talk and the slide show – Alfred Perry (who had come for the day from Virginia) and I inspected the cellar thoroughly. Then the remainder of the group came in and all took their assigned seats.

The build-up of the necessary energy took some time, during which we were entertained by the caustic wit and light-hearted charm of 'Emily Bradshaw' from the other side. Then, clearly audible, the overture: the jangling of the cowbells on the luminous string over the table.

At the same time I felt several 'swishings' of cold air across my forehead, accompanied by a cold draught. After this 'ringing in' there were diverse, discreet drumming noises while the first unseen protagonist entered the scene: I felt the probing fingers of what I took to be the hand of a little girl of about three or four years old shyly exploring my right knee and thigh. 'She' then moved on to Ellinor on my right, as if to convince her that I had not fantasised, and then on to Alfred, whose wristwatch came in for special attention.

Next on the programme were the fireworks performed, first by one, then by several, orange-yellow points no larger than fireflies. What struck me was the great variety and ever increasing inventiveness of the displays. There was a flywheel gyrating at great speed on several changing planes, a circle as well as a semi-circle held in place against all natural laws. And the climax: a number of spirals, none quite like the other, all ending in a flame-like upward reach and dissolution at the ceiling. The thought came to my mind that these 'intelligent' formations might hold the key to the still unsolved mystery of the crop formations [crop circles].

The last part of the sitting was devoted to a conversation between the two realms. 'Emily Bradshaw' asked for several delegates by name (or their home towns) in order to pass on messages or to give encouragement in difficult private situations.

'Edwin' tried to answer Alfred Perry's very specific question about new energies that might become available to man after the exhaustion of fossil fuels to be expected in about twenty years' time. A team of scientists on the other side was consulted by 'Edwin', who then referred to the amplification of low voltage electricity as one of several yet to be discovered sources of power.

Robin Foy had placed an empty tape recorder on the north side of the table, from which cracking noises came throughout the sitting until it was audibly shoved from its original position. When the lights finally came on again after the two-hour session (to most of us it seemed it had lasted no longer than about thirty to forty minutes) we were all in for a last surprise. The tape recorder was now seen at the other (south) side of the table, with the four batteries piled up neatly and in appropriate order some distance from it.

Ellinor and I were not alone in feeling the strong uplifting energy that supported the entire sitting and stayed with us for hours after this remarkable event came to a close.

As mentioned earlier, the spirit team had proposed a four-part plan to progress the work. One element of this plan was the chronicling of developments in a bulletin format. By winter 1994, the first issue of the new bulletin, *Spiritual Scientist,* was able to report on the further successes with the photographs. Also, various objects had been apported into the large dome during experimental sessions. There had been loud discharges of energy from within both domes, accompanied by 'sparks of light' and sounds 'resembling the tearing of material'.

On Friday 13 January 1995, the team attempted to transmit an image onto a factory-sealed, 35mm Polaroid 'Polapan' black-and-white instant slide film. They thought there had been a successful transmission, so the film was developed using the special Polaroid instant slide-processing machine. As predicted, an image had been transmitted onto the film. This was a clearly written verse in what they later discovered to be Romanised Sanskrit (see Plates 8 and 9). Diana explained:

> We had no idea what this language was in actual fact until, at a later session, we were told that this particular verse came from the book known as the *Srimad Bhagavatam*. This is a very ancient book of sacred Hindu texts, originally written in ordinary Sanskrit. About thirty-five years ago it was translated into Romanised Sanskrit for the first time by a Krishna devotee, and then published by the International Society for Krishna Consciousness in that form, which is the way we received it on the film.
>
> At this point, we had no idea as to where to find this book, or its more modern translation. Clairvoyantly, I received a message to 'Go to the Oxfam shop.' So I went and was amazed to find a copy of just one of its eighteen volumes on the shelf. It just so happened that this was the *very* volume that we needed, and it contained a full translation of the photographic verse of the *Bhagavatam* we had received.

In the volume Diana found, the preface states:

> Material science has tried to find the ultimate source of creation very insufficiently, but it is a fact that there is one ultimate source of everything. *Srimad Bhagavatam* is the transcendental science not only

for knowing the ultimate source of everything but also for knowing our relation with HIM and our duty toward perfection of the human society on the basis of this knowledge.

The original verse on the photograph reads:

> *yad atra kriyate karma*
> *bhagavat – paritosanam*
> *jnanam yat tad adhinam hi*
> *bhakti – yoga – samanvitam*

The translation of this verse is as follows:

Whatever work is done here in this life for the satisfaction of the mission of the Lord is called *bhakti-yoga,* or transcendental loving service to the Lord, and what is called knowledge becomes a concomitant factor.

A fuller explanation following the text goes on to say that when work is performed to satisfy God, the performer becomes gradually purified. This purification means attainment of spiritual knowledge. Therefore knowledge is dependent on karma, or work done on behalf of God.

'This was truly an inspiring work,' said Diana. 'We were so grateful to our spirit team for bringing us such an illuminating text, so that we, in turn, could share it with others. After all, that was what the work done during the Scole Experiment was all about – sharing spiritual science with the world.' Diana concluded with a point we might all ponder on. She wondered how the spirit team was able to transmit this interesting text, in a clearly 'hand-written' format, onto the film.

Alan explained another image that had at first puzzled the group. This was a diagram of an unusual device, which looked almost like an aqualung with pistons. The image appeared to be a page from a scientist's notes, as it also contained faint writing, which was too blurred to read. Initially, the group had no idea what this drawing represented. However, by discussing the matter with a number of scientists with whom they were in correspondence, they did eventually learn that this was, in fact, a drawing of an early electrical cell, known as a Western Standard Cell. This may well have been a piece of standard laboratory apparatus with which the spirit scientists within the team at Scole were very familiar during their lifetimes. Because its voltage is so constant, this same cell is still used in laboratories today, for the purposes of calibration.

Visitors from Polaroid were due to attend a session. Raji said that the team would like the visitors to be offered the opportunity to fully examine the room. He said the group members should also submit to being searched prior to the experimental session. In addition, he referred to the picture of a good-looking young man that had been received at the previous session. The group was told that this gentleman was a member of the spirit team and that he 'had a big heart' for helping others. His name was Kingsley Fairbridge, and he had been born in South Africa, educated at Oxford and had then moved to Australia, where he had set up Fairbridge Farm Schools, teaching underprivileged children a trade. His health had not been robust, and he had died young from cancer. The group had never heard the name before, and made a great effort to try and find out more details about this man. Initial investigations proved fruitless. In frustration, they published the man's name and the details they had been given in the new bulletin, asking subscribers to help.

One of the subscribers was a crop-spraying pilot in California, USA, and he had a female friend in Australia, to whom he passed on his copy of *Spiritual Scientist*. It came as a complete surprise that this friend knew Kingsley Fairbridge's daughter, who was still living in Australia. The daughter subsequently wrote to the Scole group, and they sent her a copy of the photograph they had received, together with the information they had been given about her father. The daughter confirmed the accuracy of details and also commented that the photograph was a good likeness of her father.

From this point onwards, much more was accomplished with the photographs. Experiments with Polaroid films had been very successful to date, in that transmissions had been received on four types of film:

- Polaroid 600 Plus (flat instant films used in the Polaroid cameras everyone is familiar with)
- Polapan 35mm (slide films, black and white – ISO 125)
- Polagraph 35mm (slide films, blue and white – ISO 400)
- Polachrome 35mm (slide films, colour – ISO 40)

The 35mm films were supplied with a disposable cartridge of chemicals so that they could be developed using the Polaroid processor and then turned into individual slides in a Polaroid slide-making machine. This equipment enabled the group to quickly find out whether transmissions had been successful. If so, they could create the slides themselves for showing to audiences.

With the instant Polaroids, a diverse set of images had been received. The first included star clusters and a good portrait of Sir Arthur Conan Doyle, (see Plate 10), who was a serious investigator of the paranormal. Another showed three French airmen from the First World War standing in front of their aeroplane. There was also the title page from a piece of sheet music, which the team explained was meant to convey the joy they experienced during Scole sessions. The music was entitled: 'When We're Together.'

Some of these images posed more questions for the group and they invited readers of *Spiritual Scientist* to assist in answering them. For example, they had tried in vain to track down the composer of the music and had absolutely no idea who the airmen were or why these men should be on the transmissions. In another instance, the signature of the composer Ivor Novello was printed on a film. This image proved to be the *same* as Novello's signature.

Other pictures resembled underwater seascapes containing what looked like some sort of life. The detail in these pictures is outstanding, showing minute feather-like tentacles and coral-type structures (see Plate 11). The spirit team had previously told the group that they would be showing them pictures from their side of life and so the group therefore wondered if these images could be from some other plane of existence, where plants and other forms of life might be found.

The team also transmitted 'something very different' on the 35mm rolls of film. One film was colour, the other black and white. On the colour film, the images resembled distant galaxies, although they contained abstract features and the group thought this 'reduced the possibility that they were from our known universe'. The team said that they depicted 'areas of existence'. On the black-and-white film, there were easily distinguishable faces amongst a 'mass of splodges'. One image showed a young woman's smiling face mirrored along the plane of the top of the head. Another showed a man's face, with a chunk missing. Parts of other faces were also visible amongst the splodges (see Plates 12 and 13).

The group learned that the communicators were part of a spirit 'photographic department' and that this department was a specialist part of the team. This was the team's own description. It intrigued the group that the spirit people had organised themselves into specialist divisions. The group also learned that the members of the photographic department were sending their own thoughts as 'transmissions', with the intention of 'influencing' the films to achieve the face images. The team explained that 'some images are very personal to the communicators involved in the experiments, especially when faces are manifested'. Some transmissions had been more successful than others; the splodges could now be understood as 'failed attempts'.

In early April 1995, the team decided to focus most of its efforts on dome experiments. Much of the creative energy gathered together during sessions was to be concentrated in the larger dome. The team soon asked that the smaller dome be removed from the cellar. A light with a blue hue was produced within the dome. Unfortunately this was not particularly bright, certainly not enough for the group members to see one another clearly. The team scientists explained that it would take a number of sessions to gradually build up the charge of energy within the dome and that no-one should touch – or even come within one foot of – the dome between experiments. This was to avoid a 'premature discharge of energy', which could set the team back by several weeks.

In searching for rational explanations as to why a dome should be used in these experiments, the group consulted specialists in our own dimension. Scientists suggested that the dome might behave like a Leyden Jar, the earliest form of capacitor, in that it might store up the energy generated within the cellar and thus remain charged for some time. Such energy could be discharged through a body to earth if somebody were to touch the dome. It was also suggested that domes are efficient at energy storage because the dome shape encloses the greatest amount of volume relative to its surface area.

By mid-April 1995, the dome was lighting up like a giant light bulb. There were two tiny bright points inside the top of it and what appeared to be their reflection at the bottom. The group was told by the team that the illumination was brought about by the passage of spiritual energy between these two points. The top of the dome seemed to act as a lens, which projected a disc of light, about three feet in diameter, onto the ceiling. This experiment lasted thirteen minutes. A spirit scientist told the group that this was the first of many such experiments and that the light would become more intense and last longer in the weeks to come.

'We could hear the emotion in the voice of this scientist,' reported the group. 'He was clearly thrilled with the success of the experiment. For a brief moment, as he mentioned the words "more intense", the light in the dome became visibly brighter.'

The scientist then said that it was the team's intention to illuminate the whole of the room in this way, so that all proceedings could be clearly observed in future. A short while later, the team said they had now found a way to recycle the energy in the dome, thus dispensing with the need to build up the energy within it over a period of time. At the end of April, the team was able to light up the dome for a period of fifty-two minutes. The spirit scientist who explained this said that the team would continue to experiment with the lighting until they had achieved the optimum effect.

The group said there was then a further change in the lights. They became red and varied in type. The first was a very thin 'pencil beam', which shone from underneath the dome and illuminated the surface of the table. The second was tubular, about an inch in diameter, four inches long and slightly curved. This was stationary at the top of the dome and resembled a neon light. While this tubular light was shining, there appeared to be a dense smoky haze within the dome. A smoke ring appeared just above the dome, which was visible for a split second as the area was momentarily lit up by a flash of bright red light. A slight burning smell accompanied this phenomenon. A third type of red light took the form of numerous patches which each flashed on and off, for a second at a time, all around the room. At one point, it looked as though definite attempts were being made, with this lighting, to illuminate one of the solid spirit beings in the corner. However, these attempts were not successful as the team seemed unable to sustain the patches for long enough.

Then another pencil beam appeared, emanating from a bright source at the top of the dome. It started to rotate, shining a strong beam all around the room, creating a lighthouse effect. Each time the beam shone on a face, it paused for a few seconds and lit up the features brightly enough for others to see. The light was so bright that it dazzled each of the group members in turn. It was like looking directly at a red sun. The team explained that these were 'spiritual lights' and it was only with this type of lighting that visiting solid spirit beings could be seen. Any form of physical lighting which we have on Earth would be detrimental to them and they would not be able to sustain their physical presence in our environment.

Other things happened during the period of the early 'light and dome' experiments. First, the group made some changes to the base of the dome. They placed the flat wooden base on a clear Perspex platform. This was then set on Perspex supporting legs, each about one inch in diameter. The aim was to enable a clear view of the base of the dome and the space between it and the table surface. A number of times during the dome experiments, the lights would enter the plastic legs and illuminate them.

Early on during the experiments, the group began taking photographs of the lights as they appeared both inside and outside the dome. They also managed to photograph the red light within a semi-opaque sealed Tupperware tub. This was illuminated 'almost as brightly as a table lamp'.

Having already experimented with the blue and then red lights, the team introduced yellow and green at the end of May 1995. There were three or four flashes of a brilliant yellow light before a green light established itself in the legs of the dome stand.

The green light was developed further at subsequent sessions. Its source appeared to be a small solid crystal sitting inside the dome on the base. The group assumed that this must be an apport but were told that while the crystal appeared solid, it was in fact not so. The team said that they were using crystal energy to produce the greenish light. What was being witnessed was the 'spiritual essence' of a crystal, brought specially for the purpose. The overall effect was similar to limelight. It was not very bright and the team told the group that it would not produce beams, but during the evening, it gradually became bright enough so that the group members could vaguely see one another. During experiments in June 1995, the green light was sustained within the dome for 112 minutes and a yellow light, which travelled all around the group, appeared intermittently, giving a sheet lightning effect.

SOLID SPIRIT BEINGS

By early summer 1995, the group was becoming aware of solid spirit beings walking and shuffling around the room during sessions. These visitors found spare chairs at the perimeter of the cellar and could be heard dragging them across the floor. A few members of the spirit team then sat with the group at the table. The fabric of their clothes could be felt as they moved in front of each member in turn and the luminous tabs on the table disappeared and then reappeared as the forms of the visitors momentarily obliterated them.

Manu said that there were problems manifesting physically at first because the spirits were 'familiarising themselves with the process of teleportation and stabilisation of the resultant high-density spirit bodies on a sustained basis'. This needed a great deal of practice if it was to be achieved regularly at will.

Further dialogue with the spirit team at these sessions revealed more about the visitors. They were 'volunteers who were dedicated to their task of achieving solid form for reasonable periods of time'. Apparently this was very difficult to accomplish. They were also 'acclimatising themselves to the physical environment of the cellar in readiness for further experiments'.

One of these experiments involved using the brighter of the red lights emanating from the dome on the central table. These bright lights served as background illumination, against which solid spirit beings were able to show the group their animated fingers, hands and arms. As well as the lights emanating from the dome, individual red lights started to appear around the cellar. One solid spirit visitor actually picked up a red light, which was resting on the central table, in his hand and carried it around the table so that the group got a good view of his digits and palm. They report that the light shone *through* the hand, outlining its features quite clearly. Another solid spirit visitor picked up a red light and took it back to his seat. He sat down and moved the light around as he tried to show the group various parts of his body. On that occasion the group saw his legs, his arms and, even, briefly, his face.

The group also reported other occurrences during the red light experiments. They saw a variety of what were called 'sustained visible objects' – objects from the spirit world brought for the group to see (see Plates 30 and 31). The SVOs would build up in front of their eyes in what appeared to be a solid form. The group assumed that they were made of spirit light or creative energy. As such, they were hard to describe in earthly terms and, as we have mentioned, this led to some problems during the Scole Experiment – there was simply no established vocabulary to describe such phenomena.

One object seemed to be attached to the outside of the dome. Light appeared to be pulsating from within it and it constantly changed its size and shape. Generally, it resembled some sort of see-through crumpled material, the size and shape of a sea-urchin, divided into segments, much like an orange. The most dramatic manifestation of this period appeared both inside and on top of the dome, when energy built itself up into the shape of a delicate flower (see Plates 28 and 29).

Now and then the group asked whether they could bring a camera back in for a particular session; not for using in the experiments, but just to take pictures of what they were witnessing every week. They have a number of photographs capturing these numerous and varied phenomena.

SOLID SPIRIT VOICES

Once it became clear to the spirit team that they had been successful in their experiments with the spirit lights and the manifestation and illumination of solid spirit beings, attention was turned to experimentation with 'solid spirit voices'. If these voices could be achieved, they would enable the group to have a two-way conversation with the manifested spirit beings. The group had been frustrated prior to this, because although there had been some considerable success with 'trance', 'energy' and 'extended' voices, they could not see who was speaking. Now they could see their visitors, but no direct verbal intercourse was possible. Vocal contact from the manifested beings had previously been restricted to lip-smacking noises, whistles and perhaps the odd 'yes' or 'no' in answer to a question.

The group told us more about this phenomenon. It was not long after the team began the 'solid voice' experiments that the group heard whistling coming from the direction of one of the solid spirit visitors, who had been sitting on a specially provided chair. This whistling continued and developed into what sounded like low, murmured speech. It was incomprehensible. However, the communicator later managed to say *'Sorry'* quite clearly, in apology for his inability to do better at that time. By the end of this particular session, he turned to one of the group and, speaking just inches in front of her face, was able to say, *'Thank you for my chair.'*

Over the next few weeks the group noticed that several of the solid spirit visitors were making a great effort to practise their communication skills. Two of them, Cecil and Maurice, were able to provide their names. However, in the main, the whispered voices were not yet clear enough for the group to understand much of what was being said.

By the end of June 1995, there was a marked increase in the volume of the voices from the manifested beings, although clarity was still sadly lacking. One of the spirit scientists explained they had been trying a new method of voice production. The team reminded the group that the solid spirit visitors who were trying to speak had no human organs such as larynx or lungs, so they needed an alternative method of voice production.

The real breakthrough came in early July, when the group had several solid voice communicators speaking to them clearly for a good part of the session. The first of these, who introduced himself as John, soon cottoned on to the idea of picking up the Tupperware tub on the table and speaking into it to give his voice extra depth. This made his voice quite clear and audible. John told the group that he would tell the other communicators to do the same. As each finished speaking, the Tupperware tub fell back noisily on to the table, from where the next communicator retrieved it.

A number of team members became adept at using the solid voice technique and regularly visited the cellar to practise. Within a few sessions, the Tupperware tub became obsolete. Jimmy and Teddy soon followed John, and then Dorothy became the first female solid voice communicator to be heard and seen at the same time. One of the solid voice communicators, Leslie Davis, spoke with the same stammer he had had when on Earth.

MORE PHOTOGRAPHIC DEVELOPMENTS

There were more developments with the photography, with the team transmitting another image containing more text from the *Srimad Bhagavatam*. Once again, the experiment involved a factory-sealed, black-and-white Polaroid 35mm Polapan film and, as usual, it was developed and made into slides immediately after the session, using the slide-processing unit. The text appeared on three slides: one in the normal way, one back-to-front and the third was sideways on. The back-to-front, or mirror image was the first example of a picture 'brought' by the team in this way. Interestingly, the handwriting was totally different in every way from the earlier text – 'more primitive and rather childlike', according to the group. The text was numbered '31' (see Plates 8 and 9). The group wondered if this was a clue to the verse. Would it be from the same volume as the first text, the one Diana had found in the Oxfam shop? Sure enough, this proved to be the case. The translation reads:

> Clouds and dust are carried by the air, but less intelligent persons say that the sky is cloudy and the air is dirty. Similarly, they also implant bodily conceptions on the spirit self.

The explanation of the text continues:

> We cannot see the Lord, who is all spirit, with our material eyes and senses. Similarly, we cannot detect the spiritual spark, which exists within the material body of a living being. So we have to accept the living being's presence by the presence of his body. Some people cannot conceive of anything beyond matter, but the Lord is within and without all things.

Intriguingly, the message of the text seemed to correspond with some of the teachings the group had recently received.

These photographic images sparked off further discussion among members as to the meaning behind all the transmissions received on films during the Scole Experiment. They wondered whether some of the images that were being projected onto the films were glimpses into the lives and cultural backgrounds of the team communicators, perhaps from a time when they were themselves living on Earth. The faces, of course, invited speculation about whether they really were likenesses of people who once lived here.

The group had been told that some images related to a spiritual environment and represented what the team called 'areas of existence' and 'areas of communication', but it was stressed that these were only as perceived by the particular team member transmitting them. One of the most interesting things the group was told was that the images could not be transmitted before because the spirit team had only now found a way to convert their thought forms into images on the photographs, using the special 'creative energy' they had spoken so much about. The group commented on this:

> In our estimation, they were a tangible, repeatable way of receiving intelligible transmissions from the spirit world. Perhaps understandably, we began to think that the photographic experiments might be the best method yet devised by the spirit world to provide evidence for the survival of the human personality beyond physical death.

As it turned out, the group members were not the only people thinking along these lines at that time. Montague Keen, a man with a lifelong interest in paranormal phenomena and a member of the Society for Psychical Research (SPR) since 1946, was also taking an interest in the photographic experiments being carried out at Scole. He had been following the reports in the early issues of *Spiritual Scientist* very closely. After preliminary discussions, he and several of his SPR colleagues were invited, as individuals rather than representatives, to attend a number of experimental sessions with a view to setting up a series of scientifically controlled experiments. This would lead to a two-year investigation, which culminated in *The Scole Report.*

The first experimental session to be conducted under scientific scrutiny was arranged for 2 October 1995.

CHAPTER FIVE

SCIENTIFIC SCRUTINY

**Politics and religion are obsolete. The
time has come for science and spirituality.**
Pandit Jawaharlal Nehru

One of the most striking features of the Scole Experiment was
the group's willingness to invite stringent scientific scrutiny.
Individuals with credible academic, specialist and scientific
knowledge were welcomed to sessions. Some of these
investigators belonged to organisations such as the Society for
Psychical Research.

The Society for Psychical Research is a conservative institution,
with no collective view, dedicated to objective, scientific research.
Its ranks have included members of the government, lords, knights,
professors, doctors, and scholars from a wide variety of disciplines.
Much of its earlier work was centred on testing the 'survival
hypothesis', the proposition that the human consciousness survives
bodily death. Its methods are necessarily thorough.

Senior members of the Society attended many of the sessions
of the SEG, although it should be stressed that they did so as invited
individuals, not as official representatives of the Society. The
investigators were principally Montague Keen, an office-holder
in the Society for many years, and two past-presidents, Professor
Arthur Ellison and Professor David Fontana.

Montague Keen had begun investigating paranormal
phenomena in 1946, when he joined the Society. He was
Honorary Media Relations Officer of the Society and Secretary
and Vice-Chair of its Survival Committee. A former parliamentary
lobby correspondent, agricultural administrator, technical editor
and farmer, he was to be responsible for much of the detailed

work associated with the investigation and the preparation of *The Scole Report,* the comprehensive and scholarly account of the findings of some of the independent investigators, which we can commend to readers interested in the intricate details of the scientific investigation.

Montague had become intrigued by the Scole Experiment in 1994, when he saw the first issue of *Spiritual Scientist.* He had not heard of the group before and went along to Scole to investigate. In February 1995, he had a two-hour meeting with the group. He felt it was important to establish a rapport with them, although initially the group was cautious and a little suspicious. For his part, Montague was surprised that the Scole group actually welcomed serious open-minded investigation. This made them different from other groups he had met previously and certainly made their work more impressive. For this, and a number of other reasons, the Scole Experiment was, for him, unique:

> At the first meeting I was shown many of the fascinating photographs. My interest here was that, if genuine, they were solid physical objects with which to experiment. This would enhance the possibility of checking the circumstances in which the phenomena were produced. As an investigator, I have a duty to observe objectively and take all precautions that other researchers would expect me to take, even though I might think them unnecessary. I felt these people were genuine – and they certainly didn't have the characters of con artists. It is, of course, always advisable to be cautious, no matter how much you trust or believe in people. I made a detailed initial report for those of my colleagues who were also involved in this type of investigation. As a result we arranged for a series of six meetings, which started in October 1995.

The initial investigators were all long-established members of the

Society for Psychical Research. One was Ralph Noyes, who attended the first two experimental sessions and subsequently acted in a consultative capacity. A man described by his colleagues as a dispassionate but cautiously sceptical analyst, he had a distinguished career in the civil service as an Under-Secretary at the Ministry of Defence, where he was in charge of a department responsible for monitoring UFO reports. Investigation into this subject gradually introduced him to psychical research. At the time of the Scole investigation he was not in good physical health and at the end of the second session he attended, he announced his intention of retiring, while confirming that he was satisfied that what he had experienced at Scole was authentic.

Another key investigator was Professor Arthur Ellison, DSc (Eng), an Emeritus Professor of Electrical Engineering at City University. Professor Ellison had twice held the office of President of the Society, and took an active and senior part in several of the Society's committees. He had many years' direct experience of almost all types of physical and mental phenomena in the field of psychical research. He was also a member of the Parapsychological Association, and a Vice-President and founder-member of the Scientific and Medical Network. He had first-hand experience of the out-of-body and lucid dreaming states, and was particularly interested in altered states of consciousness, especially the possibility of human survival of bodily death.

The third main investigator was Montague Keen himself.

Towards the end of 1996, it was agreed that prominent researchers, mainly those on the Council of the Society, might be invited to attend as individuals after briefing by Montague Keen. Other SPR Council members who subsequently attended sessions were Professor Robert Morris, Professor Donald West, Professor Archie E. Roy, Professor Bernard Carr, Dr Alan Gauld, and Dr John Beloff. Two non-Council SPR members attended single sessions. They were Professor Ivor Grattan-Guinness and Dr Rupert Sheldrake. Ingrid Slack, a psychologist with the Open University, an SPR member and an experienced investigator of mediumship, attended three.

A number of other investigators, representing a wide variety of disciplines and backgrounds, also attended experimental sessions. These included Dr Ernst Senkowski, Dr Hans Schaer, Dr Kurt Hoffman, Dr Russell Targ, Dr Marilyn Schlitz, and Dr Bernard Haisch. Many of these independent researchers have wide and relevant experience of paranormal investigation.

The investigations involved individuals from organisations such as NASA, the Institute of Noetic Sciences and the Scientific and Medical Network. The work was conducted in a number of international locations, including Germany, Ireland, the Netherlands, Spain (Ibiza), Switzerland, and the USA. Here, other investigators assessed and reviewed the work, including Dr Ulf Israelsson, Dr Hans-Peter Stüder, Dr Theo Locher, Dr Andreas Liptay-Wagner, and Dr Pal Kurthy.

For some investigators, the Scole group's phenomena appeared, in many respects, to constitute the most important development ever encountered in the long effort to demonstrate the existence and permanence of the soul and the survival of human consciousness. Montague told us he considered it an opportunity not to be missed. The investigators all felt a great responsibility to look at this evidence objectively and thoroughly. They felt privileged to be given this opportunity.

The group also felt privileged to have these distinguished witnesses to some of the phenomena that occurred during the Scole Experiment. So it was that professors in such diverse fields as psychology, electrical engineering, mathematics, astronomy, physics, parapsychology, astro-physics and even criminology, all took part and contributed in some way to the investigations.

Dr Hans Schaer, a member of the SPR, had considerable experience of the Scole Experiment. A Swiss lawyer and businessman residing in Kusnacht, near Zurich, and the owner of a holiday home in the Mediterranean island of Ibiza, Dr Schaer sat with the Scole group on thirteen occasions, in both his homes, on the premises of the Parapsychological Society of Zurich in Zurich, and at Scole itself. The group were his guests for sessions in Ibiza in October 1995 and were subsequently invited back the following summer (see Plate 14).

PERSPECTIVES

DR HANS SCHAER

I am a down-to-earth person, a die-hard realist and businessman with, due to my legal studies, a very critical and analytical mind. I am not psychic. All my life it has been my intention to find out – if possible – whether there is life after physical death.

My research has involved visiting the Scole Hole on various occasions and I have participated in certain film and video tape experiments. I have personally conducted some experiments which have taken place under test conditions. I have been witness to a number of highly interesting phenomena.

I invited the Scole group to my old country house on the island of Ibiza. If they had ever faked anything within their own cellar, they had no chance whatsoever to do this in my home...

Just before one experimental sitting, I came up with the idea of asking the spirit team if they could provide 'evidence' by playing a musical instrument. The Scole group had neither the opportunity nor the time to prepare anything before the sitting began.

The result of this request was fantastic. The trumpet which I had placed on the table started playing, even though the mouthpiece was removed, and later on someone else started playing a drum solo on the wooden table, despite the fact that there were no drumsticks or other suitable objects available.

We also arranged a sitting for the group in Zurich, at the meeting-place of the Parapsychological Society. A large basement room was provided for the occasion, which was unfortunately not completely darkened. There was a higher than normally accepted number of guests present (twenty-two). Above us were about thirty apartments, all with a mixture of electrical equipment such as televisions, computers, record players, telephone lines, etc. Despite all these unfavourable circumstances, trance communications were achieved and personal messages given to some of the guests, and a number of them were touched by materialised hands.

At none of the sittings had the group the slightest opportunity to install any equipment of their own which could have been used to generate fraudulent phenomena. I can therefore guarantee that the results of the Scole group are in every respect 100 per cent genuine.

In assessing the paranormal Montague stressed that the standards of the normal are not applicable. Paranormal phenomena should be judged by paranormal standards. This is very difficult for people of a scientific bent to accept. The spirits state they aren't in a 'place' or 'time' and that is fundamentally very difficult to get across. We humans have no capacity to conceive of anything else than our familiar time and space in our physical world. This is why *physical* paranormal phenomena are so interesting to the psychical researcher: the influencing of the physical dimension by discarnate entities is a form of evidence that they do exist.

In order to support this survival hypothesis, the evidence collected during the Scole Experiment had to refute the competing explanations, which we could call the 'anti-survival hypotheses'. The first cry of sceptics is usually: 'Fraud!' To counter this, the investigators consulted a specialist in deception, psychologist Dr Richard Wiseman. In addition, the group themselves invited a member of the Magic Circle to scrutinise their work.

James Webster, a surgical chiropodist and podiatrist, is a former stage magician and member of the Magic Circle. He and his wife Shirley were invited to join the SEG, as guests, for one of their experimental sessions in October 1994.

PERSPECTIVES

JAMES WEBSTER

The experimental sitting took place in the cellar, which had a single door entrance/exit, with one centre light which when turned off left the cellar in total darkness. A ping-pong ball with fluorescent markings was placed in the centre of the table on a small plinth. A cube of balsa-wood, similarly marked, was on the floor near the table. The two mediums sat in as part of the group.

After opening prayers, tapes of sing-along music were played to create the right conditions. The two mediums soon went into trance and their guides came through to communicate with us. There was much lively conversation and plenty of good humour.

I received a very evidential communication – via Mrs Bradshaw – from a member of my family who had been in the etheric world for many years (Earth time). I was given his name and information regarding something of which I alone had knowledge.

Then followed a fine demonstration of spirit and energy lights, which I had never before witnessed. A pair of lights hovered around my head and then stopped just inches in front of my eyes, as though looking intently at me. There was such a feeling of love and intelligence in them.

Shirley, sitting on my left, felt several gentle but firm nudges on her leg and hand. I watched a light gently touch my left leg and then my left hand, which I undoubtedly felt.

The perennial question is: how does one convey such phenomena to convince the critics and sceptics? As a past member of the Magic Circle and a professional stage magician for a number of years, I have some understanding and experience of how trickery can be employed by the unscrupulous. It has kept me on my guard throughout over forty years of serious study and research.

With today's technology, it is easy for a stage magician to present, with the help and advice of electronics experts, a very convincing 'light show', complete with pseudo-séance effects, and the gullible will fall for it as they always have.

One such *modus operandi* might be the employment of long hollow strands of fibreglass with laser light projected through them. But this requires a previous set-up of props and gadgetry in the room and/or on the persons themselves, which would immediately fail the test conditions that are required to be met by the genuine medium and sitters.

Shirley and I have known Sandra and Robin Foy long enough to be aware of their genuine desire to find and share the evidence for proving the continuance of life after 'physical death'. They would not waste their valuable time with parlour games and people of questionable intent.

As far as we are concerned, what we have witnessed to date with the SEG has been positive and we will be observing with great interest each step.

If fraud cannot be proven, the catch-all explanation for the apparently paranormal events is that they are a product of the individual or collective psychic abilities of human participants, the so-called 'super-PSI' effect. Some commentators might say, for instance, that the images received on the photographic films during the Scole Experiment could be the result of 'thought transference' from the group members' own minds. If shown to be the case, this would be an indication of some previously unknown power of the mind but it would not necessarily support the survival hypothesis. It is probably fair to say that, depending on the initial perspective of the reviewer, a different interpretation of the same evidence is possible and this could be used to either champion or challenge the survival hypothesis.

Another, less immediately apparent, explanation is the schizophrenia or 'alter ego hypothesis', which proposes that the medium is suffering from a dual- or multiple-personality disorder.

In this scenario, the alter ego(s) of the medium take(s) over and give(s) the answers to questions on diverse subjects that the ostensible or dominant personality would not 'normally' know about. In the case of the Scole Experiment, however, this hypothesis is hard, if not impossible, to support. There were two mediums involved, working in tandem, and they were able to answer detailed technical, scientific, historical, and even philosophical questions in a simultaneous dialogue with external investigators from a wide range of specialities. The likelihood that the alter egos would be able to jump from the intricacies of celestial mechanics (a subject on which there are perhaps a handful of people in the UK who could be described as genuine experts) to the subtle interpretation of the classics, in the context of little known historical events, is slim to say the least. To quote one observer: 'There is a greater likelihood that discarnate personalities are communicating through them.' Nevertheless, all possibilities must be considered in any attempt to explain paranormal events.

It has often been hard to test the claims of mediums because they have not readily welcomed protracted scientific study. There have been notable exceptions to this, but, although much evidence has been gathered, a number of critics have considered this evidence insufficient to defeat the alter-ego, fraud and super-PSI explanations and so survival has remained unproven. Logically, of course, there is an equal chance that we do or do not survive bodily death. The anti-survivalists have no monopoly on common sense, as is often assumed by what we could call the 'consensus opinion'. This is why the SEG and their spirit team have tried so hard to achieve a scientific protocol and thus defeat the anti-survival hypotheses.

We now pick up the story in early October 1995. Ralph Noyes, Arthur Ellison, and Montague Keen have joined the SEG in the cellar for the first time. The group was 'understandably a bit nervous':

> And we were worried this would affect the session, because the close harmony of the group is paramount. The other thing is that the scientists were bringing

different energies in for the spirit team to deal with
and we wondered how they would cope with this.
Needless to say, we need not have been concerned,
as within five minutes, Manu came through and it
was business as usual.

Manu welcomed the guests and urged them to be relaxed and to
open their hearts and minds to the work in order to allow the
energies of all present to blend together. Patrick and Mrs Bradshaw
also came through, both in their normal good humour. Contrary to
the group's fears, the team was able to demonstrate bell ringing,
shooting-stars, illumination of feet, lights passing through the table,
audible rapping, an arc of light, a circle of light, a light entering a
crystal, a light passing through an investigator's hand, touches,
energy voices and static electricity effects.

During the 'lively' first session, a spirit scientist discussed a
number of topics at length with the investigators. The team
proposed a regular programme of experimentation and the
investigators accepted this.

Montague acted as a convenor and host on Scole experiment
days, putting his colleagues up overnight at his home nearby. After
each meeting, the investigators returned there to discuss, far into
the night, what they had experienced that day. Then Montague
would write a detailed account of each session, supplemented by
the transcript of the session's tapes that Diana Bennett produced.
He would also make commentaries on the transcripts. All the
investigators were very conscious of the significance of what the
Scole group was claiming. Montague said that if it was more than
a collective hallucination, then they were onto something that was
of real and substantial importance.

A report of the first sitting stated that the responses of the spirit
communicators were 'immediate, apposite, unevasive, and
humble'. The nature of the light was 'distinctive, purposeful, and
intelligently directed'. It changed direction much further and faster
than would have been possible were it to have been subjected to
manual manipulation.

This first session allowed the investigators to become familiar with the phenomena. As they grew to be on much easier terms with the spirit personalities, more attention could be devoted by the team to the production of the physical evidence the investigators were seeking to examine.

It was by no means a straight run. Not all of the original expectations were satisfied. The spirit team had clear ideas about what they wanted to do and the investigators also had a clear idea of what they wanted the team to do. The two did not always match. It soon became apparent to the investigators that the team itself was on a learning curve, subject to trial and error.

A central issue for the investigators was the absence of light. They had envisaged the eventual use of video or infra-red equipment which would enable them to see what anyone was doing at any time, but had to be content with the group's assurance that it was the intention of the team to 'bring their own light'. To compensate for this shortcoming, the investigators took other precautions against deception, freely discussed with the group and the team.

At the second session, held on 16 December, the atmosphere changed after the usual preliminaries, and a light show soon began. Joseph, one of the spirit scientists, explained that the energy was being used to create something visual. Suddenly, a flash of light was seen. A short while later, the glass dome on the table lit up. A full-size materialised face and hand were illuminated by this light. The hand picked up the table tennis ball on the central table and bounced it in the bowl on the table. It then picked up a quartz crystal and moved amongst those present.

Joseph said that the team wanted to try an experiment. He asked everyone to place their hands on their knees and apply a little pressure towards the floor. All enjoyed the surprise when this joint action caused the light to brighten considerably.

The investigators asked whether the spirit lights would register on a spectrometer (which measures wavelengths of light) as being in the visible range of human sight. The spirit scientist answered that they probably would. He added, however, that most of the spiritual light was not emitted as photons. There were only enough photons present to enable human witnesses to see and photograph it.

According to *Spiritual Scientist,* investigators who observed the spiritual light said that:

> There appears to be no way in which it could be generated by any normal means; it appears to be capable of being photographed, from previous evidence; it appears to have no focal point of emanation but can change from a fairly concentrated spot to a generalised glow; it appears to be intelligently guided; and it appears to be associated with some form of psychokinetic power.

Back in the session, the subject of 'negative vibrations' was also discussed with Joseph. All agreed that a small proportion of scientists would openly show suspicion and deep hostility towards anything that was so overtly and intentionally paranormal as the work of the Scole group.

The investigators wondered if sceptical visitors to the group might inhibit the phenomena and whether the production of a permanent paranormal object was feasible. This might be two interlocking rings made of different wood with no join. Since there would be no earthly way of creating such an object, it would be irrefutable evidence of paranormality. A discussion followed about the difficulties for the team of producing such an object and sustaining it afterwards. The team thought that they could perhaps produce a permanent paranormal object in the ideal conditions of the cellar, but it would be hard to sustain it beyond the confines of the experimental room. (This object would be different from the apports, as these already exist in the physical dimension and are transported to the cellar, so there is no need to 'sustain' them physically.) However, the spirit team emphasised that they were determined to create overwhelming evidence to prove that the spiritual dimensions do exist.

Joseph went on to say that the experiments the team had embarked on had been carefully thought out by a team of spirit people, but up until that moment, they had always thought it sufficient to provide their own evidence of the afterlife. Joseph asked the investigators to understand that their suggestion of other experiments would pose some minor difficulties on the spirit side. He said that in-depth discussion might sometimes be needed in regard to just how these experiments could be carried out. He also said, however, that the main objective of any experiment was to achieve successful results and this is what the team would wish to do. They wanted to perfect any experiments to the point where they could produce repeatable, successful results.

The investigators felt that visual displays such as sporadic lights and levitations were interesting but did not constitute the best subject matter for scientific scrutiny. The photographic work was more suitable. The team said that it was their intention to produce some exceptional photographs that would not easily be explained away. These would be unique, and modern technology would assist in proving their authenticity.

Piers Eggett, a government scientist, was invited to a sitting.

PERSPECTIVES

PIERS EGGETT

Although I have been interested in psychic phenomena for most of my life, I have only been a scientist for twenty-eight years. Nevertheless, during this time spent studying the propagation of radio waves through the Earth's atmosphere, I have come into contact with many different aspects of science and technology, including radio, electronics, acoustics, ultrasonics, mechanics, lasers and optics throughout the visible, infra-red and ultraviolet spectrum. I would like to think that this experience has given me a good insight into how things work, and how various effects can be achieved, and so puts me in an ideal position to observe psychic phenomena calmly and honestly.

I was invited to sit with the Scole group and have put

together the following thoughts on some of the technical aspects of the phenomena witnessed. The sitting itself has already been reported, so I won't repeat the whole description here, and although I am admittedly a firm believer in Spirit, I trust that any gullibility was outweighed by my natural curiosity and open-mindedness.

In conclusion, I would like to say that it was a most exciting meeting, with many different phenomena witnessed, any one of which ought to be sufficient to convince any thinking person. Hopefully, other groups will soon be encouraged to begin working in this new way, to provide the proof of Spirit which is so needed in the world today.

Luminous Tabs These were attached to a number of items in the room, including the wrists of the regular sitters, but I am here referring to four tabs fixed to the top of the central table. These were clearly seen to become obscured at times by something opaque.

These tabs are by necessity quite small and, therefore, rather dim, but not so dim that they can only be seen using averted vision. This is a technique widely used by astronomers for observing faint stars. Peripheral vision or 'looking out of the corner of your eye' is more sensitive than looking straight at something, and so faint objects can sometimes be seen in this way, which are invisible when staring straight at them. Faint lights could, therefore, appear to come and go by scanning the eyes around the room. The luminous tabs at Scole were too bright for this to occur.

Also, examination showed that there were no hidden lights fitted in the table. The phenomenon seems to be perfectly genuine.

Spirit Light This was a small ball of white light which moved around the room in all directions, sometimes at great speed, leaving a trail like a firework by persistence of vision – the length of time an image will remain on the retina after the light that caused it has been removed. (It is this feature of the human eye which allows us to see TV and movie films without flicker, and why a rapidly moving spot of light leaves a trail.) At times the light hovered in mid-air, and then touched some of the sitters, giving them a small electric shock.

There was no beam of light (scattering from particles in the air) coming from a fixed source; the ball of light was the source. I have no explanation for this phenomenon, except the one given, i.e. that it was produced and controlled by Spirit. I defy any conjurer to reproduce it.

Energy Voice A man's voice was plainly heard emanating from the central area of the room. Of course, we are all familiar with electronically produced stereo sounds moving from left to right and back, between a pair of loudspeakers, but it is a much more difficult feat to position a sound in three dimensions.

I am convinced there were no hidden loudspeakers anywhere in the room, and in any case, this voice had a crispness and clarity to it which would be difficult to replicate.

Also, it was clear from what was being said that the speaker was present with us in the room. I have no doubt whatever that this phenomenon was genuine.

Levitation On the central table was placed a white Pyrex bowl with a table-tennis ball inside it. The ball had a luminous tab on it. At times the spirit light entered the bowl, illuminating it, and the bowl could clearly be seen moving around, with the ball rattling about inside. At one point, the ball was lifted by the light and was held close to the ceiling, from where it was later dropped onto the floor. It remained there until the end of the sitting.

There was no sign on the ball of its having been attached to anything. I can see no physical explanation for these phenomena and believe them to be genuine.

Apport A picture postcard appeared on the table towards the end of the sitting. This was clearly heard to land on the table, so it was certainly dropped there. The only place a card could have been concealed, therefore, was on the ceiling, but there was no mechanism on the ceiling capable of doing this.

In any case, if a card were dropped from this height, there is no guarantee where it would land; it could go anywhere. I am in no doubt that this phenomenon was completely genuine.

As we have seen, even before the investigators arrived, the group was already imposing certain procedures and carrying out some tests. Luminous armbands were worn by all the members so that they could be seen if they attempted to move around in the dark. These armbands were initially fixed with pins but later had Velcro straps so that they would be heard if removed. Highly sensitive flat microphones were used on the walls and floors to pick up and record the slightest sound. Temperatures were measured and monitored by the group on sophisticated equipment to see whether temperature changes corresponded to the time during the session that phenomena occurred. Thermometers were placed at ground and ceiling levels in the cellar, and on the porch outside the house for comparison.

Temperature records were kept for each session starting on 26 June 1995. The temperature was recorded in the cellar at the start of each session, both at floor level, and at the height of the probe. This exercise was repeated at the end of each session. By use of a sensitive instrument, the group could also determine the maximum and minimum temperatures throughout, and the deviation. The variation of temperature was only slight, measuring just plus or minus 1.0°C. When apports were received in the cellar they noted that the temperature at 1.82 m rose by 2.5°C and the floor level sensor also rose by 1.3°C.

It seemed to the group that the best way to convince the critics would be to conduct more and more controlled experiments. To this end, a supportive scientist loaned them 'a highly sophisticated precision instrument', an air flow meter. Its prime function was to measure the movement of air over a given area. As we know, during numerous experimental sessions, the group members experienced flows and even gusts of cool air, sometimes referred to as 'psychic breezes'. To determine whether these experiences were subjective or objective the group was advised to place the instrument where they thought the breezes were most intense. During sessions when breezes were not experienced, no movement of the air was registered on the meter. However, on one notable occasion, when a spirit helper was actively present and in the vicinity of the meter, it recorded a significant volume of air movement. Instruments help to confirm that something is a fact rather than the result of imagination or desire for something to be true.

So, the importance of recording data was recognised during the Scole Experiment and record keeping is likely to be adopted during further experiments by other groups around the world.

When the independent scientific investigators first became involved, they went to considerable lengths to ensure scientific protocol was observed. These included bolting all external doors, searching the cellar and adjacent rooms, and checking for hidden entrances and equipment. Nevertheless, as is standard practice in science, colleagues of the investigating scientists made some criticisms of the procedures adopted. For example, one of the criticisms was that the group members were not invasively body-searched prior to sessions. In the past, with ectoplasmic methods, the medium could be accused of secreting muslin or similar material in a bodily orifice, which when produced would look like ectoplasm. Therefore a very invasive body search was required, usually undertaken by a female nurse, since most mediums were female. This and many of the other criticisms are addressed in *The Scole Report*. Regarding body searches, one reason given in the *Report* was that these were not necessary for the Scole group because ectoplasm was not being produced and most of the physical phenomena witnessed could not be directly associated or attributed to group members.

This brings us to an important point about scientific scrutiny during the Scole Experiment. Those who were experimenting, investigating and reviewing, whether champions, critics or dispassionate observers, were all limited by a lack of common vocabulary and past experience with which to assess the new spiritual science phenomena. The new energy-based experiments were unique and, as such, there were no procedural precedents. Apparently rational criticisms, such as requests by reviewers for body searches, may illustrate a less-than-complete understanding of the innovative nature of the work undertaken at Scole.

To a certain extent of course, we are all scientists, examining any evidence of 'reality' which life sends our way. We have various natural and man-made instruments as well as accumulated knowledge and experience at our disposal. However, 'public opinion' is generally more swayed by the findings of scientifically trained (and thus 'qualified') people. Most of us require such qualified people to investigate on our behalf. It was therefore important to the SEG that the independent investigators implemented acceptable scientific procedures so that the Scole Experiment would be taken seriously by both the scientific and lay communities alike.

Initially, the main aim of the investigators was to establish control over certain parameters of the experiments, especially the timing and method of production of the photographic films. Montague Keen explained their intentions:

> We were first out to see whether the phenomena, in the conditions in which they were produced, could have been accounted for by 'natural' man-made means. If not, we then wanted to ascertain whether any apparent paranormal force was derived from the group's psyches or from discarnate entities.

The 'discarnate entities' explanation would, of course, support the notion of survival, although in theory these entities could still be beings who had never lived on Earth but enjoyed some other type of existence. All in all, though, if every other explanation could be defeated by the thoroughness of the procedures adopted, some might say that this was an important step towards proving that the images on the films must be evidence of survival.

Sceptics who do not want to accept *any* evidence of survival have attempted to *infer* that the evidence is not paranormal. If all the unique phenomena that the investigators came into contact with during the Scole Experiment were 'normal', then it would imply that the Scole group were performing an elaborate hoax and deliberately lying to the huge number of people who attended sessions and the experts who came to verify what was occurring. So far, the investigators have been unable to produce *any* evidence of fraud. *The Scole Report* attempts to answer all criticisms in full.

In the absence of a permanent paranormal object (due to the spirit team having their own itinerary), the investigators (and, it would appear, the team) judged that, of all the phenomena produced at Scole, the photographs constituted the best repeatable physical – and potentially 'cast-iron' – evidence available for their scientific scrutiny.

Piers Eggett wrote an article for *Spiritual Scientist* on the question of acceptable evidence:

PERSPECTIVES

CONVINCING THE SCIENTIFIC MIND

People I meet are often surprised to learn that I am both a government scientist and a committed Spiritualist. Somehow, the two don't seem to go together, but I am by no means unique. I think of myself as following in the footsteps of the pioneers, some of them far better scientists than I will ever be, such as William Crookes and Oliver Lodge, to name but two. Scientific people, however, are notoriously sceptical, so what can be done to help convince them of the truth?

We rely on our senses to tell us about the world around us and although I know they can be fooled, I would say that if our senses of sight, hearing, touch and smell simultaneously indicate that someone is present in the room with us, then it must be a fact. We normally accept a person's presence with less sensory input than this, after all. We don't have to touch someone to prove they really are there. This proof, however, is personal to the recipient, being specifically tailored to their particular need, and obviously does not constitute proof to anyone else.

Similarly, the small gifts apported to us either in circle or directly into our homes are quite meaningless to those not present at the time, no matter how precious and undoubtedly cherished they are to those who receive them. I have been privileged to receive a number of gifts this way, and my scientist friends are always keen to see them and examine them closely, but at the end of the day, they have only my word as to where they came from. In any case, what exactly do they prove? They show that it is possible to dematerialise an object in one location and rematerialise it somewhere else, but do they prove the existence of Spirit?

One of the main ways in which a scientist verifies a theory is by testing it repeatedly with a suitable experiment. When we put Spirit to the test in this way, we immediately run into difficulty. First, many effects have been observed, but do we really have any idea of why and how these things are brought about? Second, results are not consistent.

It is important, therefore, to have experimenters who have at least some experience of the work. Even then, results are likely to be very variable, since no two circles are ever the same. Care must also be taken not to influence the results. I was aware of this possibility as a young experimentalist, over twenty years ago, when I used to ask not to be told what results to expect, because I knew that if we were looking for a subtle effect, I could sometimes influence it just by thinking about it.

How, then, do I go about convincing my sceptical colleagues? The best proof of all is, of course, the kind of personal proof, which I have had, and I am sure that anyone who is genuinely seeking conclusive proof will eventually be given it. Meanwhile, there must be something I can do to whet the appetite of the scientific mind.

I put this problem to Spirit one day, and was immediately

shown the inside of a library. The walls were covered with bookshelves to the ceiling and in the foreground stood a group of scientists from the past. One or two faces were familiar, but most of them I didn't know at all. One man stepped forward and explained that they understood my desire to help and the problems I was facing. He went on to say that they would impress my mind from time to time with thoughts about various experiments and measurements which could usefully be made. They have already given me some ideas, which I am eager to try out. I think it is so important to work with Spirit if we can, as their task is difficult enough without having us against them.

One of the major problems with physical phenomena, at least to the sceptical mind, is that of light, or should I say, the lack of it. Most work of this sort takes place in complete darkness, which it must be said, if you don't have complete confidence in the integrity of the medium and sitters, can appear highly suspicious to an already critical investigator. Spirit tell us they are well aware of this problem and are as keen to work in light as we are. The trouble is, working in the dark is much easier for them and to develop a medium to work in light conditions takes much longer. It has been done in the past and I am confident that before long, we will, once more, have physical mediums working in perhaps not daylight, but certainly subdued light. Once people are sure that they are not being deceived, an enormous degree of scepticism will be removed. I'm afraid, though, that many scientists will still have their doubts...

We cannot force people to believe as we do, but if we can prompt them to think about our words and the evidence given by high quality clairvoyance, then we have done them an enormous service. If they can just admit to themselves that the existence of Spirit is a possibility, then when they are ready for their own personal proof, they are less likely to turn their backs on it or to look around for signs of trickery. They are much more likely to say to themselves 'This really is true!'

The investigators' third session, on 13 January 1996, was different from the first two in a number of ways. Due to ill health, Ralph Noyes, the SPR's Honorary Secretary, had stepped down and invited David Fontana to attend in his stead. Professor David Fontana, PhD, was an educational and counselling psychologist, a Distinguished Visiting Fellow at a university in Britain, a professor at two universities in Portugal and a Fellow of the British Psychological Society. He had written more than twenty books on psychology and related themes translated into twenty-three languages. A member of the Council of the British Psychological Society and Chair of the Transpersonal Psychology Section of the British Psychological Society, he was also, at the time of the investigation, the President of the SPR. He had published works in the field of psychical research and chaired the SPR's Survival Committee. He had a long-standing interest in psychical phenomena and in methods of deception and had investigated and witnessed a wide range of psychical phenomena in various settings.

The group too had undergone some change. Mimi had left some time earlier for personal reasons, and Ken and Bernette had decided to stop attending because they could no longer commit to the regular travelling. So it was that just seven people – the four remaining group members, and the three investigators from the Society – would take the photographic experimentation forwards.

CHAPTER SIX

STUDYING THE PHOTOGRAPHIC FILMS

All the evidence we come across in real
life is faulty to a greater or lesser extent;
and the only question of importance is
how good the evidence is; not whether it
is perfect or imperfect. Evidence is a
matter of degree.

G. N. M. Tyrrell

THE PHOTOGRAPHIC PROTOCOLS

In view of the anticipated criticisms relating to phenomena
produced in total darkness, Professor Fontana suggested a four-
step protocol so that the investigators could control the point at
which the photographic images were actually produced.

First, the investigators would provide the film to be used.
Second, the investigators would ensure that the film was in a
secure container, provided by them. Third, the investigators
would have control of the container throughout the session.
Finally, development of the film should be under the control of
the investigators. According to *The Scole Report,* 'Such a
protocol would remove any possibility of physical intervention.
Neither the Spirit team nor the Scole group offered any objection
to this protocol.'

We should remind ourselves at this point that the Scole group
had already been conducting experiments in photography and had
a stock of various types of film which had been kindly provided
by Polaroid.

THE SECURITY BAG

Prior to the investigations, Montague Keen had discussed with Dr Richard Wiseman the sort of protocol likely to pass muster with sceptics. Dr Wiseman was an SPR Council member and former member of the para-psychology unit at Edinburgh University. A senior lecturer in psychology at the University of Hertfordshire, he specialised in the psychology and practice of deception. He was thus considered something of a specialist consultant in regard to security procedures.

Dr Wiseman had provided a fraud-proof security bag made of opaque triple-layered polythene. The investigators proposed to place an unopened tub of 35mm film in this bag, in the hope of receiving transmissions from the spirit world in the form of images on the film.

This bag was given to the group after the first session in October 1995 and gave rise to some discussion during the second session on 16 December, when Mrs Bradshaw said:

> *You have given us an excellent bag to look at. Took it all round the room and checked it out, didn't we, and it was really very good. I don't think we are going to have too much of a problem, but what we would like to do is to start to experiment with the group and just yourselves, and not take it beyond that, just for a start, and see how we go with it.*

Montague Keen agreed. 'That was the intention – a dummy run, as we might call it.'

Later in the session, a discussion took place with the spirit team as follows:

> **Joseph:** *Much of this that we present to you and present to many people will be very hard to prove and it will be hard to use some of these physical demonstrations as evidence... That is why these specific experiments, in this case the photographic*

experiments, are so perfect and so unique in the way they are done and the results achieved; and it has one ultimate aim in mind: it is not used as an experiment to attract people's attention as a trick, but to produce phenomena that will last... That is what we shall be doing in a photographic way in the next few weeks. If Monty – may I speak to you? – can purchase film rather than take it from stock, you know, Polaroid 12 pictures where we have done that before: that seems to work quite well.

Robin: A colour one or black and white?

Montague: I'll get both, so you can choose.

Mrs Bradshaw: *Well yes, we're bound to use them both, aren't we? That will be all right. But what about the speed? What have we had good results with?*

Robin: We've had good results with... there's only one speed on the colour film, that's ISO 40, and the other one that I think we have achieved the best results is about 110, but that's black and white, but I'll check up.

Arthur: Then is the idea that Monty should bring one of each kind of film sealed in the same bag: is that the idea?

THE STAR FILM

At the next meeting, on 13 January 1996, Professor Ellison took the tub containing a 35mm Polapan Polaroid film which had been bought by Montague Keen, removed the chemical cassette and placed the unopened tub containing the roll of Polaroid film in the Wiseman security bag. The chemical cassette was put to one side to be used for the development of the photographs after the session. Professor Ellison then sealed the unopened tub and took it downstairs for the experiment, placing it on the floor beneath the table.

After the session, the investigators opened the bag, removed the film tub, extracted the roll of film and put it through the electrical developer upstairs. The results, projected by the Foys on to a large screen in their library immediately afterwards, showed mainly star-like scatters with occasional lines inconsistent with any horizontal scratching which might have been ascribed to the development process (see Plate 32). However, in one section there was a small cog-shaped light with a shadowy substance behind.

The investigators considered that the outcome 'indicated paranormality', since the image was certainly not random but rather a recognisable shape. Logically, of course, there ought to have been nothing at all visible. Although the results did not match the qualitative expectations of the investigators, they could find no way in which this procedure could be faulted, because the bag had been lodged inaccessibly between the feet of Professor Ellison and Montague Keen for the duration of the experiment. Furthermore, the film had been provided by Montague Keen, and he and Professor Ellison had put the film through the developer. The recognised security bag and the film had been in the possession of the investigators throughout. This then, was how the scientifically controlled photographic experiments began – with a procedure which could not be faulted and an outcome which 'indicated paranormality'.

The following descriptions of the photographic experiments are based on those in *The Scole Report,* which provides an accurate insight into how the groundbreaking investigation of the Scole Experiment was conducted. Once again, we would like to express our thanks to the authors of the *Report* for providing us with a copy in advance of publication.

THE GREEK ON GREEN FILM

At the fifth session on 17 February 1996, the procedure was varied. The film bought by Montague Keen was Polaroid 35mm colour, purchased directly from Jessops of Leicester, the main suppliers. The package was again opened by Professor Ellison. He removed the chemical cassette and gave the tubbed film to Montague, who placed it on the edge of the table immediately in front of him in the cellar. Robin Foy explained that the spirit team had told him they were having more difficulty than had originally been expected in getting through the black polythene security bag which had been used in the dummy run of the third session.

Towards the end of the session Joseph and Emily Bradshaw contributed:

> **Joseph:** *Let's hope you find something really interesting on the film. Bear in mind these are only the early stages. Progress will be made, believe me. Those responsible have explained to me their difficulties and their confidence in achieving what they are setting out to do.*
>
> **Mrs Bradshaw:** *I do echo Joseph's words. I hope that we have been able to give you something that will make you jump up and down when you get upstairs. We'll have a small wager: if you don't jump up and down I'll bring half a crown next time!*
>
> **Arthur:** That's not legal tender.
>
> **Mrs Bradshaw:** *Oh dear. Still, you'd like to have half a crown, wouldn't you – but I don't think I'll be paying up.*

It turned out that Mrs Bradshaw's half crown was safe. When the film was developed immediately after the session, most of it was discovered to be blank. However, three or four frames contained colour images. The most significant of these images showed three lower case Greek letters set against a green background: ì **å** *í* (see Plate 15). These letters, in English, represent 'm', 'e' and 'n'. They appeared to be illuminated, as though a searchlight had been beamed on them. On close inspection, they also had very faint indications of preceding and succeeding lettering.

The investigators noted that, in this instance, there was no security bag. The tub containing the film was not marked and not visible, even though it was only a few inches from Montague Keen and was very close to the other investigators on either side of him, namely Professors Ellison and Fontana. One or both of these investigators would almost certainly have been able to detect any attempt at switching tubs by the group members, who would have had to reach across them and grope in the dark. However, the control could not be said to be perfect, since theoretical possibilities for switching did exist.

THE LATIN MIRROR-IMAGE FILM

On 25 May 1996, at a seminar attended by ten people, a Latin message was produced on film. The main investigators were not present on this occasion. However, a detailed account of the proceedings was given by Mr Denzil Fairbairn, a businessman:

PERSPECTIVES

DENZIL FAIRBAIRN

I was 100 per cent sceptical of the claims that had been made within the first half-dozen editions of *Spiritual Scientist magazine.* To me it all seemed rather fanciful and somewhat exaggerated.

Prior to going into the cellar for the sitting, I was asked, by special request of the spirit team, to select and take charge of a sealed brand new 35mm black-and-white Polaroid film from amongst approximately a dozen similarly boxed and sealed films. I was then asked to remove the plastic container containing the film from its sealed outer box and to make the container identifiable to me by placing my signature upon it. The film did not leave my possession until it was placed on the large central table in the cellar room, where it was within my view until the moment that the lights were switched off.

I must mention here that this film was placed on the opposite side of the central table from where our hosts were sitting, and the glass dome in the centre of the table obscured the film from our hosts' positions in the room. Therefore, in my opinion, it would have been impossible for any of our hosts to have tampered with the film, especially when I add that each of our hosts was fitted with luminous bands which indicated their positions within the blacked out room at all times.

A welcome and some words of encouragement were in the first instance given by Manu, who then stepped back to begin the process of blending the three types of energy used in the execution of this type of phenomenon.

Next we were introduced to an Asian gentleman called Raji. The mediums were then simultaneously controlled; one by Mrs Emily Bradshaw, a delightful lady for whom I felt an almost immediate attraction, and the other by Joseph, a quietly spoken and modest man who gave the impression of being knowledgeable, albeit in a humble way.

First there were unmistakably cold breezes about the room, particularly below knee level, where it was at times absolutely freezing.

Suddenly, out of nowhere, a tiny light shot upwards from the table area. It was so fast that all one had left imprinted on one's vision was the streak of light in mid-air. This happened several more times and on each occasion the light grew more intense in brightness and remained visible for longer and longer periods.

People heard footsteps and shuffling noises upon the carpeted floor, and we were advised by Mrs Bradshaw that we had two spirit visitors in the room with us. We then heard, emanating from a point above the table, someone trying to speak. Initially, this first voice wasn't too clear; then a second, well-established voice, recognised by the Scole group as that of 'Reg Lawrence', spoke out from the same vicinity. He was trying to make some 'small adjustments' to help the first speaker to make himself heard more clearly.

I asked my mother whether she had felt any touches or taps, to which she replied that she had not. Mrs Bradshaw then went on to give my mother some very evidential information from my father, and while she was speaking to my mother, I felt the touch of a solid form on my wrist and stomach.

My wife, who was sitting next to me, then felt a touch on the back of her head and shortly after this my mother felt the weight of a solid hand resting in hers. She let us all know what she was feeling and then she felt her other hand being guided and brought to rest on top of the spirit hand. Both of her hands were then lifted up and kissed on the finger-tips. This was instantly recognised as something which my father had often done prior to telling my mother that he loved her.

We were then advised that the spirit photographic team might have had some success in impressing something onto the blank film and I was again asked to take charge of the film from when the sitting had finished until it was time for the developing to take place.

The roll of film was put into a mini developing machine provided by Polaroid Ltd and we all waited in anticipation for the final prints. It was pure delight to discover that two out of the twelve frames had something quite remarkable on them. There was actually a printed message in Latin which was not only mirrored within one of the frames, but also the whole of that frame was mirrored in the second frame, so that the whole message appeared in various states of mirroring four times.

This message was: *Reflexionis, Lucis in Terra, et in Planetis* (Of reflection of light on the Earth and the planets) (see Plate 33).

The investigators noted that, although they did not supervise this experiment, the obvious normal explanation of the results would appear to involve the switching of the film by a member of the group. This could have been done by either removing the film from its container and replacing it with a previously prepared film or by substituting the entire tub, with its contents. However, the investigators considered that neither explanation could be reconciled with the existence of the paper seal which Mr Fairbairn had applied to the tub before the experiment began. This was because it would be extremely difficult to remove and replace the seal *in situ,* in complete darkness and undetected. The group members would also first have had to remove or obscure their luminous armbands during the session in order to pick up the tub, remove the seal noiselessly and without damage, snap open the lid unheard, replace the film with another, close the lid silently, reseal the paper and then finally replace the tub in its original position.

Alternatively, said the investigators, Mr Fairbairn, despite the testimony of other independent witnesses, most of whom he had never previously met, could have been in secret collaboration with the group, a hypothesis which would also have to be advanced to explain similar results when other experimenters were involved.

THE GOLDEN CHAIN MESSAGE

The investigators themselves made the next attempt to obtain photographic evidence, on 13 July. In addition to Professor Ellison and Montague Keen, this session was attended by Professor Archie Roy, a specialist in astrophysics, who had brought an unopened package of Polachrome 35mm 12-exposure colour transparency film.

On this occasion, Professor Ellison cut open the sealed package, removed one carton, broke the seal and extracted the black tub, leaving the chemical cassette behind as usual. Montague Keen then affixed a luminous adhesive tab to the side of the tub. Professor Ellison put the tub in his pocket, later placing it on the cellar table between one of the four luminous tabs on the edge of the table and a crystal, which was pointing towards it. The tub was in the same position at the end of the session.

Development of the film revealed a large scrawled message which seemed to read: *Perfectio consummata feu quinta Ellantia Universalis* (see Plates 16 and 17).

This was followed by a roughly drawn circle with a dot in the centre. Professor Roy pointed out that this was a symbol for the sun, theories about which had been mentioned in the astronomical discussion he had been having earlier with the spirit team.

A friend and neighbour of Diana's, Beverley Dear, later found a book, *Magic Symbols* (F. Goodman, Trodd, 1989), which reproduces illustrations contained in a German publication of 1747, *Aurea Catena, oder eine Beschreibung von dem Ursprung der Natur und Natürlichen Dingen*. This contains an illustration of the Golden Chain of Homer (*Aurea Catena Homeri*). On this chain are attached or suspended a number of symbols, one of which has a circle with a dot in the centre and a small cross below. At the base is: *Perfectio Consummata seu Quinta Essentia Universalis* (From chaos to the highest summit of mankind).

According to *The Scole Report,* this was translated by one adviser as above, but Dr Gauld, a member of the SPR, considered that it was better interpreted as 'completed perfection or the fifth universal essence: part of the highly symbolic device which begins the chain with chaos and confusion and ends with perfection, representing man's progress towards the light'.

So, from the evidence of *Magic Symbols,* what the investigators had initially supposed to represent the sun was now seen more clearly to match the bottom symbol of the *Aurea Catena Homeri.* It might be considered worthy of note that a film with this subject matter should be received when a professor of astrophysics was present, especially since what was found to be on the film after the session pertained to discussions during the session.

THE GERMAN POEM

In a similar vein, the next successful film session resulted in a message in German being received when German investigators were present. During an earlier session of 31 May 1996, for which both Walter Schnittger, a consultant automotive engineer, and his wife Karin, an interpreter, were present, the unopened film in its plastic tub was held by Karin Schnittger throughout. It appeared that the team had made an obvious attempt to put a German poem onto the film, though the result was blurred and only partially legible. This blurring was apparently because Karin had shaken the tub during moments of excitement or laughter during the session.

The next session attended by the Schnittgers was held on 26 July 1996. It is important to note that Walter Schnittger this time held the tub containing the film in his hands throughout the session, neither putting it on the table nor allowing anyone else to touch it. He then supervised the development procedure.

This time, the transmission was much more clearly visible on the film (see Plates 20, 21 and 22):

> *Ein alter Stamm mit tausend Aesten*
> *Die Wurzeln in der Ewigkeit*
> *Neigt sich van Osten hin nach Westen*
> *In mancher Bildung weit und breit.*
>
> *Kein Baum kann bluthenreicher werden*
> *Und keines Frucht kann edler seyn*
> *Doch auch das 'Dunkelste' auf Erden*
> *Es reift auf seinem Zweig allein.*

> An old trunk with a thousand branches
> The roots within eternity
> Bends over from East towards the West
> In many forms far and wide.
>
> No tree can become more richly blossomed
> And no tree's fruit can be more noble
> But even the 'darkest' on earth
> Ripens on its branch alone.

This film also contained symbols representing the planets and Chinese ideograms, all 'precisely drawn, clearly visible and in brilliant colours'.

According to the *Report,* there were three interesting features about this film. First, the poem was written in what the Schnittgers and other German speakers considered good German in a style characteristic of the period around 1840. Secondly, it was a poem of high quality and, despite extensive inquiries made in Germany by the Schnittgers, Dr Kurt Hoffman and others, its authorship remained unknown. Thirdly, according to Robin Foy, the team had suggested that it was written or found by an ancestor of Walter Schnittger's, thus providing further possible evidence of a link between a participant and film content.

According to a footnote in the *Report,* Dr Kurt Hoffman informed the investigators that German experts he consulted had identified the poem as characteristic of the style of Friedrich Rückert (1788-1866). It was noted that Rückert was a popular poet and the inspiration for many of Gustav Mahler's songs. He was also famous for translating the Koran into German and was greatly interested in Eastern mysticism. Although Rückert was a probable candidate, extensive inquiries made of leading German scholars in sixteen UK universities failed to confirm the authorship. No record of publication has been found. The poem is not among the anthology of Rückert's verses available to scholars and is considered 'very obscure'.

The investigators considered that all this may be thought to have a bearing on the general fraud hypothesis, to the extent to which this hypothesis relies on relatively easy access to material already in the public domain.

THE *WIE DER STAUB* FILM

Although the protocol at the sessions at which the first and second German poem image were produced each had a single weakness (the film was selected from the Foy stock), this weakness was removed for a later session which the Schnittgers attended, at which another message *Wie der Staub in... Wind* (Like dust in... wind) was produced. This film result seems to have been achieved with 'perfect protocol', i.e. no chance of fraud whatsoever (see Plates 18 and 19).

PERSPECTIVES

WALTER SCHNITTGER

The week before our sitting, Robin Foy telephoned to inform us that a film experiment was planned for the following week. He asked me to buy a Polaroid Polachrome 35mm colour slide film and a padlock. He asked us not to handle the film more than was necessary.

I bought a safety lock, packed in its original sealed container and ordered three such films, one with twelve and the other two with thirty-six exposures. All remained in our exclusive possession until our arrival, with the films in a plastic bag, for the sitting on Friday 22 November 1996.

At the Foys' home I carefully examined the very solid wooden container placed on the coffee table of the living room, noting that it could just accommodate one film roll in its plastic tub. I removed the padlock and two keys from their package and placed them on the table in front of me. I selected the twelve-exposure roll, removed the developing cassette and tub from their packaging and immediately placed the tub with the unopened film in the box, which I padlocked right away. I left the chemical cassette in the room.

I took the locked box with me to my car where I deposited the two padlock keys, then handed over my car keys to Hans [Schaer], who remained with us throughout. All members of the group witnessed this procedure.

From the moment of locking the box until the time the film was processed after the sitting, the box was solely in my hands. It was never allowed to stand alone and was not even touched by anyone else. In the cellar I held the box on my lap, with both hands, until, having told him I was right-handed, I was asked by Edwin to place the box in my right hand in such a way that my forefinger was on the lid with the lower part of the finger feeling the locking mechanism. With my hand in this position, Edwin asked me to place the box on the table so that the base rested on the table. My right arm, from hand to elbow, rested on the table while my left hand remained on my left knee.

During the several minutes which followed, with my hand in this position, the table vibrated several times, sometimes so strongly that the crystals on the table started to rattle. On one occasion the pullover and shirt on my right arm were pulled up and a finger circled my wrist; then the clothes were pulled down again. It felt as though at least five hands were touching my right arm at the same time, some of them quite powerful, as if they were seeking to pull my fingers away from the container (which I did not allow) or to apply force to the container, so that some effort was needed to keep it in place. I once experienced a sensation of coldness as though a piece of ice had been placed on the back of my hand.

I was then asked to replace the box on my lap and hold it in both hands until after the sitting, when I retrieved my car key from Hans, took the box to my car to pick up the padlock keys and returned to make a close examination of the processing machine to ensure that it was empty. I then inserted the cartridge containing the chemical gel and finally unlocked the box, removed the plastic tub, extracted the film and inserted it into the processor.

This I then closed and started the clearly audible processing mechanism, which took about two minutes. I removed the film, which we all inspected. This showed text, symbols and lines over the whole length of the film, together with some German words like *wie* and *Staub* in handwriting and strange mirror-written text.

THE X-RAY FILM

A similar protocol was followed by Walter at another session on Friday 6 December 1996. Walter put the padlock keys in his car, locked the car and retained the car key. Again the box was held in his right hand on the table, when he was touched several times, although less force was applied to his hand than on the earlier occasion. What emerged from the processor had the appearance of a series of X-rays of Walter's fingers and thumb.

THE DRAGON FILM

On 17 January 1997, a further sitting was held with Karin and Walter. The procedures were the same, except that the box was under Karin's observation while Walter went to the car to lock up the padlock keys. It was not touched by anyone else during that brief period.

This time the group remained upstairs while Walter went into the cellar and placed the box in the centre of the table in such a way that the opposite corners of the box were directed to the four cardinal points as indicated by the four luminous tabs. A plain sheet of A4 paper had already been placed in the centre to allow him to describe an inked outline round the box and hanging padlock. At Robin's request both Karin and Walter fully checked the room but found nothing suspicious.

Walter confirmed that during the sitting which followed none of the six participants moved from their seats, as judged from the positions of the luminous armbands worn by the group. At the end of the session he checked to ensure that the outlines on the centre paper corresponded precisely with the position of the box and its lock. Upstairs, Karin again kept the box under close observation while he retrieved the padlock keys from the car. After ensuring that the processing unit was empty, he marked both the chemical processing spool and the film with his special shortened signature and, with Alan's assistance, placed both into the processor, after which he identified the signature on the film, which contained hermetic symbols (see Plates 23, 24 and 25).

The images were all traced to a single published volume. This is not unusual. It might make sense for the spirits to transmit material from a single, traceable source in a session rather than using several different texts which would simply complicate the procedure without affecting the overall outcome: evidence that the spirit team could produce recognisable images on film.

THE WOODEN SECURITY BOX

The wooden security box used in these experiments had been introduced at the team's request, to improve security (see Plates 34 and 35). It was given up for scrutiny and came back with all the seals broken – thus suggesting that it was impossible to open the box without breaking the seals. Had the investigators opened it without breaking the seals they would have shown everyone how it was done. Some of the experts who attended sessions held the box themselves for the duration of the sitting. They agreed that it was a physical impossibility for the mediums to tamper with the box. For someone to open the box in the dark conditions of the cellar they would have to hold it down with one hand and open it with the other. All this without moving the box or the padlock from their positions which were marked with pencil at the start of a session.

The team had been experiencing a few problems, as the photographic work was experimental for them as well as for the group and the investigators. A discussion was held during the 10 August 1996 session as to the nature of the energy transfer and the problems experienced. Albert, speaking through Alan, attempted to explain what happened:

> **Albert:** *These forces are being used much like a carrier wave is used, transmitting, and these forces can penetrate material in our world and your world...*
> *The thought process or imagery is carried by this* [carrier] *wave, that's how I think of it. These carrier waves are* [used] *to carry signals like modulation, frequencies modulating.*
> **Arthur:** Correct. Radio waves, making a high frequency, go up and down. The high frequency will carry the energy and the lower frequency is the intelligence being carried.

Albert: *I'm glad you said that. This is what I feel is a good example. When I use the analogy of radio I get into trouble. You will agree that there is some material that radio waves have difficulty with.*

Arthur: Yes, metal.

Albert:... *They do have difficulty penetrating other substances, not necessarily metal. As* [these forces penetrate different materials] *a change takes place. These transformations during this* [process] *are lost sometimes; part of the information is lost and is unpredictable. We have nothing to gauge our findings on because of the unpredictable nature of this phenomenon. Now added to this complication, the different substances affect these waves themselves, and we have different losses, and different changes taking place with different materials. In relation to the films, the films are in a metal container. Can you confirm this?*

David: Yes.

Arthur: I thought it was plastic.

Montague: It's in foil.

Albert: *It's not in foil; it's metal, about ten thousandths of an inch thickness.*

Arthur: That's fairly thick.

Albert: *That's no matter. We have adjusted for it long ago, but what caused us problems is when the films are placed inside other objects. At the moment there are two layers. Black, too, is a problem. There is no problem now, but it does give us a problem from time to time, but when other layers were used, this caused problems, to be overcome with further experiments. This is why we had a negative result when faced with another layer. In time it could have been rectified, but it was thought we'd return back to where we started* [and] *move forward in a slightly different way.*

The team hoped the box would maintain security while eliminating some of their difficulties. They wanted it made with a hinged top lid and a sturdy hasp. The aim was to place the film securely in the box and thereby reduce the possibility of accusations of fraud in regard to those occasions when it might be necessary to leave the film unattended for some days or longer for the team to work on. The need to do this might arise because the team could not always achieve a result in one session.

This wooden security box was also used as a padlocked container for the films during sessions. As outlined by Walter Schnittger, the investigators added further precautions such as retaining the keys to the padlock, placing the box on a piece of paper and drawing round it and the padlock to show it had not been moved, and even holding the box throughout experimental sessions. Images still appeared on the films placed in the box.

For reasons already explained, the investigators felt that the best evidence would be obtained if they could establish that they had total control over when and how the photographs were produced. However, this does not mean that all their experiments involved just the photographs.

For example, in 'The Crystal Essence' experiment, the investigators were asked to verify that they could see and touch a visibly glowing crystal in a bowl on the central table. They could see the bowl because of a light created by the spirit team in the otherwise pitch darkness of the cellar. The investigators confirmed that they could both see and touch the crystal. Then they were told by the spirit team to try again. This time, although they could still see the crystal, they could no longer touch it. Then the spirit team told them to try once more. Now they could both see and touch the crystal again. (Once he realised what was being attempted, Professor Ellison put his chin so close to the rim as to preclude any human interference with the crystals in the bowl.)

The spirit team had apparently created something akin to a hologram of the crystals. They said they had done this to illustrate what happens to the physical human being at death. The 'physical' or earthly element of a person is no more, but the essence remains and moves on to 'another place'. In this case, the team had removed the physical and left the essence of the crystals visible in the bowl. Needless to say, the scientists found this demonstration fascinating, not least because it appeared to be evidence of a new type of manipulation of matter and energy.

Even though the investigators made every effort to adhere to scientific protocols, each one of the experiments they supervised fell short of perfection to a certain extent. This is true of any experiment where the scientists cannot have total and complete control over all of the variables. If this concerns you, we should point out that this is as true of many experiments in biology or medicine as it is of those that were carried out during the Scole Experiment. The lack of total control of all variables does not necessarily negate the value of an experiment.

The group always allowed the experts to include any amendments to the procedures to enhance security. Although the spirit team suggested the sort of box which might be appropriate, they did not lay down the protocols. It was the investigators who introduced security bags and other checks to eliminate the possibility of tampering.

On the same theme, a particular strength of the Scole Experiment relates to the 'thread and rope' argument. Any piece of thread has a weakest point and it will snap there when the thread is tugged from both ends. However, if you put 500 pieces of thread together and intertwine them, you have a rope, which will not snap. The weakness of each thread is overcome by the unified strength of all of them put together.

This is also true of the 500 experiments conducted at Scole over a five-year period. Each one had its weakness but, taken together, the overall result is strong and convincing evidence that human consciousness may well survive bodily death: some form of intelligence really did appear to be attempting to communicate from 'somewhere'.

If a fraud was being perpetrated, this must of necessity have involved the whole SEG, all working together. They would have to have planned, to the last minute detail, all of the conversations that took place during the sessions. This plan would have included who was going to say what, when and how and do what, when and how. They must also somehow have known, in advance, whether, for example, Professor Ellison was going to be delayed by the trains (as happened) and therefore if he was going to be involved in the forthcoming conversation at all.

The group members needed to be able to skip, seamlessly, from discussions of their experiments without the investigators to those with the investigators. The members of the group, especially the mediums, would have had to know what Montague Keen, Professor Fontana, and Professor Ellison (and other investigators) had been researching, and when, and where, and how far each had progressed. The skills and powers of information gathering which would have been needed to perpetrate a conscious deception on this scale become so great that we have to ask ourselves whether communication by discarnate entities (with access to this information on 'another level') is the more likely explanation.

Along these lines, it is clear, in our opinion, from the tape transcript of the session on 16 August 1997, that the spirit team appeared to know a great deal about Montague Keen's interest in Rachmaninov and the special significance to his early life of one of this composer's works. This musical work was heard coming from one of the audio-tape machines (the one without a microphone) during the session. As Montague told us:

> There was not only the familiar 'white noise' coming from the microphone-less recorder, but also music and a voice speaking over it. I almost immediately recognised the music was part of Rachmaninov's Second Piano Concerto. I was deeply moved because the music meant a great deal to me. It was one of the earliest pieces of classical music I knew – I listened to Rachmaninov's own recording on 78s before the war. It took me back to boyhood days as an evacuee. I was certain that I had never mentioned this fact to anyone, least of all to the members of the Scole group, none of whom appeared particularly interested in classical music.

Interestingly, both the music and the voice speaking over it were recorded on the blank tape, but none of the voices or the background music from the room itself. Professor Fontana had personally marked this blank tape and put it into the machine at the beginning of the session. He was also careful to ensure that none of the group had access to the tape or the microphone-less machine at any time.

We weighed the strength of the fraud hypothesis in the light of what happened at this session. On the one hand, Montague Keen has testified that he had told no one in the group, or elsewhere, of his interest in, and youthful connection with, the work 'performed' by the spirit source. On the other hand, it has been suggested, by some critics, that Montague *must* have told the group all the details and that he had then somehow mysteriously forgotten that he had done so. The logical extension of this argument is that the critics who make this charge would have to make it for *every* other instance of apparent 'knowledge' on the part of the spirit team. All evidential information would have to have been collected by the group in advance and then they would have to wait for an appropriate time to bring it into the conversation.

For many who take the trouble to actually review the comprehensive evidence pertaining to mediumship over the past 100 or so years, this charge of 'information gathering' for the purposes of fraud on the part of mediums falls into the category of 'absurd'. Those who suggest the absurdity of the fraud charge often also say that this is the main reason why the super-PSI hypothesis is preferred by most critics: since super-PSI is inherently unprovable, it is a perfect dump-bin for all unexplained happenings.

It sometimes appears that any proposition, however far-fetched, is preferred to contemplation of the survival explanation. Some seem to find it totally unthinkable that there really *are* personalities who have survived death and are now in another realm of reality, still self-aware, with a memory of their Earth life and the ability to communicate with those of us who are still here, given the right conditions.

However, and this is important, whether the survival hypothesis offends some theological, sociological, logical, or other human bias is not really relevant to its claim to truth, even if it offends our current beliefs. If the spirit team is able to prove the case for survival, we will all eventually have to accept this 'new' truth and adjust to the implications.

Keith McQuin Roberts has a scientific background. He was invited to attend an experimental session at Scole.

PERSPECTIVES

KEITH MCQUIN ROBERTS

I have a scientific outlook by nature and by training. It seemed then, and it seems still now, that enlightening others about survival needs a different, *scientific,* approach if it is to have any chance of better success than previously.

We went down into the cellar, known as the 'Scole Hole'. This room had been converted to exclude all light and contained just chairs and a table. Robin encouraged us to examine the room and explained the operation of equipment used when visitors from the scientific community were attending a demonstration. He explained the steps and security measures taken to avoid any risk of claims of fraud or manipulation of the proceedings.

The phenomena were much as expected, as this was a demonstration rather than an experimental sitting but this did not detract in any way. It gave me more time to observe and consider and, although I knew what to expect, I was still greatly impressed.

One phenomenon was that of a small, seemingly ball-like light which moved around the room. It acted as though it were a solid object and appeared to be deliberately moving from one person to another.

I was intrigued by the way that I was able to feel a slight

pressure when it touched me. Even more astonishing was the way it made a noise as it descended *through* a heavy table-top, yet was able to come back up through the top completely silently. This all seemed to be a demonstration of scientific laws presently unknown.

The highlight of the session for me was being touched by a materialised hand. I had hoped I would get the chance but was almost overwhelmed when it happened. I recovered my wits sufficiently to show good manners and asked if it was OK to touch back. But, in the excitement, I forgot to say 'Hello' and ask who was with me. The demonstration began to draw to a conclusion shortly after this.

Although the phenomena I experienced intrigued me, I feel they are not important in themselves. Rather, they are important waymarkers along the path which we all hope may lead to results that are repeatable and reliable under controlled conditions.

In time perhaps there will be the promised breakthrough and the message from the spirit realms may eventually reach much more of humankind than at present. I am not convinced, however, that this will occur in the foreseeable future. Nor am I convinced that this world is anywhere near ready. I hope I am wrong though, because my own outlook was transformed by what I have learned and I wish that others could have the same opportunity.

If experiments do result in reliable, repeatable phenomena which can be tested by scientists, and if these do irrefutably demonstrate existence beyond death, humankind would be confronted by concepts possibly more challenging than anything ever faced in this world before. There could be massive implications for science if Earth and spirit scientists work together.

The group told us that some of the investigators involved in the Scole Experiment freely admitted to looking forward to the sessions and recognised the potential for future experiments, given co-operation from both sides of life. The group found it useful to learn from these experienced investigators just what was required as evidence to convince their more sceptical peers. Of course, the group could only ever conduct experiments and provide evidence within the limits of what was achievable by the spirit team using their 'energy based' methods of communication.

At the more speculative end of the explanatory scale, it has even been suggested that the spirit team was able to make contact 'using the science of atoms and molecules' because it is only in relatively recent history that individuals with the relevant knowledge have died and become available to do the work 'from the other side'. We can do no more than proffer this explanation as one that has been put forward.

It is also interesting to note that a number of eminent scientists, academics and other scholarly investigators have been heavily involved in paranormal and parapsychological research in the past; some suffered derision at the hands of their 'more realistic' colleagues but, nevertheless, carried on regardless because their results were so intriguing. However, there is now a burgeoning interest in paranormal events that defy normal explanation. A section of the psychology department at Edinburgh University is now dedicated to the study of this subject.

Professor Fontana has commented that physical paranormal phenomena could lead us to rethink some of the most cherished laws of science. Many distinguished researchers have personally witnessed and scrutinised the circumstances in which these phenomena are produced. Other scientists around the world are beginning to review the Scole Experiment and even examine the new experimental work that is now being done by other groups which are following the Scole lead.

CHAPTER SEVEN

AUDIO EXPERIMENTS

Mediumship in all its forms is a crude makeshift which we must use until our engineers perfect a mechanism we can use automatically. This is possible and will doubtless be the next step after television. You are within a short distance of two extremes: annihilation or illumination. If you will spend the time and money in seeking to reach us that you now spend in developing some military devices, you will soon give us a device for communicating with you.

William Brandon (via a medium) in 1935

The spirit team eventually asked the group to set up a foundation, known as the New Spiritual Science Foundation, to study 'spiritual science', which was best explained as 'the science of life and the afterlife'. This new field of investigation widened the parameters of what we would normally understand as science. Following the formation of the Foundation in mid-1994 and the publication of the first issue of *Spiritual Scientist,* the group soon realised that there had been a substantial world-wide growth in the number of experimenters in the field of 'trans-dimensional communication' during the previous decade or so. The Foundation was contacted by a number of individual researchers and organisations working in this field. Some of them were apparently receiving regular transmissions.

Trans-dimensional communication embraces a number of different types of electronic phenomena, made possible in recent years by the advances in electronic technology not only in this world but also in the spirit world and aided considerably by the rise of the microchip. The main forms of communication now being received are: electronic voice phenomena (EVP), television picture phenomena (TPP), messages via computers, messages via radio, messages via fax and telephone calls from deceased communicators.

While, until the Scole Experiment began, the members of the group could claim very little knowledge of the last five of these six forms of communication, Robin Foy had accumulated about twenty-one years' experience in researching EVP by the time the first issue of *Spiritual Scientist* came out in winter 1994. He had obtained several thousand examples of EVP on a series of simple cassette tape recorders, ranging from single words to long sentences, with many of them being by way of direct answers to the questions he had asked the communicators.

EVP was first discovered by Friedrich Jurgenson, a Swedish artist, opera singer and producer of documentary films, in 1959. His work was later expanded upon by the German Professor, Hans Bender, of the University of Freiburg. The Latvian psychologist and philosopher, Konstantin Raudive, then wrote a book about EVP called *Breakthrough*. It was so widely read that Raudive was associated with the phenomenon and the voices were known as 'Raudive voices' for a brief period of time.

In the past Robin has run many workshops on EVP and helped others to achieve it for themselves. The procedure requires a minimum of equipment, together with patience and dedication, and the voices appear as 'extras' on tape recordings. The speech can often be faster than normal human speech, although the style and timbre of the voices varies considerably. They often manifest in a peculiar rhythm on the tape, making it difficult for those not familiar with the EVP to detect at first. However, once a person can hear them clearly, sometimes after playing the tape several times over, they are much easier to recognise and understand.

There have been reports of similar phenomena for a number of years. Tom Sawyer, a visitor to Scole, reported his belief that the BBC has banned broadcasts at twenty-nine megacycles/second because spirit voices were heard on this frequency when people were taping from their radios. Robin continued by telling us in more detail about another development within the group: two-way audible communication between the dimensions using modern equipment. This had been called 'trans-dimensional communication', or TDC, at the spirit team's suggestion. Using this technique, the group was able to conduct conversations with personalities in other dimensions and record them on a cheap and simple battery-powered tape recorder.

On Valentine's Day 1996, screeches and weird noises started to come from the tape player the group was using to play background music during a routine experimental session. At first they thought that the tape recorder was about to seize up. However, a member of the spirit team told them that this was in fact a new form of communication with which they were experimenting. Robin was asked to turn down the volume control to blank-out the music, but the interesting thing was that the 'weird noises' did *not* decrease in volume. The group members gradually became aware that they were listening to words, although these were partly inaudible on this first occasion.

The technique was further developed, a few months later, at one of the group's seminars. The team had asked them to provide a simple battery-powered tape recorder from which the microphone had been removed. After a few crackles and whistles, a whispered voice said *'Hello'* through the amplifier. With eager encouragement from the group members, the voice gradually became stronger. A short conversation then took place. The communicator addressed one of those present by name and went on to talk about the many possibilities of this new form of communication. The group was then told that the silicon chip in the tape recorder was the 'point of entry' for this contact.

Shortly afterwards, the experiment was repeated at a seminar for German delegates. This time, the female voice coming out of the amplifier greeted everyone loudly and clearly with *'Guten Abend'*. The team said that the trans-dimensional communicator was a German *Fräulein*. She gave her name and spoke several sentences in German. According to the German delegates present, there was no trace of a foreign accent in the spoken words. They were quite convinced that this clear communicator was in fact of German origin.

At a seminar in the late summer of 1997, the emphasis was again placed on this new form of communication. One of the invited delegates, Tom Sawyer, operated the recorder. Soon after it was switched on, a voice was heard. The music was turned down so all could hear the voice better. The communicator asked: *'Is that you, Tom?'* Recognising the voice of his father-in-law, who had died less than a year previously, Tom responded immediately. The two had a personal conversation for several minutes.

THE GERMANIUM RECEPTOR

Trans-dimensional communication had been achieved using a simple tape recorder. However, the group was soon asked to build another device, a 'germanium receptor', to use alongside the recorder. The receptor employed a crystalline substance known as germanium. In addition to being a semi-conductor, this substance is also classed as a semi-rare metal. The receptor was plugged into the microphone input socket of the tape recorder.

There were several teething problems for the spirit team in achieving successful communication but they said: *'When you hear the results, we think you will agree that we have certainly made spectacular progress.'* To their amazement, the group found that using the receptor with the tape recorder allowed clear conversation with a number of 'personalities' from what were believed to be distant dimensions, that is, not from the spirit world as we would understand it. The team explained to the group that some of the dimensions were so far removed from our own that it had never been anticipated, even by many evolved souls in the spirit world, that any form of direct communication would ever be possible.

We first saw the germanium receptor at Lyng. All present were asked to gather round a table at the front of the seminar room. On the table sat a rectangular glass box with a wooden base.

'We call this box, the fish tank,' explained Alan. 'Visitors have witnessed lights passing *through* its glass sides during experiments.' Inside the box, sitting on the wooden base, was the germanium receptor itself. Alan told us that it was not kept inside the fish tank during experiments, but normally placed there for protection. 'It looks a bit Heath Robinson, but I can assure you it works!' he laughed.

We learned that, during the early germanium receptor experiments, scientists and researchers worked closely with the group. In the initial stages of experimentation, the spirit team asked the group to ensure that the compass crystals on the table were aligned exactly with north, south, east, and west. The group often heard spirit team technicians moving around the table area where the receptor and recorder were placed. The technicians were constantly re-adjusting the equipment and re-aligning the energised crystals. This led the group to believe that the crystals played a very significant part in the TDC phenomenon, a fact which was later confirmed by the spirit team.

As the experiments progressed, the group started to receive very unusual signals using the germanium receptor. They had been told that these contained large amounts of information that would be useful to mankind. The signals sounded a little similar to data being downloaded through a computer modem. During the seminar, the group said they anticipated instruction from their communicators on how to decode these signals.

The group explained that the spirit team was constantly pushing back the barriers of spiritual science with their pioneering TDC work. We were told that a communications network was being established between the many dimensions, including our own. Once established, the network would give humanity permanent access to the 'distant dimensions beyond the spirit world'.

It was not the case, however, that anyone could immediately achieve trans-dimensional communication just by building a germanium receptor. The process seemed to involve creating the right conditions within an experimental group and co-operation with a spirit team. For other groups, this might even involve the use of different equipment from that used at Scole, or even a different technology altogether. The SEG did not make a conscious decision of any sort to experiment in this way. The motivation came from the spirit team.

During their early experiments with TDC, the group had continued in the only way they knew how, along the same lines that Robin Foy had been using for many years. Then, on 14 September 1996, at the twelfth session with the scientific investigators, spirit scientist Joseph came through and asked if the group could get germanium. Professor Ellison was present and explained to everyone that germanium was a semi-conductor that had been used for making 'chips' before silicon. Joseph then asked if a small amount could be obtained. Arthur Ellison agreed to try and get a small amount.

Later in the session, after a light display, Joseph asked out of the blue: *'Did someone mention a coherer?'*

No one had. What was it? Professor Ellison explained to the group that the device had been invented by Sir Oliver Lodge and used in radio before crystals such as germanium and silicon but for the same purpose, as a semi-conductor. The professor also explained that a coherer was used in conjunction with radio (electromagnetic) waves. As these waves pass through the coherer, parts of the coherer stick together, conduct and rectify.

Joseph then returned to the germanium, explaining that only enough to cover a fingernail was required. This prompted an interesting discussion, which would lead to a new phase of experimentation in trans-dimensional communication:

> **Arthur:** If you can do things with a germanium crystal, electronic voice production might be possible.
> **Joseph:** *That's right; it might well be.*
> **Arthur:** That's the end product, perhaps?
> **Mrs Bradshaw:** *Don't spoil the surprise, Arthur. Put your logic away. Wait and see.*
> **Joseph:** *It's very interesting how things have parallels in other dimensions. What you term 'electrical fields', 'electrical energies', 'magnetic energies', all have parallels in other dimensions...*
> **Arthur:** If you can move a piece of germanium around and press it in a certain way, you might produce electric charges which might be used to speak, when amplified and put through a speaker.
> **Joseph:** *Yes, we know.* [Laughter.] *We've done it!*

For the next session, on 9 November 1996, Professor Ellison brought a very small quantity of germanium. This was placed in a saucer and left on the cellar table. A spirit scientist took charge, although he said he was relaying messages rather than speaking from his own knowledge. In response to Professor Ellison's query as to whether silicon would have served instead of germanium, the spirit scientist immediately said that it would not, explaining that the germanium had special properties intended to enhance communication. However, he stressed that this was to be communication of a totally different nature, 'communication that has never, we believe, been attempted or achieved before, voices from other areas or dimensions of life... but not necessarily of the afterlife as you think of it'.

The members of the Scole group found this conversation fascinating, as it linked to previous sessions when a personality who had recently come through the trance state of one of the mediums had explained that he was not familiar with the physical environment of the Earth. It was quite clear that the communicator had never lived on this planet. Normally, most spirit communicators were quite 'at home' when they spoke to the group. However, this particular 'being' seemed to have difficulty understanding time, light and colours. Human physiology appeared to confuse 'him' as well. The group stressed that they used the word 'him' loosely because gender was uncertain. This communicator had told the group that 'far off' dimensions would be attempting to communicate with them. The group therefore found it exciting when the team started giving instructions on how to put together equipment which might enable this promised trans-dimensional communication to occur.

Apparently, these communications would form 'trans-dimensional links' or bridges, enabling 'chains' to be established. These chains would then remain *in situ* for other communicators to use. The spirit scientist said it was hoped to transmit messages through the germanium 'using it as a focus, but not simply a focus'. The experimenters learned from the team that they would not be dealing with electromagnetic waves, but rather pure spirit vibrations. In other words, it was made quite clear that the group and investigators were not to think in terms of radio waves, which are, of course, a part of the electromagnetic spectrum.

Having confirmed that radio reception was not to be the means of communication, the spirit scientist continued to discuss, apparently with reference to another communicator, the device for receiving the 'spirit vibrations':

> **Spirit scientist:** *Someone has already volunteered their help in the manufacture of small devices... something will be needed to hold the germanium.*
> **Robin:** Oh right.
> **Spirit scientist:** *And I see he's referring to a piezo* [Greek: to press] *effect.*
> **Arthur:** Yes.
> **Spirit scientist:** *He wants you to mount the germanium and apply a degree of pressure, a constant pressure between the two threaded screws. These can be used as terminations.*
> **Arthur:** Yes. Should they have points or flat ends touching the germanium?
> **Spirit scientist:** *One flat and the other pointed.*
> **Arthur:** Like a crystal radio set.
> **Spirit scientist:** *There's some polarity involved.*
> **Arthur:** Yes, when the radio waves hit it they are rectified, when they can be made audible.
> **Spirit scientist:** *Well, I don't know if we can rectify anything because I don't anticipate the need here.*
> **Arthur:** Rectify means take out half the waves; it doesn't mean put something right.
> **Spirit scientist:** *Very well. Robin, I'm asking you if you could... mount the crystal as has been suggested.*
> **Robin:** Yes, we'll get it done.

The spirit scientist then requested a device be brought to the cellar to amplify what would be transmitted.

> **Arthur:** With a microphone or speaker?

Spirit scientist: *No, I don't think so. No, not a microphone but purely an audio input; but a relatively high impedance input.*
Arthur: Yes, I understand.
Spirit scientist: *The gain does not have to be a considerable amount.*
Arthur: The gain is the number of times the output is of the input.
Spirit scientist:... *The two terminations upon the germanium will be used as an input.*
Arthur: Yes, I see.
Spirit scientist: *Hopefully the output will be heard.*
Arthur: There will be a small loudspeaker.
Spirit scientist: *Yes, we are now talking of voltages. There is some concern as to the amount of electricity. Could this be of low voltage?*
Arthur: I should think this would be.
Spirit scientist:... *Unfortunately you will not be able to use any other electrical equipment.*
Robin: Right.

Professor Ellison then established that the team required amplification operating on an extremely low voltage, millivolts to be precise. Further discussion about the technical aspects of the experiment puzzled Professor Ellison because he considered the equipment and techniques being suggested as 'wholly outmoded'. Since Professor Fontana was having a special session two days later (on 11 November), Professor Ellison asked his colleague to raise the matter.

At the following session, Professor Fontana raised Professor Ellison's query, asking if it were possible to substitute the germanium rectifier with a silicon diode. Joseph was adamant that it was not a rectifier and should not be thought of in that way. He and other members of the team stressed that germanium was necessary because it had spiritual and healing qualities. It was also explained that the proposed device was not essential to the desired effects, but helpful, much like the function of the glass dome on the table. Professor Fontana mentioned the problem of the fragility of the germanium and inquired if pressure from a pointed screw was necessary. Joseph replied that it need not be too pointed and stressed that they should not think in terms of 'cat's whiskers' or rectifiers.

The investigators did not consider that the degree of technical know-how displayed by the team during discussions about the germanium receptor would be within the normal knowledge of the group members. The *Report* noted that prompt and detailed technical responses were given through the mediums to spontaneous questions put by a professor of electrical engineering.

After receiving the information from Professor Fontana, Professor Ellison advised the SEG on how to build the germanium apparatus. He suggested the use of a pointed conductor resting lightly against the metal, around which was placed a small insulating frame, with strips of copper to make connections to the underside of the germanium, and the pointed steel screw resting on the top. Professor Ellison was concerned that the pointed screw might crack the germanium when screwed down on it. To overcome this, he had considered making the point of the screw rest on the end of a piece of coiled wire to add a measure of resilience. Then he realised he was reinventing the crystal detector from the early days of radio and designing a rectifier, which allows the current to pass in only one direction. He asked the communicators whether a modern, more reliable silicon diode would not be better. The team informed him that the device was not to be used as a diode and should be made exactly as described. A piece of rubber was therefore placed under the germanium to give it the desired resilience.

Despite Professor Ellison's continuing reservations about the viability of the germanium device as an instrument of communication, by the session of 3 January 1997 it was ready, having been constructed by the group under his supervision. To this session, Professor Ellison took a box containing an amplifier with a tape recorder built into it, the whole having been constructed by one of his PhD students. He attached this box to the germanium device, which was now known as the 'germanium receptor'.

The finished device was actually quite small, about 2.5 inches by 1.25 inches, and had a short length of cable to connect it to the input of the amplifier box (see Figure 2). The amplifier box had a tape recorder built into it, which enabled recordings to be made directly from the source (the germanium). Since there was no microphone connected, the result would be a recording of the communication only, not the voices of those present during the experiment. There was, however, an output to a speaker so that any sounds coming out could be heard. The whole session was, of course, recorded on a separate tape recorder, giving valuable information to correlate with the trans-dimensional communication achieved via the germanium receptor.

On the evening of 3 January, the group was joined by Professor Bernard Carr, an astrophysicist, as well as the other investigators from the SPR. When the device was switched on with the volume control at maximum, there was, as expected, no sound from it. However, when the spirit scientists began their experiment, crackles and bangs, a bit like electrical sparking, came from the speakers. A sound like a steam train accelerating from a station was also produced and finally the rushing sound approximating to white noise. When asked, Professor Ellison explained to the group that this white noise was the sound that could sometimes be heard between stations on a radio. Professor Ellison and Professor Carr were particularly intrigued by the source of the noise, since they said that no normal explanation could account for it. Professor Fontana and others present also reported hearing 'whispers'.

Edwin then spoke. He emphasised that the team was still at the exploratory stage but that they were confident that the combination of amplifier and germanium would soon result in clear speech. Edwin even said that eventually it should be possible to communicate via technology alone, without employing human mediums at all. Very few people display either an interest in or an aptitude for mediumship, so this would mean that far more people could receive trans-dimensional communications.

At this stage, it was apparent that the team's attempts to communicate were encountering considerable difficulties.

Although there had been a good deal of muttering, whistling sounds and even some musical notes, the communicators concluded that there was something wrong with the amplifier. Edwin said that a message about these difficulties could be expected soon. Somewhat intriguingly, he said this message might take the form of a sketch on one of the films to be used at the next session on 11 January.

At this next session, Ingrid Slack, a psychologist with the Open University, was present. There were two films (Kodachrome 200 35mm 36-exposure) and two security boxes. The first security box was named the 'Alan' box because it was made by the Scole group medium. The investigators considered the Alan box susceptible to tampering because of its exposed screw heads. To overcome this potential problem, the investigators asked the group to seal over all the screw heads with a lacquered paint. The investigators believed that this paint would fracture if any attempt were made to open the box by interfering with the hasp in order to open the lid. This lacquering was carried out and the painted seals deemed satisfactory by the investigators. The second secure container was named the 'Keen' box. This had been built under Montague Keen's direction and had no exposed screws.

Before the experiment, Professor Fontana and Ingrid Slack removed two films from their packaging and placed the unopened black tubs containing the film cartridges in the Alan and the Keen boxes. They had secretly marked both film tubs. The investigators then closed the lids and Montague Keen padlocked both boxes. Professor Fontana held the Alan box, which had a combination lock. Ingrid Slack held the Keen box, which had a key-operated padlock. Only Montague Keen knew the combination lock number of the Alan box and he also retained the keys of the Keen box. The boxes were then taken downstairs to the cellar by Professor Fontana and Ingrid Slack and placed on the circular table close to where they would be sitting.

Immediately after the session, Montague Keen unlocked the two boxes. Professor Fontana and Ingrid Slack checked the secret markings on the tubs and placed each in a separate Jiffy bag. Ingrid Slack then made a mark externally on the Jiffy bag containing 'her' tub, to distinguish it from that which had been in the box held by Professor Fontana. She sealed each bag on the gummed flap with sealing-wax, on which she imprinted the chasing of her ring. She repeated this sealing-wax procedure on a separate sheet of paper so that the person opening the Jiffy bags could be satisfied that the seals had not been broken and that the ring impressions in the wax seals matched the one on the paper.

Next morning, Montague Keen faxed a message to Ralph Noyes, the then Hon. Secretary of the SPR, in order to have dated confirmation of the above facts, and in particular of the predictions made by the spirit communicators. The essential passage read:

> It was made clear by the spirit communicators that their intention was to link the message on the films with the events of that evening, and more particularly with the problems of the electronic equipment, possibly including a diagram, or some message or request to or affecting Professor Ellison. This was a response to a request I had made at a previous sitting for such an evidential link.

Montague Keen arranged for the two films to be quickly developed at Kodak's works in Wimbledon, where the production manager, David Cobb, inspected the seals and satisfied himself that they had not been broken or interfered with. He also checked that they matched those stamped on the paper and then signed the authentication note. Before Montague Keen returned to collect the results, Ingrid Slack telephoned Mr Cobb to find out whether there was anything on the films. This was an additional, previously agreed, safeguard to ensure that Montague Keen could not be accused of substituting a faked for a blank film. (It would appear that the investigators even scrutinised themselves!)

On one of the films, in the middle section of the fifty-inch long roll, there was an electrical diagram (see Plates 36 and 37) together with a clearly written message, under which was a monogrammatic signature, which could have been 'FOX'. The message related to the diagram and had one short word crossed out (here written as 'xxx'):

A represents the Germanium, B and C Coils of high Resistance.

The whole being xxx enclosed in Box.

This could help *[reception?]* Considerably

Another monogrammatic signature at the far right of the film was: *TAE*.

At the same 11 January session that this film was received, the experiments with the germanium receptor continued. There was much adjustment by the spirit team during the session.

After a prolonged attempt at communication via the device, it became clear that the team was attempting to improve reception and eliminate faults. Edwin explained that a contact had been made and asked Robin, whose hand was on the amplifier – in order to make volume adjustments as requested – to press the recording button. Robin did this but, despite much encouragement and the sound of a voice, Edwin had to inform the communicating personality – whose name was said to be Thomas and who appeared to be *within* the trans-dimensional communication device – that no one in the cellar could hear him properly.

Robin turned the volume up. Mrs Bradshaw then announced that Thomas was making a further attempt. However, every time Robin pressed the recording switch to obtain a permanent record, the switch flipped back. Edwin, who seemed to be able to hear Thomas and Thomas's problems clearly, made assurances to Thomas that his message was understood by those in the spirit realm and that there would be something in writing on the film for Professor Ellison. This turned out to be the case.

The Scole group commented:

> As predicted, we did indeed receive valuable information on that sealed film and, at the same session, there was the strange attempt at communication by 'Thomas'. From what the spirit team said, he seemed to be *inside* the machinery. We were intrigued to learn that Thomas was trying to form a link in a chain of communication and that he

was not from the same 'place' as our regular communicators such as Mrs Bradshaw and Edwin. They could hear him, but we couldn't, and that was the reason for all the adjusting and the instructions on the film. We later came to believe that Thomas in the machine was *TAE* on the film. During his lifetime on Earth, he was a famous scientist and inventor.

The film showed the germanium receptor and its connections to the amplifier but, in addition, two coils had been added to the circuit. The text explained how these two coils were to be connected and their positions in relation to the germanium. Again the SEG enlisted the help of Professor Ellison, who assisted them in finding the necessary components.

At the next session the team explained that an interaction or 'effect' took place between the germanium crystal and the coils. The relative proximity of the coils, and their polarity, were important factors in the reception of communications. A coil produces an electromagnetic field around itself. This field has a direction. It also has polarity, that is, north and south poles (see Figure 3).

The group explained this further:

Just to confuse things, remember that in this instance we are not actually referring to electromagnetic fields but energy fields or patterns. This can, of course, give rise to some misunderstandings about the nature of the communication, because it is beyond our current knowledge. We knew very little about the new spiritual science technology and so tried to remain open to all new ideas. We were therefore prepared to be guided by the team every step of the way.

The team told us that these energy fields, associated with the coils, behaved in much the same way as their electromagnetic counterparts with regard to direction and polarity. A void is formed where the two fields around the coils oppose each other. We all probably remember trying to push magnets together in physics lessons at school where the like-poles repelled. This void was described to us as 'non-spin energy space'. It is in this void that the germanium is situated, in other words, right in the heart of the opposing fields (see Figure 2), where it can detect and absorb the fluctuations in the energies. These fluctuations cause the interaction or effect on the germanium crystal to take place and it is this that opens the link to far and distant dimensions. So, the void can be imagined as a *doorway* leading to other areas of existence and the germanium is the key that unlocks the door.

Although the investigators were concerned that the suggestions on the film would be likely to attenuate (weaken with distance) rather than strengthen any signals, if normal physics applied, Professor Ellison nevertheless reassessed the design of the germanium receptor according to the instructions on the film and obtained the relevant coils.

It was during the weekend of 18/19 January 1997 that Walter and Karin Schnittger visited the Scole group. Walter, whom you may remember is a consultant engineer, instructed the group on the correct soldering of the wires. Once the germanium receptor was modified and the group had corrected some minor difficulties they were having with the amplifier, they were all set to continue with the experiments. They did not have to wait long for a spectacular result.

At the next session, on 21 January, the first noises were familiar: crackles, clicks and white noise. The group members were straining to hear, almost banging their heads together as they leant forward to get nearer to the loudspeaker. Then, suddenly, a faint voice was heard: *'Hello.'*

'You can imagine the excitement as the voice grew louder,' reported the group. 'It was a man's voice. He was definitely trying to make himself heard. He kept repeating: "Hello, can you hear me? Hello, can you hear me?"'

Plate 1: Street Farmhouse in Scole, near Diss in Norfolk - the venue for the experimental sessions.

Plate 2: The cellar known as the 'Scole Hole' where all the paranormal activity took place. On the table are the dome, a 35mm film, and a cassette which were used to record the phenomena.

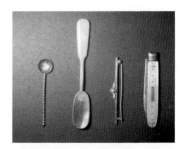

Plate 3: Various apports, including several of the gifts from the sessions held on 3 January and 14 February 1994. All the items were teleported using the new form of creative energy which the team developed.

Plate 4: This famous picture of St Paul's Cathedral during the Blitz was captured on 35mm film using a conventional camera during a session held on 28 February 1994. Is this an actual memory from one of the spirits who lived in London during the Second World War, or their memory of seeing the actual picture in the media?

Plate 5: Photograph from 28 February 1994 of the front page of the Daily Mirror, 16 December 1936. A copy of the original was obtained. It was almost identical to the photograph, with some minor differences which indicated it might have been from another edition on the same day.

Plate 6: An image of the River Seine taken from the Notre Dame Cathedral which was captured on film on 28 March 1994.

Plate 7: Another image from 28 March. Is this man an Afghanistan tribesman, or perhaps someone's spirit guide? The group thought it might be Raji, one of the spirit team, but the spirits told them later it was not.

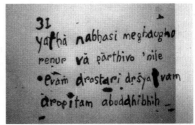

Plates 8 and 9: The *Srimad Bhagavatam*. These photographs were transmitted by the spirit team on to factory-sealed, 35mm Polaroid slide film – the first on 13 January 1995, and the second a few months later. Diana Bennett later found a Sanskrit text in an Oxfam shop which was one of the eighteen volumes of the *Bhagavatam*. It turned out to be the one which contained the translation of the transmitted text. Coincidence?

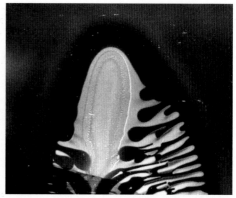

Plate 10 (above left): This very clear portrait of Sir Arthur Conan Doyle – a renowned investigator of the paranormal – was received on Instant Polaroid film during one of the sessions held in 1995.

Plate 11 (above right): The group described these strange shapes as seascapes, but also wondered if they were from some other plane of existence where plants and other life forms might be found. Notice the energy field or aura in the centre.

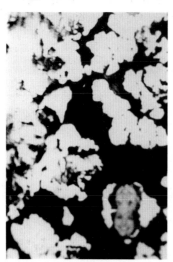

Plates 12 and 13: The spirit photographic team transmitted images on to the rolls of 35mm film. Here we see two unmistakable faces; there is mirroring with the woman's face [left]. The other image of a man [right] is so clear that you feel you should recognise him. If you look very closely, you can just see other faces in the process of development.

Plate 14: The experimental sessions in Dr Schaer's finca (farmhouse) in Ibiza, 29 June and 1 July 1997. The two mediums are sitting in the foreground of the picture. Recording equipment was placed on small tables between the chairs, and in the niche in the wall at the back of the room. Phenomena were observed in a number of venues other than in the cellar in Scole.

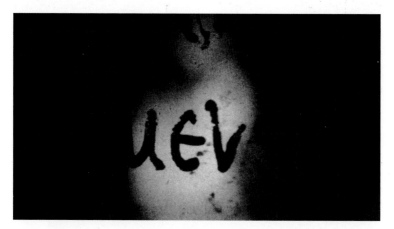

Plate 15: Greek on Green, 17 February 1996. Investigators from the Society for Psychical Research monitored the session in which this appeared. The letters translate as 'm', 'e', and 'n'. A Greek expert said that in today's language this does not represent the word 'men', but would probably be an abbreviation of a Greek name.

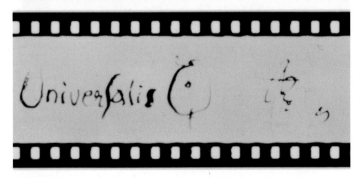

Plates 16 and 17: Perfectio consummata seu Quinta Essentia Universalis (From chaos to the highest summit of mankind). This phrase was transmitted on to an unopened roll of colour film during a session attended by Professor Archie Roy, a specialist in astrophysics. The symbols allude to the Golden Chain of Homer (*Aurea Cantena Homeri*), which symbolises a journey which begins with chaos and confusion, and ends with perfection, thus representing Man's progress towards the Light.

Plates 18 and 19: Wie der Staub in... Wind (Like Dust in... Wind), 22 November 1996. This film was produced in conditions described by investigators as following 'perfect protocol', i.e. no chance of fraud whatsoever.

Plates 20, 21, and 22: The German poem in three sections. This is one of the most intriguing and important of the Scole films which was transmitted by the spirit team during a session on 26 July 1996, attended by German investigators. The author has not been identified although there is speculation that it might have been written by Friedrich Rückert (1788-1866) who was famous for translating the Koran into German. There is no evidence to suggest the poem has ever been published. It is written in the style typical of c. 1840. Note the Chinese symbols and possible celestial allusions on the final section.

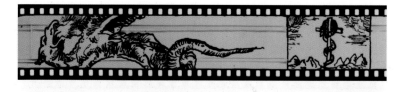

אהיה אשר (Hebrew)   QVADRANS MVRALIS

Cassiel

Plates 23, 24, and 25: The Dragon Film, 17 January 1997. The dragon [top left] can mean earth energy in Chinese philosophy, or it could represent the serpent or devil cast into the bottomless pit. The serpent and cross symbol [top right] could represent the Old and New Testament or an allusion to the mix of Man's bad and good nature on Earth. The Hebrew name for God appears on the left of the middle section – each letter stands for one of the names of God. Cassiel [bottom left] is an angel associated with Gabriel.

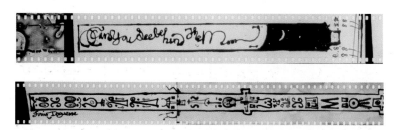

Plates 26 and 27: Daguerre and Can You See Behind the Moon – this photographic image was one metre in length! It is not known what this phrase means. Louis Daguerre, an early pioneer of photography, is famous for Daguerreotypes. This image bears his name, but it is not his signature. Why is it on the film? What do the glyphs mean?

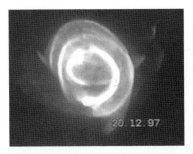 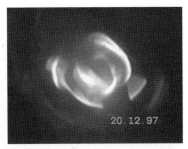

Plates 28 and 29: These dramatic flower-like energy forms manifested on video following experiments which took place on 20 December 1997.

Plates 30 and 31: These creative energy forms appeared on video on 13 March 1998. They were from a variety of materialisations known as 'sustained visible objects' which were brought from the spirit world for the group to see.

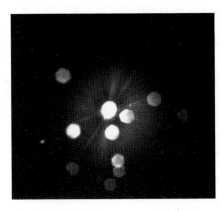

Plate 32: Images such as this 'starburst' were captured on film which was sealed in a security bag, and watched by an independent scientific observer during the experiment. The investigators said the films could not have been accessed or tampered with during the experiments – which led to the conclusion that the images produced must be paranormal.

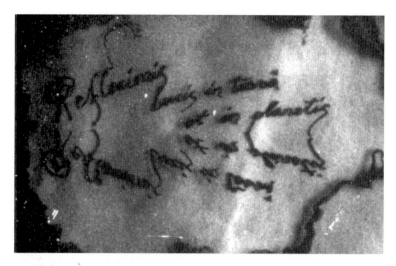

Plate 33: The Latin Mirror image – *Reflexionis, Lucis in Terra, et in Planetis* (Of reflection of light on the Earth and the planets), 25 May 1996. The notion of mirroring and reflection was a recurring theme during the Scole Experiment. In esoteric philosophy, it is sometimes said that the physical universe mirrors or reflects the spirit realm.

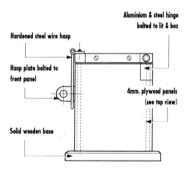

Fig 1. Solid Wooden Security Box.

Plate 34: The wooden security box in which the unopened films were placed.

Plate 35: The diagram shows the security measures taken to ensure the films could not be tampered with during the sessions.

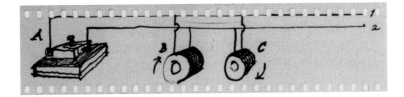

Plates 36 and 37: The Germanium receptor and instructions received on 11 January 1997. The electrical diagram was to help Professor Ellison assist the group in altering the receptor to enable verbal communication between the Scole group and the spirit team. Spirit voices were first heard on 21 January 1997 – a milestone in trans-dimensional communication had been achieved.

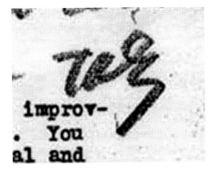

Plate 38: The TAE signature appeared on the far right of the germanium receptor film during a session at Scole on 11 January 1997. It is not known what the 888 means.

Plate 39: For comparison, the group obtained a copy of Thomas Edison's mono-grammatic signature from an original document dated 25 May 1925 from the Edison Institute in the USA.

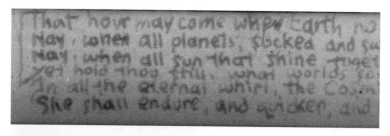

Plates 40 and 41: *Diotima, Ce n'est que le premier pas qui coûte*, poem by Frederic Myers. Diotima is a fictional prophetess who, according to Plato's *Symposium*, taught Socrates all he knew about love. The items on the film all related to an encomium (tribute) to Frederic Myers – after his death in 1901 – by Sir Oliver Lodge and others. Is the evidence sufficient to conclude that the spirit of Frederic Myers did indeed transmit the information received on this film?

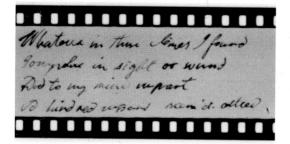

Plates 42 and 43: The *Ruth* 1 [detail and mongram] and *Ruth* 2 poems were compared by investigators with the little-known original document in the Beinecke Rare Books and Manuscript Library at Yale University in the USA. The handwriting on the film bears a strong resemblance to the original. It would have required someone with specialist knowledge to even be aware of the original – so was it Wordsworth himself, his sister Dorothy, his biographer Myers, or some other communicator who transmitted the messages onto the two films? We may never know.

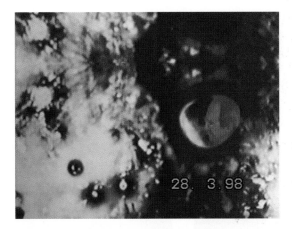

Plate 44: This image is from a video experiment on 28 March 1998. You can just see a man's face in the bubble-like sphere on the right – he appears to be wearing glasses. Another face is just in the process of forming begind him. The group was told by the spirit team that these pictures showed other areas of communication or existence, i.e. not from within our known universe.

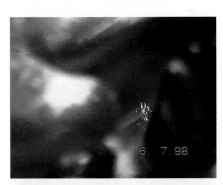

Plate 45: Project Alice. Despite the filming taking place in complete darkness, dramatic surges of colour were captured on video on 6 July 1998.

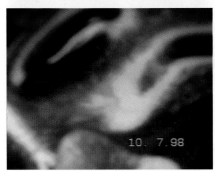

Plate 46: Project Alice. These spectacular moving lights were caught on video on 10 July 1998. During these sessions the camera zoomed in and out of its own accord in order to focus on the images it was recording.

Plate 47 (above left): Cancer. The Scole Experimental Group was told this image closely resembles a cancer cell. The characters 'T21' can just be seen in the bottom left corner. Perhaps this refers to the 'T' cells.

Plate 48 (above right): Project Alice. A video taken in fully lit conditions showed the edge of a square screen. As the image rotated, a fully animated face was revealed. This inter-dimensional friend was named 'Blue'.

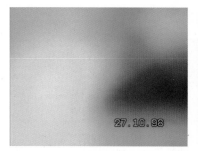

Plates 49 and 50: Project Alice. The experiment on 27 October 1998, recorded in darkness, showed two very bright red lights and a large green light moving across the screen.

Plate 51: This picture from a video experiment on 21 September 1998 clearly shows some pyramid formations.

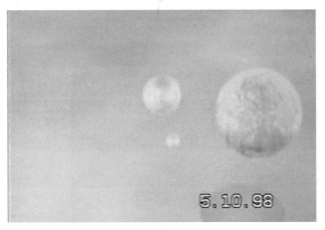

Plate 52: These 'worlds' appeared on film on 5 October 1998. Could they represent planets from an unknown universe in another dimension of existence?

Plates 53 and 54: A profusion of spirit lights captured on video, 2 November 1998.

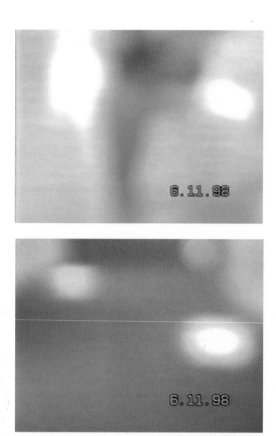

Plates 55 and 56: Two of the amazing moving-light phenomena caught on video 6 November 1998. Were these glimpses of the spiritual dimensions, or attempts by the spirit team to manipulate earthly lights?

Plate 57: Alpha and Omega – the beginning and the end. Could this be an allusion to the polarity necessary in a physical three-dimensional universe? What do the symbols and shapes in the middle mean?

UNITED KINGDOM MEDIA COVERAGE

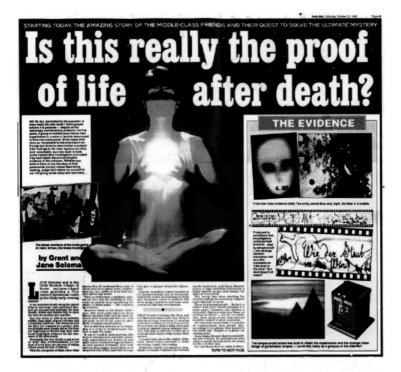

Daily Mail, Saturday 22 October 1999 by Grant and Jane Solomon

UNITED KINGDOM MEDIA COVERAGE

Time Out, October 1999

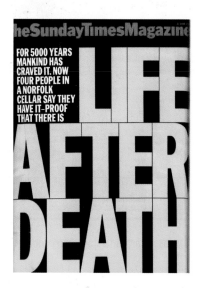

Sunday Times Magazine
front cover, 1999

Eastern Daily Press, 1999

WORLDWIDE MEDIA COVERAGE

Japanese Super Mystery Magazine *MU*, Winter 2000

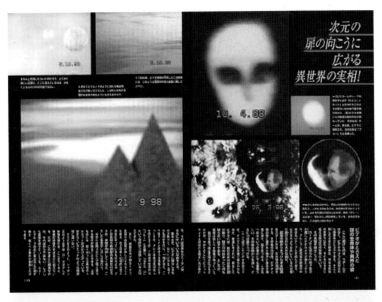

UNITED STATES INTEREST

George Dalzel, author of the book, *Messages*
and contributor to *The Scole Debate*

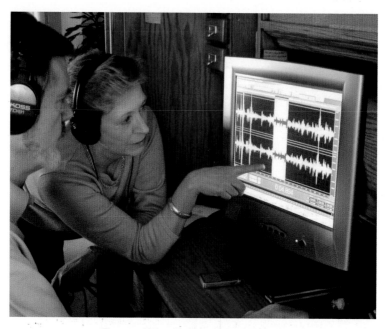

Tom and Lisa Butler of the AA-EVP
American Association of Electronic Voice Phenomena

THE NORFOLK EXPERIMENT

THE ISIS EQUIPMENT

An image being captured via digital video camera with the ISIS system

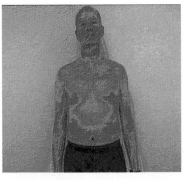

A 'filtered light' image of the man seen having his ISIS scan [left]

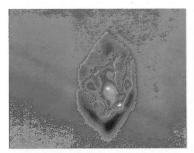

Above left: ISIS scan of quartz crystal.

Above right: ISIS scan of same quartz crystal whilst being used for healing. Note changes in colour and intensity.

Left: ISIS scan (different light filter from above) of interaction between human light fields.

THE NORFOLK EXPERIMENT

CPE – CRYSTAL PHOTOGRAPHIC EXPERIMENTS

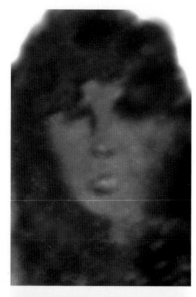

Left: Early 'new work' of Diana and Alan.

This is the first image received. Diana and Alan were 'instructed' as to how to set up the equipment during an early session.

Below left and right: These two images were received as a 'pair' during the same session. The left image shows what appears to be an old white-haired man, and the right shows what could be a white owl.

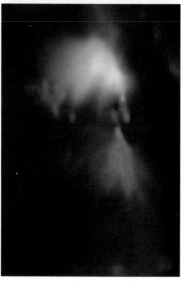

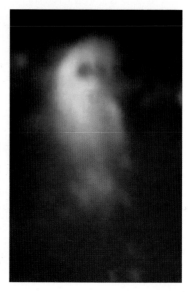

THE NORFOLK EXPERIMENT

CPE – CRYSTAL PHOTOGRAPHIC EXPERIMENTS
MORE IMAGES

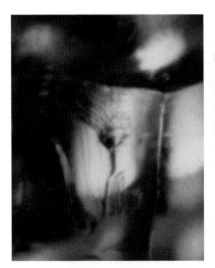
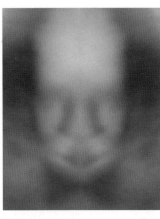
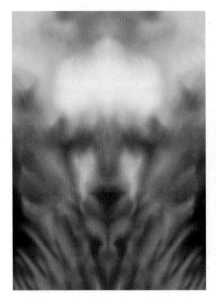

THE NORFOLK GROUP – FIRST SESSION

THE EXPERIMENTAL ROOM

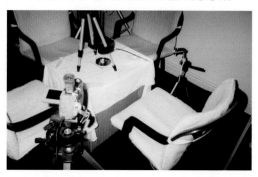

Four comfortable chairs surround a central table on which sits a digital still camera mounted on a tripod. There are clear quartz crystals at the four corners of the table. A spotlight shines a beam of light into the crystal. Images are captured at intervals. Lighted conditions.

A video camera records some of the events, providing images as a permanent record and for analysis with the ISIS light imaging system. This part of the experiment aims to find a 'frequency band' that the communicators can utilise to repeatedly 'reveal' themselves on film.

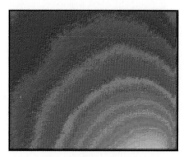

Plain wall
ISIS Filter 001 applied

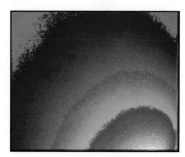

Same wall
ISIS Filter 010 applied

Then he succeeded:

> *I shall continue this transmission in the hope that you can hear me clearly. You understand, my friends, that we are experiencing some difficulties, but we feel sure that these will be overcome. However, we feel we have made considerable progress upon the last attempt to communicate with you. We have, for some time, been involved in an experimental communication system and it is this system that we are using now. It is hoped that, in the future, this system will enable us to communicate with those distant dimensions and, if all goes according to plan, you will be part of these experiments. I shall repeat myself and say I do hope that you can hear this communication. We will stay here for a little longer, please be alert.*

The communication paused for a short time, then continued, becoming clearer:

> *At some time in the near future, there will be many attempts made to communicate with you in this way. There are many people here who feel, as I do, that this work is of the utmost importance to mankind and therefore are willing to put their hearts into these experiments.*
>
> *Thank you, my dear friends, thank you for co-operating with us and giving us this moment of your time.*
>
> *May peace be with all of you.*
> *God bless you.*

The communication then ended, having lasted approximately twenty minutes, the whole having been recorded on the tape recorder. A milestone in trans-dimensional communication had been achieved.

Further discussions with the communicators on the subject of inter-dimensional links ensued. One very interesting conversation concerned man's use of semi-conductors. (As we know, germanium and silicon are semi-conductors.) This discussion provided insights into the use of other materials, such as carbide, in the future. The team told the group that the possibilities were almost unlimited, given the right circumstances. They explained, as best they could, why semi-conductors would play an important part in future experiments and how some of the links between the dimensions would be made.

At the team's suggestion, the group carried out several experiments without the germanium receptor attached to the amplifier. This set-up apparently still allowed some communications to take place, but only with 'near' dimensions. Some of the two-way conversations in experiments without the germanium were witnessed by members of the Society for Psychical Research and recorded on tape.

The team explained that the 'closer' dimensions, such as the spirit world related to Earth, did not have the same difficulties in communicating. However, some of the communicators from the distant dimensions could speak only through the germanium receptor, as this provided them with a clearer channel than other methods. It also helped them to be understood, as some form of translation took place. This was essential since some of these personalities were not familiar with language.

The team also told the group that it would be possible to receive messages via computers, faxes, telephones and tape recorders in future. Apparently, any type of electronic equipment is open to possible interaction, even television and video recorders. The group was told they would soon receive evidence supporting this prediction but, to get to that stage, they would have to work in closed session – just the four of them – on the trans-dimensional communication experiments. The team said they wanted to work on establishing the links with the distant dimensions and it was best if only the four familiar energies were present during what they thought would be the 'most difficult set of experiments we have tried to date'.

Dr Ernst Senkowski joined the Scole Experiment in 1995. He studied experimental physics at the University of Hamburg in 1946 and gained his doctorate at the University of Mainz in 1958. He worked for UNESCO as a physics expert in the National Research Centre, Cairo, Egypt, before being appointed as a professor training engineering students in physics and electrotechniques in 1961. In the mid-1970s he started his own experiments on unexplained voices on tapes. After a few months, the results 'showed the reality of audible contacts with the apparently, so-called "dead".' After obtaining his own independent results, he discovered that others, such as Jurgenson and Raudive, had made similar observations. He retired in 1988.

Given the above, we considered Dr Senkowski to be something of an expert witness in regard to the Scole Experiment. In November 1998, he sent us an account of his experiences at Scole together with other relevant information.

PERSPECTIVES

DR ERNST SENKOWSKI

I and my wife had the opportunity to take part in two sessions of the SEG in 1995 and 1996.

My own observations as well as later personal reports of my colleagues, the Schnittgers, left me convinced of the genuineness of the phenomena. I considered a number of them to be physical anomalies that cannot be incorporated into the current scientific framework. Nevertheless, it is possible to integrate these (and other) 'paranormal' effects within broader proposed systems which arise from the results of modern consciousness research, particularly the interactions of mind and matter.

The following considerations are based on my twenty years' experience in the lesser known field of Instrumental

Trans-communication, or ITC. [Dr Senkowski coined this term in the 1970s to describe 'electronically supported contacts with other ranges of human consciousness' including 'the beyond'.]

Given a wider view of the nature of the laws which may govern the universe, the many-faceted Scole phenomena may enlarge our always limited vistas of life and may one day appear quite normal.

Throughout history, 'mediums' in 'trance' states have expressed 'transinformation' and performed 'trans-communication' through speech or automatic writing. Since the 1950s, all types of electronic apparatus (audio-tapes, video tapes, radios, telephones, TVs, computers) have been used in this field. Each piece of apparatus constitutes the final link in a hypothetical translation chain. They delivered messages from no-where into now-here and allowed dialogues with otherwise hidden 'virtual transpartners' or 'communicators'.

Unlike telecommunications devices that function in the hands of any user, transcommunication appears to be subject to the psychic faculties of the operator (and perhaps other less obvious factors).

In spite of the remarkable observations collected by private persons – including the SEG – no 'official' scientific verification of ITC under laboratory conditions has been undertaken. We are still left with many open questions. However, the results of the current research could bring us *nearer* to significant answers.

The Scole Experiment presents itself as a combination of mediumistic and instrumental single and two-way transcommunication. Additional extraordinary effects were manifested and documented. These carried less direct information but demonstrated the possibilities of astonishing mind-matter interactions.

I believe we should clearly differentiate between extraordinary facts and their interpretation. We should also avoid separating the currently mutually exclusive materialistic and spiritualistic views and instead consider a holistic cosmos.

The materialistic-spiritualistic controversy appears to be a consequence of an historical split in ways of thinking. This split could possibly be overcome by a new perspective as expressed by the renowned psychologist Stanislaw Grof, who said that the comprehension and classification of paranormal phenomena is not yet possible in the light of an, as yet, unfinished world-view into which mysticism, modern physics, neurophysiology, consciousness research, information theory and theory of systems may converge.

═══

It appears from Dr Senkowski's use of words that a whole new vocabulary is being developed to describe these new phenomena in search of a new understanding of the relationship between (conscious and subconscious) mind, body and spirit.

It seemed to us that his approach is consistent with many of the ideas contained in the new spiritual science that the spirit team said was soon to be much more accepted by scientists and lay people alike.

CHAPTER EIGHT

VIDEO EXPERIMENTS

In my father's house, there are many mansions.

Jesus Christ

Another set of experiments began towards the end of May 1997. This work was called 'Project Alice', as it involved the use of mirrors. This was a reference to the famous book, *Through the Looking Glass* by Lewis Carroll, which featured Alice. Guided by the team, the group began using a video and mirror arrangement to capture moving images sent from the spirit world. Project Alice went far beyond any other work of which the group was aware, because the images were being captured on video film. Like many other experiments, Project Alice was conducted alongside a number of related and unrelated trials. The germanium receptor and microphone-less tape recorder experiments ran concurrently, overlapping on some occasions.

So how did these video experiments come about? As we know, at the end of Patrick Night in February 1994, Patrick told the group that they would soon be asked to bring a still camera and perhaps just photographic film on its own into the cellar for the planned experiments. At the same time, the group had also asked if they could bring a video camera into the sessions. Patrick said that if they brought it in for the next session, a one-off experiment might be permitted by turning the video camera on for a period of about five minutes. But, since it was felt that there 'may well be a problem with interference from the camera motor at this stage', the team would let the group know. At the next session, five minutes' filming was allowed but produced nothing. On 11 April 1994, the group asked when they would be able to record with the video camera again. The team said they had examined it thoroughly but, at this point in time, it had been decided not to do any specific work with it. The group was therefore asked to remove it until further notice. This further notice came much later, in the first half of 1997. Having sought the agreement of the team, the group started to use their video camera during experiments on a regular basis, but they were not sure how the spirit team would eventually work with it. At the end of the 27 May session, a new communicator came through and told the group that the time had come to construct a 'double psychomanteum' in the cellar to link in with the video work. The psychomanteum would consist of two mirrors. One of these would be behind the video camera, so it could catch and reflect the 'electron luminosity' (the coin-sized circle of light emanating from the viewfinder) back towards the other mirror, which would be situated in front of the camera. The whole arrangement would form a 'loop' with the camera in the middle, and so aid in the creation of a 'doorway' to and from other dimensions. The aim was to capture, on video, the spirit team members entering the cellar through this doorway.

The original forms of the psychomanteum were known as 'oracles' and were operating many centuries ago. People would gaze into highly polished surfaces, which gave the same effects as mirrors, in order to communicate with their 'dead' relatives and loved ones. This ancient practice would now be combined with modern technology to achieve remarkable results.

Initially, the camera was allowed to run in the darkness for forty-five minutes, the duration of the video tape. It was during these preparatory sessions that the group was able to record, for the first time, objective phenomena such as moving lights and sustained visible objects from another world.

During the preparatory stages of Project Alice, on 5 June, the video camera was set up – with no mirrors as yet – and a brand new blank tape was started *before* the room lights were turned off. On playing back the tape afterwards, the group saw a very distinct face at the beginning of the video film. It was clearly a man's face, smiling happily. Where had he come from? He certainly wasn't physically in the room. This footage was historic for the group because it had been recorded in the light. There was no question of it having been recorded at any other time, as the date of the session was clearly visible on the tape, together with the image. This meant that future experiments, with investigators present, could probably be conducted in lighted conditions, which would of course answer one of the main criticisms of the sceptics who said that the group's work was some sort of magician's trick in the dark.

For the session of 9 June, the group had been asked by the team to hire a second video camera for use in a special experiment. This they did, and both cameras recorded such fantastic images that the spirit team asked the group to keep them 'under wraps' until such a time as they were cleared to share them with the public at large.

The final instructions in the preparations for Project Alice came through on Friday 13 June. The group was asked to set up a practice experiment at the next session, using only one small mirror. The instructions received from the team were quite specific. The dimensions for this mirror were to be one unit of length across to two units of length down. The mirror was to be set up portrait fashion, as opposed to landscape. This was important, because it would produce the approximate shape of a door. The mirror had to have a dark, matt surround, so as not to give off any reflection. It was to be set up at the southern point of a table, with its top inclined back slightly. The camera was to be at the north side of the table, a few inches higher than the top of the mirror. The camera was to be focused into the mirror but, most importantly, it should not actually be visible in the mirror when one looked through the camera's viewfinder (see Figure 4).

The group was very excited by these developments, especially when Mrs Bradshaw went as far as predicting that they would be likely to get some good images the first time that two mirrors were used.

The group set up two mirrors and a camera as instructed. On 17 June the first proper experiment of the project took place. The camera did not run for its full forty-five minutes, as the group was told to turn it off, using a remote control, after about half an hour. The team told them to watch the resulting video carefully. They predicted that, if there were no results during the first twenty minutes, then there would be no results at all.

The group was not to be disappointed. Something had indeed been recorded at the beginning of the tape. Once again, it had been taped in lighted conditions at the start of the session. The four members of the group were blocked out visually and audibly, while coloured patterns and interference appeared on the film for a few moments, followed by images of what appeared to be a being from a far distant dimension.

Edwin came through with refinements to the experiment: *'The set-up of the mirrors is not ideal. Next time, please put the camera below the table, instead of above. It will also be necessary for you to provide a totally matt-black screen behind the camera.'*

Thus began a series of experiments that comprised the early days of Project Alice. The progress of the project was to be kept secret until the results were adequately consistent. The team was not sure just how long it would take for regular results to come because this project involved what they called 'pure pioneering work'.

Some of the early experiments of Project Alice took place in darkness with the camera positioned between two mirrors, creating 'a loop' for the team to work with. The group made many minor adjustments to the position of the camera and the two mirrors during this period, as the team tried first one set-up and then another, constantly improving their technique. It was not long before the group was asked to record in the light for a few minutes at the start of each session. Then it was requested that the video camera be moved to the rear of the cellar and curtained off from the central table and the group. This was so that the camera was no longer in the vicinity of the group, as Project Alice and the TDC experiments were interfering with one another to a certain extent. From then on, the video camera – on its tripod – was focused in a line parallel to the rear wall of the cellar, where it was set up with the two mirrors, the camera forming the base of a triangle with the mirrors forming the two sides.

Over the following months, the group noted surges of colour on the video tape when viewed on a television screen, but no other result was apparent during this period of intense development. During the sessions, however, the group constantly heard spirit technicians coming from behind the curtains in the area of the video camera. When the videos were played back, they saw that the camera had repeatedly zoomed in and out on its own – a physical impossibility without the help of manual manipulation of the camera itself.

The team felt that positive results would be achieved, but the timing was a matter of speculation. Project Alice and the TDC experiments that were running in parallel were the hardest experiments they had ever attempted.

In early August 1997, the team asked the group to stop all visitor sessions for the foreseeable future. The group had to inform the scientific investigators of this decision. The investigators, who attended for the last time on 16 August 1997, had not been aware of the progress of the trans-dimensional experiments or the nature of the video experiments. Montague Keen stated:

> We went along to sessions knowing that the group were experimenting during closed sessions with the germanium receptor and other instruments for trans-dimensional communication. However, there was a curtain rail at one end of the cellar, behind which, we assumed, other things were going on in our absence.

Visitors were excluded as it was important for the team, at this crucial stage of the new experiments, to keep up the momentum of their work from session to session. Whenever there were visitors present, the energy balance changed and this retarded the vital development. On the advice of the spirit team, the group also stopped the seminars at that time. With just the four of them and their 'known' energies present, there was much more scope for rapid advancement.

As Project Alice and the other trans-dimensional communication experiments progressed, it became more and more obvious that the group was leaving behind some of the basic phenomena they had previously witnessed. The energies were changing as they linked into distant dimensions beyond the spirit world they knew so well. Consequently, it became more and more difficult for the team to repeat aspects of phenomena that had previously been commonplace.

A few exciting results began to show on the tape and the group started to make out indistinct figures moving across a blue light. Since the room was in darkness – after the initial few minutes of filming in the light – there should have been no blue light. They also saw a hint of body parts, such as hands and arms, moving across the screen in a red light. Again the light should not have been present... and certainly not the limbs. The average video camera, like the one used by the group, requires a certain small amount of light (a minimum of three lux) to produce any images at all. Logic therefore suggests that there should have been nothing at all on any of the tape shot in the dark. But the images were there.

On 26 September, a recording in the dark produced a very interesting video. When the group viewed it afterwards, they saw a large well-defined luminous green circular 'patch', which appeared on the screen several times. This was animated. It moved across the screen and sometimes popped up from the bottom.

After this the team gave instructions for modifications. They asked the group to take one of the mirrors away, so that only the large mirror remained in front of the video camera, with the camera focused into it. Using this new set-up, on 16 October, a light suddenly shot across the screen like a comet. Later, on the same tape, a light moved randomly around the screen.

The last experiment in October was also productive. The early part of the session, recorded in the light, behind the curtain, showed a couple of hazy figures moving briefly onto and off the screen. Later on the tape, which was recorded in darkness, two very bright red lights appeared and then a large green light moved across the screen (see Plates 49 and 50).

At this stage, the team explained something of their methods:

There are two separate 'photographic spirit teams' working on Project Alice. The 'early' team is trying to introduce results onto the tape during the short period when the camera records in full light. There is also a 'late' team, which is trying to project results onto the film during the dark period.

The group later became aware of a third team trying to produce images during the middle part of the session.

There was a breakthrough from the 'late' team on 14 November 1997. It was a short session, as Edwin and Mrs Bradshaw wanted to give the group time to watch the video recording carefully. The group considered the result to be 'truly amazing'. The last eight minutes of the tape, filmed in total darkness, showed images of various objects unlike anything they had seen before. These constantly moved and turned on the screen as if displaying themselves. Hazy forms also moved about all over the screen. One was similar to quartz crystals. Another, popping up from time to time from the bottom of the screen, resembled some sort of glove puppet. The scenes stopped only when the tape ran out. Edwin and Mrs Bradshaw explained that these images were connected to the TDC communications in some way and that the group would soon learn more.

At the next session, they saw something different again. The team said that this was a background 'screen', developed specially by the photographic department. In the future, the group would be seeing definite images on such a screen, maybe even in mid-air, without the need for a video camera.

Over the next few weeks, Project Alice continued to surprise the group. On 4 December, there was a good result from the early team. The group had been told during the session that they should see colours when playing back the tape. Afterwards, they saw a series of red and white images on the video. The rest of the tape showed shots of rectangular moving shapes in many colours, interspersed with occasional coloured layers.

As we know, the TDC experiments with the germanium receptor were continuing in tandem with the video experiments. In early December 1997, this work took an interesting turn as it appeared that the receptor and video recorder were being used as two halves of the same experiment. On 8 December, the group received trans-dimensional communication from a personality who was transmitting from a location he described as 'West 3'. He referred to himself as 'a friend'. The group commented: 'It was clear from the conversation, via the receptor, that this friend had obviously had input into the film work done during the session.' He also said that there were several personalities at his location who were aware of what had been happening with the video tape experiments. He asked the group to look very carefully at the tape after the session. If he and his colleagues had been successful, the colour blue would be prevalent on the images received. He assured the group that once good results had been achieved on the video tape, success would build on success, and they would get more and more images. This was only the beginning.

This was obviously a very busy session. Edwin and Mrs Bradshaw told the group that they thought some success had been achieved on the video, this time by the late team. They were, as usual, correct. On playing back the video, the group members first noted a sort of smoky haze, like a flame, developing in the centre of the picture. Then they saw a marvellous sequence of moving images. These images moved in and out of focus, but a bright blue colour predominated, just as predicted by their trans-dimensional friend. At the time, the group members had no idea what they were seeing, but the sequence went on for five or six minutes until, once again, the tape ended.

The session of 20 December 1997 again produced some wonderful video images, which lasted about six minutes. It was the day before the winter solstice and Manu had said that the dimensions would be very close to one another at this time, which would for some – not explained – reason be of great help to the video work. During the session, the video camera was switched off by a spirit technician, with a loud click, well before it was due to finish. Mrs Bradshaw said that the photographic department felt very optimistic about the result and Edwin added that there should be lots of colours and images on the video. He advised the group to look deep into the colours.

The group was not disappointed: 'We witnessed a myriad of

colours, together with incredible animated images. These colours were all those of the rainbow, together with vibrant mixtures of pink, turquoise and many more.'

The video camera experiments continued in the New Year of 1998. The early shift was successful on 2 January, with the video camera recording in full light. It was during this session that Emily teased the group by saying that one day they might get to see some faces on the video and that the image of a 'light worker', with dark hair, a headband and very red lips, appeared.

After this, the group recorded for fifteen minutes at the beginning of each session in full light and from Friday 16 January 1998, the team asked that this be extended to thirty minutes, with the video camera still focused on the mirror, behind the closed curtains. This period was to be made up of ten minutes of 'chatter' and twenty minutes of 'meditation'. Sandra volunteered to put together an audiotape of meditation music that was exactly thirty minutes long, in order for the group to time this period precisely. This experiment was to run in parallel with the germanium receptor experiment, which, the team stipulated, should have an audio-tape in it of thirty minutes duration each side. This represented a progression as far as the group could make out, as they would now be allowed to record some of the results of the trans-dimensional communication directly through the germanium receptor and recorder apparatus. There were, however, occasions when, for one reason or another, spirit technicians would turn the recording part off.

Successive sessions often seemed to be related, each building on previous experiments. The group explained that since the video tapes were of forty-five minute duration, this allowed the last fifteen minutes of recording to take place in darkness. This was tried a few times and, on viewing the start of the tape of the 26 January session, the group clearly saw the shape of a square pink and gold screen.

It was at their next session, on Friday 30 January, that the real breakthrough came. Towards the latter part of this session, Edwin asked the group to watch the start of the video carefully. Mrs Bradshaw said that if she had not given up gambling, she would have had half-a-crown on the evening's video result being a good one. She was right. At the beginning of the video, there was a single pink and gold line running from the top to the bottom of the picture. This was obviously the screen the team had mentioned, viewed side on to show that it was flat. Gradually the line turned sideways and the square screen came into view, now seen from the front.

The amazing thing was that, as the screen rotated, it had an image on it. This was a very clear view of 'an animated inter-dimensional friend, whose features, to say the least, were not exactly as our own'. This 'friend' has been named 'Blue' (see Plate 48). We leave you to judge for yourself whether the image is at least thought-provoking. The group had no doubts. For them this was a fantastic result which had been achieved in fully lighted conditions.

After this important session, the set-up for Project Alice was changed again. On 2 February 1998, the group began to work in a new way. The first thirty minutes of each session continued to be in full light, with video recording taking place. However, the mirror was now placed higher up and the top was tilted further back. The video camera was set up even higher than the mirror and focused into it. Between the video camera and the mirror was a low chair, facing the mirror. The curtains which had divided the main cellar from the area of Project Alice were no longer closed while the light was on during the early part of the session. The team told the group that they should, one after the other, sit on the chair and look at the mirror. However, it was important that anybody who sat on the chair facing the mirror must not be able to see any part of themselves in the mirror.

Now that the video experiments had progressed to this stage, the group and team felt able to invite Dr Hans Schaer to scrutinise a video session, part of which would be in fully lighted conditions. The date was set for Saturday 28 March 1998. Dr Schaer reports that the first part of the session took place in excellent visibility. He noted that the curtains at one end of the cellar were drawn back. Alan had bought a duo-pack of two sealed video-camera tapes from a local shop. They were packed together in a sealed plastic wrap and were forty-five minute JVC type EHC (extra high grade) cassettes. The unopened package was handed to Dr Schaer.

Having inspected the package, Dr Schaer opened it and selected one of the cassettes, which he signed and dated. Alan showed him how to insert the cassette into the video camera. Dr Schaer was careful to do this himself, making sure that nobody else present touched the cassette. The camera was a JVC compact VHS camcorder, model GR-AX600 registered at 3 lux (1 lux in slow shutter mode), with an F1.6 lens, which Dr Schaer had earlier supplied to the group. It was already mounted on the tripod when he inserted the cassette and was pointing towards the upright mirror across the room, which was inclined backwards slightly and positioned approximately eleven feet from the camera lens. The electric light in the cellar was on at this stage and conditions were described by the doctor as being 'bright'. In these well-lit conditions, he switched on the video camera.

Dr Schaer and the four members of the group then sat round the central circular table outside the curtained off area where the camera was situated. Robin put on the tape of Sandra's meditation music. After exactly five minutes' meditation, Alan got up and sat in the chair which had been placed between the video camera and the mirror. He gazed into the mirror for five minutes. He then returned to his seat and Diana took her turn to gaze into the mirror. After five minutes it was Dr Schaer's turn, then Sandra's and finally Robin's. Robin then closed the curtains, returned to his seat and switched off the light.

The five participants remained seated in the dark for about another three-quarters of an hour, during which time Alan and Diana went into trance. There was the usual type of trance conversation through the mediums, with Manu, Mrs Bradshaw and, briefly, Patrick McKenna coming through to address the group. Then a new entity from a faraway dimension introduced himself. Nobody could clearly make out his name and even though they listened to the tape several times after the session, the closest they got was 'Shariness Darti'.

During this session the spirit team indicated that the phenomena which had been produced in the past would not be continued, because the energy would be used for the development of new phenomena. Towards the end of the session, Mrs Bradshaw said that she believed this experiment had produced a remarkable result and that if there were anything on the tape it would be near the beginning. This meant that it would have been produced during the first thirty minutes, when the video camera had been running in full electric light.

At the end of the session, when the light was switched on again, all were surprised to find that the curtains, which had been closed prior to starting the dark period of the experiment, had been opened by about twenty inches.

Dr Schaer removed the video tape from the camera, checked his dated signature and carried the tape upstairs, where he inserted it into the video player in the Foys' sitting room. At the very beginning of the tape, they all saw in the lower right part of the television screen the clearly recognisable 'profile of a man aged between fifty and sixty, slightly bald in front, with dark black hair and possibly a black moustache, wearing metal-rimmed spectacles'. This portrait appeared as if it were inside a water bubble (see Plate 44). It lasted for about six seconds. There were many coloured 'slurs' (Dr Schaer's word) on the tape, some of them animated. One of the slurs started to move towards the bubble, entered it and formed a second man's head behind the first one, but still easily recognisable. The second man wore something like a Russian fur hat. His face remained there for about three seconds and then both portraits vanished.

Dr Schaer concludes his report of these events as follows:

> We were not that evening, and still are not, able to identify these two men. No specific explanation as to their identity was given by the spirit team either. The Scole group were kind enough to produce a postcard-size enlargement of one sequence of this video tape which shows these two men in profile very clearly.

It was soon after this that we attended the seminar in Lyng. During the afternoon, having just shown us 'Blue' manifesting on the screen, Alan explained more about the evolving video experiments. He said the special meditation tape for background music was exactly thirty minutes long. Using a small clock in the lighted room, the group timed the experimental periods precisely. The first five minutes in the light, with open curtains, was used for a short meditation. Then each member of the group in turn sat on the chair and gazed into the mirror, with the video camera recording constantly behind them. As each person sat below the inclined mirror, looking up, they were unable to see their own reflection. The four group members doing this in turn, for five minutes each, together with the initial short meditation, accounted for twenty-five minutes of filming in the light. When the last group member left the chair, that individual drew the curtains behind them, and the final five minutes in fully lighted conditions would be taken up with a further five-minute meditation. Visitors to the group in the future would be invited to take part in the psychomanteum experiment, each spending five minutes on the 'hot seat'. The final fifteen minutes of filming then took place in darkness. Alan explained that the group understood that exciting results lay ahead of them in connection with Project Alice.

Further experiments did produce an array of images. There were things that looked like shrimps, an orange and yellow flower unfolding, a comet, eyes, lips and even a beak. Another image resembled a rotating doorway. Articles about the video experiments continued to appear in *Spiritual Scientist.* The June 1998 issue of the magazine reported on 'The Open Doorway':

> The interdimensional doorway is now well and truly open and we have been privileged to welcome loving beings to the group from many different dimensions, some of which are very far removed from our own earthly dimension. At recent sessions we have had 'physical' interaction with beings who are quite different from us. While they could not understand our language, we were told by the spirit team that they were reacting to our emotions, particularly the

love and welcome which we were mentally extending to them. We were also told that much knowledge was passing between us during these interactions. Such beings come partly to learn from us, but mainly the purpose of such visits is to bring help and information to mankind at this time. This generous purpose, of course, far outweighs anything we can give to them. When, on one occasion we commented on the loving nature and gentle touches of these interdimensional beings who visit us, Emily Bradshaw asked us to share this information with others so that all may know that there is absolutely no reason to have any fear when dealing with such beings. If you sit in a group with love in your hearts and a genuine desire to help others to a greater understanding, then you only draw to yourselves those who have the same desires to help mankind.

At another session, we again had otherworld visitors with us in tangible form. After the earlier part of the video work, in full light, we closed the curtains in front of the camera and mirror before turning out the light and proceeding in darkness. Shortly after this we heard various noises and movement. The curtains were continuously swishing open and closed. We were told that this was because the visitors kept returning to the doorway within the mirror – perhaps for a recharge of energy. They also took a great deal of interest in our TDC amplifier and germanium device and could be heard pressing buttons and moving the crystals around. After the session, we discovered that the tape had been taken out of the TDC recorder. A music tape had been taken from another point some feet away and placed in the TDC recorder instead. We have certainly needed to keep our minds fully open recently to any and all possibilities.

The team's intention was to bring images of the spirit world for people to ponder on. Once again the object seemed to be to get people to open their minds. In the September 1998 issue of *Spiritual Scientist,* the group reported that they had 'already received a number of images of the spirit world'. The images were not yet very clear but, nevertheless, the group were able to make out what appeared to be grassy plains and crystal mountains in another world.

In early August, Manu commented:

> *We are continuing to try to bring you pictures of our world by using our thought focus. You may well be asked in future, 'How can you receive scenes of a world where there is no physical existence?' I should like to try to help you to have an understanding of this. When you enter our state, you cannot have a physical body or physical senses. But what you do have, in continuation, is mind. Mind and soul, blended as one. When you daydream or meditate, you can create a scene within your mind. You might see yourself walking through a wonderful natural scene of beauty; a field of poppies, perhaps, such as you have in this land. If you are working well with your mind, you will be able to project yourself into that scene. The better able you are to work with your mind, the more vibrant and real the scene will be to you. When you do not have the physical body to be a vehicle, you still have the mind to project your thoughts and to be a vehicle for your voyage.*
>
> *So you may wonder whether the spirit world is like a dream state? Well, some may say it is to a certain degree, but to us, you see, it is the true state, it is the real home of the consciousness. When you are in a physical state, part of your mind retains the ability to link with home. It is this part of you with which we can link when you are in the sleep state.*
>
> *Here, we can even visit one another. We dwell in a*

state of consciousness within our world. Our world is more vibrant and real than yours, although it is outside time – it is timeless. Unlike your world, our world does not have limitations. Our world is therefore such a creative place. There are many planes of existence and levels of existence for us to be with and interact with each other and we are able to create beauty in which to be. For ours is certainly a state of being. We will leave it there... At the moment you do not see much on the films that I can explain. But as things move forward, then it will become clearer.

When we visited the group in October 1998, we were given an opportunity to view some of their most recent video transmissions. One showed wonderful images of beautiful leafy forests, the leaves swaying in a gentle breeze. Another showed pyramids set in a great lake below orange red skies, the pyramids reflected in the calm water (see Plate 51). Two videos showed what looked like a world composed of ice.

The final transmission onto video tape during the five-year Scole Experiment involved synchronised sounds and visual images. These were received when the output socket of the tape recorder from the trans-dimensional communication device was attached to the input socket of the video camera. When the tape was played back, the group saw a man's animated face, his lips moving in time with the audible messages from him on the soundtrack. These transmissions were certainly thought-provoking.

So it was that, through Project Alice, the spirit team and the Scole group were able to create a 'doorway' through which many different types of beings were able to enter the cellar, passing between dimensions as they did so. The many beings brought a simple message of love and hope.

CHAPTER NINE

AN INCREDIBLE DETECTIVE STORY

The work the SEG is engaged in is of profound concern to mankind. It should affect the way all of us view our lives – and our death.

Montague Keen

In August 1998, we were invited to visit the home of Montague Keen, Secretary of the Survival Committee of the Society for Psychical Research and one of the main investigators of the evidence produced by the Scole group and their spirit team. We found it interesting to talk to a man who has been involved in psychical research for over half a century. Throughout the evening, this scholarly gentleman told us about the research methods employed and the findings in respect of the Scole Experiment. An incredible detective story unfolded.

As we have seen, the evidence from the investigative sessions combined a wide range of phenomena: visual, acoustic, oral and photographic. It also included discussions with the spirit team about many subjects, including the significance of the messages on the films. Montague felt that all of these combined constituted the most impressive evidence of survival ever collected to date. Furthermore, what the investigators witnessed with the Scole group appeared, to them, to be directly connected with events earlier in the century.

Montague explained that physical mediumship has always involved violent controversy. Many frauds have been uncovered, which has given all types of mediumship a bad name. Mental mediumship, too, is often fraught with ambiguities. But there are some cases of mental mediumship where the accuracy of the information communicated can be objectively confirmed. In the case of automatic writing, where a spirit takes control of the medium's pen-holding hand, the information can be checked, especially if investigators take adequate precautions to ensure the medium has no prior knowledge of the people or circumstances involved.

Some very distinguished people have been involved in the study and practice of both physical and mental mediumship. One such was Frederic W. H. Myers, the Cambridge classical scholar and William Wordsworth biographer, who died in early January 1901. A founder and former President of the Society for Psychical Research, Myers had a life-long interest in the study of psychical matters. Before he died, he made arrangements to get back in touch with his colleagues (after his physical demise) and thus prove the reality of life after death once and for all. Myers left an enduring legacy, including a message in an envelope which was not to be opened until it was thought certain by his peers that it was he who was attempting to communicate its contents by whatever means possible.

On 19 February, a few weeks after Myers' death, he transmitted a message via a medium to a close friend and colleague at the Society, Sir Oliver Lodge, the guardian of the letter. A number of similar messages followed, but none justified removing the envelope from the bank vault to discover its contents.

Then, in 1904, Mrs Verrall, a Newnham College classics lecturer and the wife of Professor A. W. Verrall, received three separate messages by automatic writing, on 13 July, 18 July and 24 November. The messages confirmed that the sealed envelope left by Myers was in the care of Sir Oliver Lodge and stated that its contents would be found to contain a passage about love from Plato's *Symposium.* Accordingly, Lodge called a special meeting on 13 December 1904, for the letter-opening ceremony. The hopes and expectations were that the messages and letter together would provide evidence for survival. However, the SPR's *Journal* (January, 1905) states: 'It was found that there was no resemblance between its actual contents and what was alleged to be contained in it.' It appeared that Myers had not succeeded.

However, Myers was apparently not to be thwarted. For a number of reasons, it soon became widely believed that, together with a number of 'colleagues in spirit', this indomitable personality had formed a team determined to provide irrefutable evidence of survival by an entirely novel device. This spirit team proposed to convey clues to various literary puzzles. These clues would be scattered among messages sent through several mediums in different countries. They would become meaningful only when put together, like pieces of an elaborate jigsaw puzzle. The aim was to show that no single medium could possibly have access to all the disparate bits of information, thus defying any other explanation than that they had been communicated by spirits who had survived death.

The messages were usually communicated through automatic writing, but sometimes through 'daylight impressions' (communications in which voices were heard and then the messages were written down by someone able to write quickly). Over the next thirty years, about a dozen mediums received them. The investigation went on so long that certain investigators, like Professor Verrall, actually died during the course of it and began communicating themselves.

Montague told us that the transmissions were complicated and allusive in that they made indirect references to people or events. Some of these took the form of mythological or symbolic events. Only when pieced together, usually by an outsider who had the ability to co-ordinate the apparently meaningless bits of information, did the message become apparent. These 'cross-correspondences' are comprised in twenty-four volumes, each of about 500 pages, making 12,000 pages of evidence collated over an extended period. There are only thirteen copies of the cross-correspondences in the world. According to Montague, only a classical scholar with ample time and a first-class brain could tackle them now. These documents have been analysed thoroughly and they constitute impressive evidence of survival.

However, for many others in the Society and elsewhere, the

evidence of the cross-correspondences can be explained in ways that do not involve survival. One counter-proposition is the 'super-PSI hypothesis', the basic premise of which is that there is a connection at some subliminal level between the minds of human beings. This explanation, which endows the mediums' minds with unlimited telepathic, clairvoyant, and precognitive powers, is difficult to falsify. However, it must always remain a matter of opinion until there is any evidence that any medium possesses such powers. There has certainly been none to date. Nevertheless, super-PSI has become the catch-all explanation which allows any apparent evidence of discarnate intelligence to be attributed to the unlimited powers of mediums who are somehow subconsciously linked together and tapping into an all-embracing fount of knowledge, perhaps a 'collective human psyche'.

The cross-correspondences ceased in 1930, with the specialists still arguing over their significance. Yet, many years later, Frederic Myers still appeared to be involved in providing evidence in support of the survival hypothesis... through the Scole Experiment. As Montague told us:

> At an early stage of the investigation with the Scole group, several references were made by the Scole spirit team to people associated with the early years of the Society for Psychical Research *and* the cross-correspondences. There were at least half-a-dozen references made to sections of the Society's reports – which were very accurate – and some of them related to the correspondences.

The Scole spirit team seemed determined to defeat the super-PSI hypothesis and any other competing explanation, by way of sending coherent messages and cryptic literary puzzles, as well as creating a wide range of other phenomena beyond earthly explanation. By way of example, the cryptic puzzles transmitted during the Scole Experiment include messages in Sanskrit, Greek, Latin, French and German, as well as a special reference to the poems of Wordsworth, with whose work Myers was very familiar. The spirit communicators were able to converse on a wide range of subjects with individual investigators who were experts in their own field. It seems the team was trying to show that the messages were of discarnate origin because the mediums involved could have had no conscious or unconscious knowledge of all these very specialist subjects.

THE FREDERIC MYERS ENCOMIUM AND THE *DIOTIMA* CLUE

The sixth session of 16 March 1996 was the start of an experiment which produced one of the most interesting, challenging – and ultimately evidential – photographic films of all. The information on the film, although cryptic, was soon considered to be very relevant to Frederic Myers.

After processing, there were a number of images along the length of the film. On the extreme left was a single Greek word: *Diotima* (see Plates 40 and 41). This was followed by a sentence in French: *Ce n'est que le premier pas qui coûte.* (It is but the first step that counts.)

Then came the following stanza, written in script across four long lines:

> That hour may come when Earth no more can keep
> Tireless her year-long voyage thro' the deep;
> Nay, when all planets, sucked and swept in one,
> Feed their rekindled solitary sun:––
> Nay, when all suns that shine, together hurled,
> Crash in one infinite and lifeless world:––
> Yet hold thou still, what worlds soe'er may roll
> Naught bear they with them master of the soul;
> In all the eternal whirl, the cosmic stir;
> All the eternal is akin to her;
> She shall endure, and quicken, and live at last,
> When all save souls has perished in the past.

The next message consisted of Greek letters: ó í ð ù å ï á í å ñ ù è ç ò é å ó ï ì å è á (It is not yet apparent what we will become.)

At the end of the film there were two names. The first was difficult to decipher, especially since it was in mirror-image. It was later confirmed by the spirit team to be 'Cora L.V. Tappan'. The second name was written more clearly and appeared to be 'Will Rallings'.

Not surprisingly, this film and its messages created much intrigue. The group and investigators discussed how they might solve the cryptic puzzles. As it turned out, they did not have long to wait for some helpful hints from the team. Before the investigators had the opportunity to probe further into the meaning and origin of the messages on the film, they were given some significant hints during the eighth session on 18 May 1996. They had not at that stage discovered any particular significance in *Diotima* and had not been able to translate the Greek, some letters of which were far from clear.

Early on in this session, Manu came through:

> *This is part of the plan: no doubt you have decided that for yourselves, for it is reminiscent of other times when spirit came and gave you something to puzzle over. That in time caused it to be a great part of the evidence for all. I think you know what I am meaning.*
>
> *I would add to the puzzle a bit more! There are more clues to come, and this will aid you. I will just say this, for it has been used in connection with the man from our side of life, who looks upon you as our ambassadors, and because he is experienced in doing this communicating work, he will be of great help to you and I do not think it will be very long before all is revealed...*
>
> *He said these words: 'Infinite progression, infinite harmony and infinite love.' I could not put it better and so I repeat these words that they may be another part of the puzzle. It will fall into place shortly, you will be pleased to know. Think of those words: they*

*have much meaning and I would like you to ponder
on them in your meditations.*

The investigators considered that Manu could only have been
referring to the encomium (tribute or memorial) to Myers
published by the SPR shortly after his death. This was dedicated
solely to Myers' memory and comprised five encomia, the first
by Sir Oliver Lodge.

The links with Myers were getting stronger and stronger as the
investigation proceeded. On page 8 of Lodge's encomium appear
the same words in Greek that were seen on the *Diotima* film: ό í ð ù
åïáíå ñùèç òé åóïìåèá (It is not yet apparent what we will
become.)

Also, the stanza on the film – later traced to a verse in one of
Myers' poems *The Renewal of Youth* (first published in 1882) –
immediately precedes a paragraph in Lodge's encomium which
he introduces with the very words Manu had given to the
investigators at the sitting:

> Infinite progress, infinite harmony, infinite love, these
> were the things which filled and dominated his
> existence.

The expression written in French on the film, *Ce n'est que le
premier pas qui coûte,* was a further piece of the puzzle. It was
later found to be a direct quotation from a passage in Myers'
monumental posthumous work *Human Personality and its Survival
of Bodily Death* (1903).

The investigators considered that this clear link with Myers
was later strengthened by a clue from Mrs Bradshaw. At the end
of a lengthy session on 9 November 1996, with regard to a
reference by Montague Keen to Myers' work, the following
dialogue took place:

Mrs Bradshaw: *While you're there have a peep at*
Human Personality *Volume 1, page 250.*
David: Page 250?

Mrs Bradshaw: *That's it, that's where you'll find another little clue for you, Monty. I know you're fond of these clues. Another little tease for you. I hope your French is good. That was another clue.*

Montague: Ce n'est que le premier pas qui coûte!

David: Your French isn't very good. [Laughter.]

Montague: I was quoting from one of the clues that was given to us.

Mrs Bradshaw: *I'll leave you with that so I can tantalise you a little longer.*

Montague Keen confirmed that this quotation does in fact appear on the page Emily mentioned. It is in the original edition, which is now fairly rare compared with the more familiar abbreviated single volume edited by Mrs Eleanor Sidgwick. Montague wondered whether perhaps it appeared on the *Diotima* film in order to hint at where Lodge had drawn the remark from.

In reference to the link between the writing on the *Diotima* film and the spirit team's verbal clues, *The Scole Report* states that the handwriting consisted of closely related messages 'which provided further possible evidence of the role, relevance and pervasive influence of a purported Frederic Myers. It constituted, in fact, the first substantial example in which the physical impression of messages on a sealed, unexposed film was closely linked with orally delivered information'.

So, the stanza, the French expression and the Greek phrase all appeared to be clues linking the film to Frederic Myers. However, the *Diotima* reference was still not solved. Professor Fontana made an interesting suggestion that, if written backwards, *Diotima* reads *'ami* to *id',* or 'friend of the spirit'. As we shall see, this proved to be an ingenious but incorrect attempt at a solution. Again, it was discussions with the spirit team, especially Mrs Bradshaw, which gave still more clues, thus allowing another part of the puzzle to be fitted into place.

At the 9 November session, Mrs Bradshaw talked about 'a test word, received before' and told the investigators to 'look in your dusty records'. Later, she confirmed that the test word was indeed

Diotima and more than hinted that it been received before in the cross-correspondences. She said that these communications had been of great importance at the time, a great step forward, and were still held in high esteem by a great many people. Furthermore, they remained difficult to explain away.

Emily then gave a very evidential clue. She said that the first time the test word appeared, according to her information, was 18 December 1902. So, there were 'Not so many dusty books to go through!' This led to the solving of the clue. In brief, the 'test word' clues referred to Plato's fictional *Symposium* (a drinking party in ancient Greece, with philosophical discussion afterwards) which was comprised of speeches made at an imaginary banquet about or in honour of (spiritual) love. One of the speakers was Plato's mentor and hero, Socrates. He said that everything he knew about love had been taught to him by a prophetess called Diotima. According to Diotima, love is not a god but a great spirit, one of a race of spirits whose function is to act as interpreter and mediator between gods and men. The implication seemed to be that all intercourse between gods and men, whether sleeping or waking, was through spirits, and one of these was love.

Montague Keen thus suggested that the word for which they had been given a handwritten clue on the film appeared, after investigation, to be 'love'. In his view, the context was consistent with the eulogy to Myers and made sense in the light of the content and purpose of the communications received at Scole. (For a full account of this complex investigation, we suggest referring to the Society for Psychical Research, where a consultation paper is available for inspection as a supplement to *The Scole Report.)*

So, the clues on the *Diotima* film were found to contain references to an encomium to Myers, published by the Society for Psychical Research, shortly after his death in January 1901. *Diotima* itself proved to be the crucial word since it was the first word on the film and was also a 'test word' given in one of the early cross-correspondences, with which the spirit of Myers gave every appearance of being closely involved. Having linked the film to Myers, the spirit team then seemed to be linking both Myers and the film to the cross-correspondences.

This was fascinating for a number of reasons, not least of which was that the cross-correspondences were an earlier attempt to prove survival by defeating the anti-survival hypotheses (namely, fraud, alter ego and super-PSI) – precisely what the Scole Experiment was trying to achieve. The investigators wondered whether the team was trying to communicate, if very cryptically, that certain aspects of the modern Scole Experiment were a continuation of the much earlier cross-correspondences.

The reason for the spirit team's clues linking Myers, the *Diotima* film and the cross-correspondences was now becoming clearer. The team seemed to be using the circumstances of one man's life on Earth to construct a series of clues to a puzzle, the solving of which would show that a sentient, *surviving* personality was involved in the transmission of the messages on the film.

An interesting aside is that the purported message from Myers, delivered through Mrs Verrall at the turn of the century, said that Myers' letter left with Lodge contained references to Plato's *Symposium*. As we know, at the time, it was adjudged not to have done so. However, a message on this subject did arrive on a film at Scole *ninety years* later.

It was certainly intriguing to the three SPR members that Myers might be trying to contact them through the new opportunity afforded by the Scole Experiment. There would soon be other messages transmitted via other films which, once again, appeared to point to Myers as a common link.

We now pick up Montague's story in January 1997. As already mentioned, at the session of 11 January, Emily Bradshaw had informed the investigators that a personality called Thomas was trying to make contact via the germanium device which was linked to the amplifier. The spirit team could hear him, but the investigators and the Scole group could not, hence the need for the electrical diagram and instructions on the film, which indicated the necessary modifications to the germanium receptor. The investigators were subsequently told, by the group, about a long communication from 'Thomas' that had occurred during a closed session on 21 January and were informed that the team had asked for further experiments with trans-dimensional communication to be conducted in closed session from then on. They needed to work only with the energies of the group members, but the investigators could still come along for other experiments. This was quite consistent with all that Montague and his colleagues had learned about what were still very experimental procedures.

The investigators were happy to turn their attention to organising sessions for the benefit of other investigators (including Dr Alan Gauld, Professor Donald West, Dr Rupert Sheldrake, Professor Ivor Grattan-Guinness, Dr John Beloff and Professor Robert Morris), analysing and solving the puzzles posed by the photographic films, and preparing to accompany the Scole group overseas for demonstrations under fresh conditions.

There was plenty to do. Original documents had to be tracked down. The contents of these documents – handwriting, signatures and so on – had to be compared with the images on the films and related to verbal clues from the team. Experts were consulted where necessary. Montague's findings, many of which stretched the bounds of coincidence, persuaded him and some of his colleagues that the communications were 'very possibly of discarnate origin'. The painstaking process of verifying the evidence became an important part of the scientific investigation.

The photographic part of the investigation, to which Montague devoted many hours of study, involves around fifteen films. The images on these films contain numerous messages, drawings and all sorts of other markings.

Montague remembers the session on the evening of 11 January 1997 as 'particularly interesting':

> This was when we received the electrical diagram film with the instructions and signatures. We had been joined by Ingrid Slack, a psychologist with the Open University. It should be noted that the main preoccupation that evening was in trying to get intelligent noises through the amplifier, which Professor Ellison had provided and which was linked

to the germanium receptor. However, the film experiments were to prove at least as interesting as those involving the germanium receptor.

The investigators, Professor Fontana and Ingrid Slack, had control of the films from start to finish. At no stage did any of the four members of the Scole group touch either the films or the boxes after the latter were handed to the investigators for inspection and film insertion. Montague had supervised the design and construction of one of the boxes. Both boxes remained very close to the investigators throughout the session and, according to Montague, could not have been removed by human hand without their knowledge. In addition, the door at the top of the stairs leading to the cellar was bolted, as was the adjoining cellar room, while the door of the cellar itself could not be opened silently. Montague explained that the theory that a member of the group might have simply leaned over and extracted a film tub from a secret panel in the Alan box or levered open the hasp without breaking the paint seals and substituted a prepared film was not supportable, as, on this occasion, there was a highly visible red LED on the amplifier. This light was sufficient to ensure immediate detection by the investigators of any groping hand.

Once the film in the box was developed, it was found to contain the electrical diagram and writing (see Plates 36 and 37). Efforts to identify the monogram below the words 'high resistance' on the film ran into immediate problems, though as it resembled the letters 'FOX' and there had been a reference to 'Fox' during the 11 January session and also another to 'Talbot', the investigators suspected that the spirit of Fox Talbot, the pioneer of photography, might have been connected with the diagram. At that stage the investigators ignored the figures '888' (which had been repeated on other films and continue to be a mystery) on the extreme right. They also ignored what appeared to be a 'squiggle' after the '888'. But, after enquiries and a comment from Mrs Bradshaw that Montague would be better employed looking elsewhere, they rejected the relevance of Fox Talbot.

The team had told the group at a closed session that Montague should look more carefully at the whole message. This led to a closer examination of the squiggle shown on the extreme right of the film, as by that time, prompted by the team's references to Thomas, the investigators had become aware of the suggestion that Thomas Edison might have been the spirit technician within the machine.

A tracing of the final squiggle signature, TAE, was sent to the Edison National Historic Site office in West Orange, New Jersey. Douglas Tarr, the archives technician, responded with samples of Edison's handwriting, including an initialled comment by him on a letter dated 1925. It proved virtually identical with the film squiggle (see Plates 38 and 39). This was the culmination of this particular film investigation.

Later films were influenced in a similar manner but under more stringent test conditions. Many were received in other languages. A number of languages were recorded, including Chinese, English, French, German, and Greek. Ancient characters (glyphs) were also received but are not yet deciphered. The group has invited readers to assist in deciphering the messages (a selection of these films can be seen in the plate section and we consider the content of many of them in greater detail elsewhere).

The TAE film was by no means the first that involved detective work. In early November 1996, the investigators and the group received the first of the two Wordsworth or *Ruth* images (see Plates 42 and 43). This was on a Polaroid (Polachrome) film. The second, two weeks later, was on Kodachrome film. Kodachrome had been suggested by Maurice Grosse, the Chairman of the Society's Spontaneous Cases Committee, as an alternative or addition to Polaroid. Montague explained that this was intended to improve the level of authenticity, as the films would be independently developed away from the site of experiments and there was only one place in the country that developed this type of film. The team agreed and the experimenters started using Kodachrome.

There was a lot of excitement when the first film was developed after the 11 November session. The image showed stanzas from a poem and included some crossings out and corrections in script characteristic of early nineteenth-century handwriting. The letters 'WW' appeared on the far right.

Montague then showed us what else was on the film. On the left is the paranormal script version as seen on the Polachrome strip on the night of 11 November. On the right is the published version appearing in Palgrave's *Treasury*. The latter is, in all essentials, identical to the wording found in other volumes and in all other editions of Wordsworth's work, save one:

The words on the *Ruth* 1 film: **The currently published text is:**

Stanza 22

Whatever in these climes I found	Whatever in those climes he found
Irregular in sight or sound	Irregular in sight and sound
Did to my mind impart	Did to his mind impart
A kindred spirit seem'd allied	A kindred impulse, seem'd allied
To my own powers justified	To his own powers, and justified
The workings of my heart.	The workings of his heart
For Ruth with thee I know	

Stanza 23 omitted from first film   Stanza 23

Nor less, to feed voluptuous thought,
The beauteous forms of Naturewrought,
Fair trees and gorgeous flowers;
The breezes had their own langour lent;
The stars had feelings, which they sent
Into those favour'd bowers.

Stanza 24

Yet in my worst pursuits I ween	Yet, in his worst pursuits, I ween
That often there did intervene	That sometimes there did intervene
Pure hopes of high intent	Pure hopes of high intent
My passion amid (?) forms as fair	For passions link'd to forms so fair
	And stately, needs must have their share
	Of noble sentiment.

WW

The currently published version was sourced and referred to very soon after the 11 November session. It was immediately apparent that the chief difference between it and the version obtained from the team was the switch from third person in the current version to first person in the film version.

During this 11 November session, and before the film had been processed, Joseph had said:

> *It's a little like what you will see on the film. There's some teasing there. I don't know what it is, if anything at all, but I do have some information. It comes from a gentleman who was very fond of words. That's all I should say... but the film, the gentleman, who is rather fond of words, says he's unable – I don't know why, perhaps because of where he is at the moment – is unable to convey what he was hoping to. He's unable to show you exactly what he wanted to show you. It's as if he's lost touch with his thoughts, I suppose. While living – that may seem strange – but he was rather evolved when he came to the Earth [and] lived, so therefore on his return I feel he's gone on rather quickly... This has perhaps caused him some... not unhappiness, because I'm sure that's not an emotion or feeling that he has. He was disappointed that he couldn't produce (that's a good word) what he wanted for you. Do you understand? I haven't made it quite clear, but it's difficult to express something on behalf of someone else.*

Several minutes later, in regard to the film, Patrick said *'someone called out "Ruth" when I wanted some clues about the film. I said "Strewth" and he said, "No... Ruth," so perhaps Ruth is on the film. Perhaps they've got it wrong.'*

For Montague, this was an exceptional occasion. Previously, so far as he knew, there had been no hint of content of films given during any session in which the spirit team appeared to be influencing unexposed film. Twice the team had emphasised their desire to ensure that any images or messages stemmed, and could be seen to have stemmed, from them, rather than from the subconscious hopes, expectations or wishes of the participants, possibly to avoid the super-PSI charge.

Once the investigators had found that the team's version of the poem on the first *Ruth* film showed changes from the currently published version, the immediate problem was to see whether there had ever been a manuscript of the spirit team version in existence. Montague had wrongly supposed this might have been part of Wordsworth's earlier, discarded draft, which the poet may have originally written in the first person but then changed his mind.

So, on the assumption that the film version had never been published, Montague looked at the text in the light of what were taken to be Wordsworth's own feelings and attitudes, a process which was to lead to a significant dispute with the team. The poem itself has an important bearing on the film message. Montague explained that the poem runs to forty-three stanzas and is an account of an abandoned orphan girl, a child of Nature, who is captivated by a dashing young American 'of green Savannahs'. This young man finds himself unable to escape from the lure of his free-roving and perhaps somewhat dissolute past, and abandons her just as they are to start a new life together. She goes mad and is thrown into prison, from which she eventually escapes to live out the wandering life of a beggar, playing on her flute, sleeping rough and ageing fast. Montague's assumption was that this first-person draft of a poem known to have been written by Wordsworth in Goslar, Germany, in 1799, may have reflected an episode in his life about which he must always have been ambivalent – his affair with Annette Vallon in France in 1791. With Annette, he had an illegitimate daughter, Caroline, but was obliged to abandon her to save himself from capture in Revolutionary France. According to Montague, although Wordsworth's conduct was fairly honourable, it is generally thought that this early love affair – he was twenty-one, and Annette a few years older – did have a profound effect on him.

Montague told us that *Ruth* is not a well known poem. During his investigation he discovered that it is not included in most of the Wordsworth anthologies. Before he had had time to check the text of all the many editions of the poem, he attended a further session with the group on 18 November, having been told by Robin Foy that the team had given the date of 1800 in connection with the poem. At that stage, Montague was still trying to discover whether there was any published version *of Ruth* that contained the first-person stanzas and, if so, what significance might be attached to that change of person.

To give an idea of how the team responded to Montague's problems, we quote from the transcript of the 18 November session. It is interesting to note that Edwin's remarks were not preceded by any reference to Montague's doubts:

> **Edwin:** *Now recently, did I say 1800? This is a question that needs to be answered. Mr Keen, you have some trouble in your mind with regard to the date of 1800. Why does this trouble you so?*
>
> **Montague:** Because the authorised version of *Ruth* by Wordsworth himself dates it 1799, the year when he was at Goslar in Germany, writing a number of lyrical poems. It seems difficult to imagine that he produced an earlier version of it after the original version seems to have been written. Clearly there is a confusion here.
>
> **Edwin:** *There does seem to be. All I know – perhaps I misunderstood – let's not worry or concern ourselves too much. I shall... yes... thank you, I'll give you what I've been told. There was a first edition to his lyric, I understand, and a second edition. I think – don't take this as 100 per cent but I think what has been misunderstood... these writings that you have are merely vibrations, thought, as you know, feelings and memories of alterations that were made to the first edition and subsequently additional verses were added, and this I believe was done. What you have witnessed was written in 1799 as well. Some that wasn't published, only a little, but he felt it was lacking somewhat. There is a certain, well, quite a lot, of change which we can't express to you – a lot of*

emotion – and a lot was changed. It isn't my place to explain. You have something which is extremely interesting and it is unlikely you will be able to find it. You may. It would be wonderful if you did. I believe it is somewhere unusual. I don't know where or I could help. We help if we can, even if it's only clues, but I'm not privileged to know where, but it does exist. It was in the family until some years ago. It isn't now. Perhaps it was... I don't know what happens to these things. Does that help?

Montague: That helps enormously.

The 18 November Kodachrome film contained what was later found to be part of the missing stanza number twenty-three, with some misplaced and muddled lines from elsewhere:

To Ruth 1880

So was it then (??) and so is now
For Ruth! with thee I know not how
I feel my spirit burn

Nor less to feed unhallow'd thought
The beauteous forms of Nature wrought
Nor less to feed unhallow'd thought
And Stately wanted not their share

Fair trees and lovely flowers
The breezes their own languor lent
The stars had feelings which they sent
Into those magic bowers

It soon became clear to Montague that the sequence of editions was crucial. So he returned to the British Library and found that *Ruth* had been first published, in 1800, among a collection of lyrical ballads, and the verses in question were in the third person. But in 1802, he discovered, a revised edition appeared in which the quoted verses were put in the first person and corresponded with the texts in the two films.

The investigators thought it highly unlikely that the members of the SEG would have knowledge of these matters, especially since Wordsworth changed his mind after 1802 and reverted, in all subsequent editions, to the third person. Montague thought it was fair to say that the footnote in Brett and Jones' textbook *(Lyrical Ballads,* Methuen, 1963) does mention the inclusion of several new or amended verses in the 1802 edition, but neither they, nor any other authority he could find, had drawn attention to the significance of the grammatical alteration or to its possible autobiographical implications.

Montague found that, after the 1802 edition, Wordsworth restored much of the original wording, along with this part of the narrative, but the next edition, in 1805, did include a new stanza:

> But wherefor speak of this? for now
> *Sweet Ruth! with thee I know not how,*
> *I feel my spirit burn –*
> Even as the east when day comes forth;
> And to the west and south, and north
> The morning doth return.

On the first *Ruth* film there are the words:

> The workings of my heart.
> For *Ruth! with thee I know*

On the second *Ruth* film, again in the wrong place, as if, in Montague's words, 'the poet or the scribe's mind is wandering somewhat', are the words:

> For *Ruth! with thee I know not how*
> *I feel my spirit burn*

Montague's research revealed that the verse just quoted disappears from all subsequent editions. So what we have, in Montague's view, are in essence some very emotive, personal sentiments, most of which appear only in the 1802 edition and which are found on one or other of the two films.

It took Montague some months to track down the original documents. First he went to Dove Cottage in the Lake District, where Wordsworth used to live with his wife and his sister Dorothy. It was Dorothy who did most of the copying and transcribing of her brother's poems. His handwriting was awful, while hers was fair copperplate. Montague soon found, from the detailed records she kept in her journal, that Dorothy had posted to the publishers the printer's proof of the 1800 edition of *Lyrical Ballads,* which includes *Ruth,* with all the amendments required for the forthcoming 1802 edition. She kept the author's copy for herself. The postal date was 7 or 8 March 1802, which turned out to be quite significant in the context of the alterations made to *Ruth.*

Then Montague got in touch with the current head of the family, Professor Jonathan Wordsworth, to ask whether he knew what had happened to Dorothy's copy of the amended proof. Montague recalled that Edwin had told him, 'It was in the family until some years ago. It isn't now.' Professor Wordsworth confirmed that it had been sold at Christie's by his uncle, Mathew, back in 1965. The manuscript had been bought by an anonymous bidder acting on behalf of the Beinecke Rare Book and Manuscript Library at Yale University, USA.

Montague explained why he attached such importance to the date when these changes were made, although he admitted that not all his colleagues were convinced. It was at this time that Wordsworth was planning to revisit his former French mistress, Annette Vallon, and their daughter, whom he had never seen. There was a temporary armistice in the war with France and thousands of English people were planning a trip to the Continent for the first time for ten years. Wordsworth must have been anxious, especially since he was proposing to tell Annette that he was shortly to marry someone else. As Montague said:

> It's in the light of these emotions that we can begin
> to see why the spirit communicators said that there

was 'some emotion involved', and I don't think it's too far-fetched to speculate that putting these confessional words into the first person singular somehow reflects Wordsworth's own struggle between carnal pleasure, or even lust, and the spirit of noble love.

Montague told us that the original *Ruth* manuscript has lodged at the Beinecke Rare Book and Manuscript Library for nearly thirty-five years. The Yale Library Catalogue index describes this proof copy as 'annotated throughout with manuscript corrections by William and Dorothy Wordsworth and an unidentified person in preparation for the edition of 1802'.

The Beinecke librarian had sent Montague a photocopy of all the changes that were introduced in *Ruth*. We were invited to compare this with the two *Ruth* films received at Scole (see Plates 42 and 43).

'Look at the first two or three lines,' Montague said:

> You can see there is a very strong resemblance in the handwriting. Certain features make it clear that whoever or whatever transmitted or created the images on the films must either have been able to see the original or to have had a clear image of it in their mind, since the crossing out and some other markings are the same. Of course, the crossed-out word didn't appear in print. It only appears here on the proof copy – *and the film* – as a mistake.

We asked whether the film handwriting could have been Dorothy Wordsworth's. Montague replied that there was general agreement that it was in Wordsworth's sister's writing on the original amendment to *Ruth,* but that there were some minor stylistic differences, in the formation of certain capital letters, between the film and the original version. This cast some doubt as to whether it was actually the deceased Dorothy who reproduced her own handwriting on the film. Also, although there were the letters 'WW' on the first film, the investigators could not presuppose that this was an authentic signature because the team often said that names on films were not necessarily signatures, nor an indication of the author of the images. What appeared was a 'thought-impression' of the communicator. However, the writing was *very similar* to Dorothy's. It seemed to Montague that this could well represent an effort to impress a visual, albeit confused, recollection onto the film. Hence the misplaced lines, the uncompleted fragments, the odd repetition. For Montague the impression conveyed by the team was that the spirit of Wordsworth himself was transmitting the images. Perhaps the poet would only have had a memory of his sister's handwriting?

The investigators carefully considered the question of whether the film scripts could have been made in ignorance of both the text and the hand-writing of the original. Montague expressed the view that, 'The most vital clue here was the similarity between the deletions on the manuscript and the film texts. In the light of this, the answer to this question must surely be "no".'

The extraordinary nature of this evidence required the investigators to examine the likelihood that there may be a normal explanation, that is, that both films were fakes. Could they say, with absolute certainty, that the manuscript amendment had never been seen by the Scole group or anyone known to them?

Montague believes that very specialist knowledge of Wordsworth would be required to even be aware of this original document. He said that even professional scholars seem to be unaware of its possible autobiographical significance. Apart from the Yale copy of the original manuscript, the only other was made in microfilm by Kodak – on the order of the Board of Trade – for depositing in the British Library, where it is available for study by approved students. He inspected this script on the microfilm projector in the British Library and found the handwriting to be 'faint and extremely difficult to read, let alone copy, especially the top verse'. Some of the words at the end of longer lines are barely legible 'no doubt due to nearly two centuries of handling of the manuscript'.

The only other possible source of information for the Scole

group, Montague discovered, was the Christie's sale catalogue, which reproduced the page on which the manuscript amendments seen in the two films appeared. Montague considers a thirty-year-old sales catalogue, with no known market value, an unlikely source, especially since there is nothing in it to indicate that the amendments are of any particular significance. But, in theory, he was unable to absolutely rule this out.

The reference to the date of 1880 above brings out another fascinating aspect of this investigation. The date written on *Ruth* 2 was 1880. Wordsworth died in 1850. Montague had originally assumed that the 1880 date was a mistake for 1800 but, when he questioned one of the spirit team, he was told that it was not.

Montague's continuing research unearthed several links between Wordsworth and Myers, whose biography of Wordsworth was first published in 1880, the date on the film. They both had close associations with the Marshall family and their home at Hallsteads in the Lake District. That was the place where Annie Marshall fell deeply in love with Myers, spent hours in his company and later committed suicide. So, both Wordsworth and Myers, for different reasons, had pangs of conscience as a result of their youthful love affairs. Montague finished his summing up by saying, 'However, this is only my interpretation. Other colleagues will disagree.'

Indeed, *The Scole Report* records that Professor Fontana thought there was insufficient evidence to attribute any paranormal involvement by Wordsworth himself. Montague told us that Professor Fontana also pointed out that, since Wordsworth deals exhaustively with his affair with Annette in *Vaudracour and Julia,* written in 1805, a communicating Wordsworth might better have been expected to have referred to this poem rather than to *Ruth,* a poem which may reasonably be accounted fairly obscure since it is not even mentioned in many of the reference books.

So was it Wordsworth himself, his sister Dorothy, his biographer Myers or some other communicator who transmitted the Ruth messages onto the two films? We may never know.

Differences of opinion about all aspects of these films, their authenticity and meaning are discussed in some detail in *The Scole*

Report and more will no doubt emerge as this controversial information, which appears to lend support to the survival hypothesis, becomes more widely known.

Given the findings of the many investigators, it is to be expected that there will be objections on many levels and from many quarters. There are already scientists who are questioning the way the evidence was gathered and certain of the results. This is part of the normal scientific process. Accumulation of knowledge designed to establish universally acceptable truths has always progressed by elimination of alternative explanations. Without the 'currently unconvinced', we would only get halfway towards the real truth of things.

This said, we would all do well to remember that some of the most important advances in history have been held up by closed-mindedness and misplaced scepticism. Albert Einstein actually changed one of his equations to fit in with peer pressure, which said that what he had proposed was impossible. More than three-quarters of a century later, new evidence from the study of the rate at which the galaxies are separating suggests that the great man was possibly right. From this we could all perhaps agree that reasoned, constructive criticisms are fine, whereas objections based on emotion, fear, existing belief structure or dogma are not.

Montague ended his fascinating account by telling us about some of the more memorable sessions during the scientific investigation.

During sessions, Montague had a notebook and took notes in shorthand. On one occasion, an apparently new member of the team asked what Montague was doing making notes and whether it was allowed. The group assured the new team member that it was all right. He then said that Montague was making a mess of it. After the lights went back on Montague found the team member was right. He had forgotten to turn the page and had written over what he had just done.

During another experimental session, on 17 January 1997, the spirit team said that their photographic department had been able to achieve some good results on what was later called the 'Dragon film'. One of the symbols on the film is generally thought to be a

Hebrew acronym, as indicated by dots above the letters, of a word meaning the name of the Lord (see Plate 23). In Hebraic tradition this word may never be pronounced. Montague recalled a conversation on 5 March 1997:

> I said to the team that the use of certain alchemical or hermetic symbols to convey messages might create the impression that the investigators were being dragged back to the occult mysteries of medievalism that enlightened science was trying to escape. I was going on to suggest that these messages might seem strange to those who were looking for messages of goodwill designed to elevate man's spiritual consciousness and so on, whereupon, in a rare display of impatience, Mrs Bradshaw interrupted me: 'So a word meaning "God" on a message on a film isn't good enough for anyone then?'

CHAPTER TEN

SPIRITUAL PHILOSOPHY

**I would not live forever, because we
should not live forever, because if we were
supposed to live forever, then we would
live forever, but we cannot live forever,
which is why I would not live forever.**

Miss Alabama
during the 1994 Miss USA contest

We may smile at this attempt at answering the question, 'If you
could live forever, would you and why?' by a young woman
unexpectedly put under pressure to speak philosophically in the
middle of a televised beauty contest. But do the rest of us really
deal any better with these important questions? If there is one
thing that the Scole Experiment does, it makes the people who
come across it think about their own perspective on life, death
and the possibility of survival.

The spirit team brought information on many important
concepts which added to the evidence of survival of
consciousness beyond bodily death. Over time, the group found
the team of regular communicators to be true and trusted friends
who were gentle, loving, harmonious and trustworthy. If they
announced that they were going to produce a particular
phenomenon, then they went ahead and tried to achieve exactly
what they had promised. There was also a band of helpers behind
the scenes, constantly beavering away in the background during
each experimental session, all with their own particular tasks to
attend to. However, these beings were not 'designated
communicators' and so group members were never made aware
of their identities.

Just like the hundreds of human participants in the Scole

Experiment, the spirit communicators all had different character-istics, personalities and perspectives. Perhaps the main difference between the spirits and the humans was that the team members said that each of them was one of 'many minds', all working together for the common good.

Apparently, each individual human is also one of the many minds in the Creation. The difference between us and spirit beings is that we are shrouded in physical form for a short time in order to have certain experiences which would not be possible in spirit form. When the experience is over, we discard the vehicle... and go *home*.

Since few of us are convinced that we have this home to go to, the team was working to prove survival so that with this understanding we might change the way we live our short lives. The idea behind the team's efforts seems to be that, if we knew what comes next, we might start working more co-operatively together *now*.

But why work together when we all appear to be separate and have different interests? The 'many minds' of the spirit team said that, since we are all individual parts of a Single Mind, it would make sense if we contributed to the progress of the whole of which we are each a part.

On the other hand, this ultimate unity does not preclude choice about our own individual experience. A very interesting point raised during the experiments was that each individual mind had total freedom of choice as to the content of the message it sent during the sessions. Thus the meeting of the many human and discarnate minds was not always controllable and predictable.

This led to some difficulties for the humans involved. For example, the scientists on the Earth side may have requested a definitive explanation of some unsolved scientific problem, but received a message about love and God instead. It is, of course, a matter of perspective as to which of these is the more important. The team said that they are both important, hence the introduction and promotion of 'spiritual science'.

Many changes took place during the course of the Scole Experiment. Not only did the phenomena develop rapidly, but there were also subtle changes in the personalities of many of the guides and helpers. The group told us:

> Over a period of time, we came to know and love our spirit team to the point of almost thinking of them as our 'extended family'. In the early days, some of them communicated in a very natural, down-to-earth way. Their humour and their sense of fun helped to unite us all together to form a harmonious and loving bond within the group. But as the months passed and the wonderful phenomena developed, we noticed a number of subtle changes in these spirit friends. They started to converse about the work on a different level. They still retained some of those personality traits we had come to know so well but seemed to be transmitting more spiritual messages.

The personalities who created this 'world within a world' were the members of the spirit team. They were real characters who had not lost their individual personalities just because they had passed into spirit form. The work carried out during the Scole Experiment was intended to show that we are *all* spiritual beings and that each one of us survives bodily death. Physical psychic phenomena are a form of communication, an interaction or 'communion' between those of us who are living a physical life at the moment on this Earth and surviving personalities who have lived a similar life to us, but now have the added advantage of having passed through the transition which we call death.

An interesting point was raised about personality by a spirit scientist, who explained that personalities are 'sometimes grouped together', like the concept of the group soul. With higher development there was less attachment to the individual personality, as a kind of merging process occurred.

The Scole group themselves also changed as the experiments progressed:

> We gained a greater understanding about the many

things we witnessed and experienced. We would like to think that each of us has become more aware spiritually and more tolerant of others around us.

Manu spoke to the group about this:

> *Your work with the spirit team at Scole is enabling you to fulfil your own predestined lives in the world. You are experiencing the presence, personalities and energies of the members of the spirit team as part of your own individual life plan. However, it is also the case that each member of the spirit team is simultaneously experiencing your own presences, personalities and energies. This helps each member of the team to fulfil their own predestined spiritual growth.*

'As you can imagine,' comments Robin, 'these were interesting thoughts for us to get our minds around.'

So it seems that spiritual science is not just about scientific proofs and evidence of survival, but also about character building and the development of new ways of thinking, being, and experiencing the world. As the group explained:

> Too often we tend to forget exactly why we are sitting in our groups. It is not just to achieve the physical manifestations, wonderful as they may be, but also to open our hearts and minds to the truth by becoming aware of our true selves, to remember that we are spirit and to remind ourselves that each of us has within us that small spark of divinity which unites us together and makes us a part of the great whole.

Early on during the Scole Experiment, the team spoke on many subjects. During one session, 'a particularly happy affair', Manu made some interesting comments during his usual introductory speech:

*In the moments before you fall asleep each night, we
would like you all to mentally ask to be linked to
'Universal Harmony' during your sleep state. This
will allow you all to meet up as a group during your
nightly rest, thus allowing the work to continue while
you sleep. Compliance with this simple request will
also help you with your daytime meditation.*

The group members started this practice and it has indeed proved
very helpful in their lives, so much so that they always recommend
it to others who wish to develop their own group harmony and
individual spirituality.

At another meeting of the group, most of the evening's
phenomena were spirit-light orientated. An object made of light,
'which looked to all intents and purposes like a steeple or inverted
ice-cream cone', was built up by the spirit team. None of the group
had any idea at all as to what it was, but Joseph said that there
were millions of them in the spirit world, growing in the fields.
They had no existence in our world as such, however, and therefore
no name could be ascribed to them.

Sandra then asked: 'Would it be possible in the future for crystal
clusters to be energised in the Scole group and issued to other
experimental groups to give them a "kick-start" with their own
tangible phenomena?'

'This might be an eventual possibility,' agreed the spirit
communicator. He went on to say that healing would be a very
large and important part of the work of the Scole group and the
New Spiritual Science Foundation. This might eventually involve
'the despatching of energised crystals to patients'.

When Manu spoke at the beginning of each experimental
session, assuming the role of first communicator, he always brought
some words of wisdom for those present. He continued to give
guidance on individual and group work, and tried to explain about
vibration, which is apparently vital for groups involved with
energy-based spirit technology:

Each of you is vibrating in space. The very chair you

are sitting on is vibrating and so is the room. All is vibration, and your own vibration is affected by your thoughts.

Be mindful of your thoughts and feelings when you come to do this work. Tell others that wish to work in this way to put aside everyday thoughts and worries and to come to their groups with a clear and happy attitude of mind. The more harmonious you are, the easier it is to blend, balance and attune the energies for our work. You are each a part of all that lives and breathes, a part of the planet itself. When you raise your consciousness, you raise others, for there is a spiritual link that binds us all together. Your consciousness can reach out and give hope to many.

Know that much is achieved in this way, much that you will never hear about, but know that it is so. Your loving thoughts and energies are used most wisely by those in spirit who blend with you. Have vision, be touched from within and strive to have heart and mind in perfect balance.

Manu spoke many times about positive thought, stressing how vital this is. Thought is very important in this and other dimensions. Each thought is 'a causal creation', 'a living thing', with both a material and non-material effect. It is therefore essential that we all 'think carefully' at all times. He explained that our minds are all part of the One Universal Mind and each of our thoughts contributes to the greater whole.

As well as spiritual wisdom from Manu, the group often had anonymous contributions from members of the spirit team. The information was no less profound because of this. Sometimes these communicators spoke about one of the most difficult subjects for our minds to tackle, that is, the concept of time and space in the spiritual dimensions.

The group once asked one of the spirit scientists whether time existed for him. 'No,' was his emphatic reply. 'There is only now.

Man invented time as you know it in your existence. It is a perception of the Earthly world, the conscious mind.'

Sensing that this was difficult for the group to understand, another of the spirit communicators gave another example. The group was told that during a very deep meditation or an out-of-body experience, clock time ceases to exist. It may seem to the person involved that they have been away for a long time, but the clock may register that the actual experience lasted only a few minutes. During those moments that they were mentally away, their sensations and their experience generally were similar to those of living in a spiritual dimension.

Similarly, just as spirit people can create actual changes around them by using thought, so it is also possible that during meditation a special 'stillness' or 'creative' moment can be attained, when there is an alignment to the Source of Creation. This moment can be used for self-healing, amongst other things. Spirit beings are more aware of being 'aligned' on a constant basis and use this feeling to be creative in many ways.

Another question that the group asked concerned the thought processes of spirit people. Did they think in the same way that we do or very differently? It was explained that humans mostly think in block thought and primarily in a particular language. On passing to spirit, after a period of adjustment, perhaps even uncertainty, one ceases to think in these ways. Everything changes as individuals then make progress towards a more 'co-operative' way of thinking. This way of thinking is non-physical; it is an unconscious 'perception'.

While living in a physical body, the unconscious mind has no knowledge of time, but some might argue that time still exists, since it continues to pass as far as the conscious mind is concerned. The physical mind is heavily programmed to such an extent that it is difficult for most of us even to believe that there actually *is* a place where everyone is able to understand one another in this way. Although it was difficult for them to describe the seemingly indescribable, the spirit team at Scole did try their very best to help the group gain a greater understanding of their world.

Dr Hans Schaer asked the spirit team a number of questions about the spirit world when the Scole group held sessions at his farmhouse in Ibiza:

What happens when we pass over? Are we met by our loved ones? Are there houses or anything comparable to our own here on Earth?

Generally speaking, most people have a moment of adjustment, a moment of confusion. What has happened to me? As this moment comes, you find yourself in familiar or comfortable surroundings. You are comforted by your loved ones if you wish.

This is a very real world to those who dwell in it. There are flowers and fields, etc. We are not able to do it justice in mere language. It is a world of beauty in which you can live for many, many Earth years. Time is not a reality, so there is no hurry!

Those you love may feel very happy with this existence but if, for example, you pass over with a greater spiritual understanding, then it may be possible to help them and together you may explore other areas of existence and go forward. It depends a lot on your needs, the life you have led and your spiritual self.

Is it possible to meet others who are on a higher level?

Yes, it is possible. Often, you can find yourselves in the presence of a teacher. There are many gatherings around great teachers. You may be guided to such an area and there you absorb knowledge, rather than listen, just by being in their presence.

Do some tell others what to do in the spirit world?

No, but you can be guided and advised.

Does each of us have a specific purpose in being here? Do we have to fulfil a task or duty?

Not exactly. You have to come to Earth for the experience. There are a few exceptions that do come to fulfil a particular task, but most people come for the experience to gain spiritually from the life.

When a pattern repeats in your life, and you say, 'Oh no, not again,' then you must look at what is happening and seek out what the lesson of that pattern is. When people begin a spiritual quest and have a spiritual awakening, then they slowly observe that they are evolving as a person and their normal thinking patterns are changing as they follow their spiritual pathway.

Sadly, the majority of mankind is not progressing well spiritually. They are not very aware. But certain energies are coming to the Earth that will help to change that. Those that are aware will be of great service in helping that energy to be used for the greater good of mankind. When man does become aware, spiritually, then he will realise that there is more to his life on Earth than meets the eye.

Is there a negative side that fights this very positive energy?

No. It is man in his ignorance that causes problems. If man lives his life without aspiring to a spiritual awareness, he lives in ignorance. Ignorance breeds negativity and negative thoughts create a negative force as, in a similar way, positive thinking creates a positive force, so we have to work on the negative forces. Not, however, those outside of man, but those within man.

What are spirit people doing with their time? Do they have tasks and duties?

Yes, we all have something to do. Don't fall into the trap of thinking we have a great deal of time on our hands. Time does not exist as you know it. Everyone does something, but not in a physical sense. You cannot, literally, work.

It is more of a mental world than a physical one. But how you conduct yourself on our side is more real than Earth life, not dreamlike or vague. It is more real than you can imagine.

Can you play music? [Dr Schaer is a keen jazz musician.]

Yes. But not in the same way as in your physical world, with the mental turmoil and continual practice, but in an instant you can express yourself in music with such joy and depth. You can also work together with others. Someone may say, 'Try it this way,' and you find it is very much easier than you thought. There is no limitation on the music, such as you have in a physical world. You have a total freedom to express your true self in music.

Do the Akashic Records exist and can we have access to them?

It is true to say that much information is stored in other realms and spheres. But again, perhaps not as much as you are led to believe. Some of the records are accessible to higher beings. There are also some on Earth who claim to have access to them, but I do not know if this is true.

Are you given a chance to develop yourself more spiritually when you pass into the spirit world?

Yes, though 'chance' is the wrong term. The overall aim is for every soul to obtain spiritual knowledge and to move towards the light itself. There are several ways you can choose to gain assistance in achieving this aim.

Remember, too, that even now, you are also a spirit, you just happen to be housed in a body, so it is important that while you are, in fact, having a life in that physical body, you use the experience of it to grow spiritually.

You have to lower your natural vibratory state to get in touch with us. Is it possible for us to raise ours for the same purpose?

It is. In so doing, there is a need for people's own consciousness to rise up and expand. Certain conditions, which can occur during the sleep state, make this possible, but it requires some training and lots of discipline.

There are also columns of energy in the world that reach from the Earth into the spiritual realms. They can assist your personal consciousness to communicate with our world.

Being in spirit is your natural state, so when you come to spirit it is like coming home. This is our understanding, but 'love' is the special word that makes everything happen.

On the subject of 'vibratory states', the team explained that even 'vibrations' is not a strictly accurate term, but is the nearest we have to the truth. There are also 'ultra high frequencies', so high that they are inaudible and invisible, at this time still beyond human measurement. As man's knowledge advances, it may become possible to develop apparatus to measure these vibrations – and so glimpse other worlds – but the information gained in this way will still be limited. The team said the whole process will need to involve physics, biochemistry, electronics, electromagnetics and other very technical subjects. But the prospect is a long way off yet. First, we must open up our hearts and minds to spiritual science.

Very special energy is apparently being beamed to Earth at present as part of a divine plan to make Man more aware spiritually. The eventual aim is to help us all transform this physical world for the better.

During an experimental session in February 1996, Manu talked about the hopes of the spirit team. He said they wanted to bring to everyone on Earth a greater understanding of who and what they truly are – their physical, mental, and most importantly spiritual aspects. The team wanted to show that we have a creative force within ourselves and that, if used wisely, it can transform not only our own lives, but the world around us too.

A couple of weeks later, at the beginning of the first of the two special group sessions held to receive the information to go into the *Basic Guide* booklet, Manu continued his theme:

> *What a joyous occasion it is tonight! For I hope that you will feel, as we feel, the upliftment of our words that will go out to reach many minds in many parts of the world. All those who wish to work with spirit in this new way, who look to you for guidance, will receive these words. Not straight away, perhaps, but in time. And you look to us to give you the words. What a splendid team we are! One cannot do without the other. And we appreciate what you do, just as you appreciate what we do, and so it should be, a co-operation of worlds, one with the other, for each other's fulfilment, for each other's wisdom and for each other's extension of knowledge.*
>
> *We wish to extend people's thinking about this, as you know. And so we hope that the words that you will be given will be enlightening and useful to others. We cannot dictate word for word, so there will be places where you will have to use your own minds also, to ensure that the language will be understandable. But we will give you the important parts, the parts that must be included to give a full picture of what must take place to get the results that people are searching for.*
>
> *I will not be too long in speaking, as I have to build a special atmosphere with the energy tonight, a special atmosphere where the words will flow freely. Those words will be given with wisdom and with much thought behind them. For I know there are those in my world who are thinking very hard about this and want it to be right, as you do also.*

The second and final special session for the preparation of the educational booklet was held a short while later. Once again, Manu set the scene for the other spirit communicators: 'You know, in a great ancient place, there were written the words across an entrance: "Know Thyself." That, of course, does not mean the physical self, but the true self, the spiritual self. And it is that which we shall help others to discover about themselves. We shall help them to truly know that they are a spiritual being, a shining being within a body...'

At an another session which was held in the presence of some distinguished scientists, Manu's opening comments were equally profound:

> *Many people will say to you that you are wasting your time experimenting like this. You know there are those who say this, of course, but it is not so. By itself, it might be a small thing to sit here and see what we can do, and to hear our words also, but combined with the energies that are coming to the Earth, there will be a great awakening in many ways. What we do is part of that plan.*
>
> *There are cosmic, pulsating energies coming to the Earth all the time. Everything is evolving, nothing stays still. At this time in his evolution, man is ready for these energies to come upon him and give him what he is thirsting for. So we shall give him the refreshing rain of knowledge, that he may drink from these waters, that he may know of his own spiritual self... for only in that way will man change.*
>
> *You cannot meet man on a physical and mental level and make him understand, but when you speak to him on a spiritual level, it is another matter. First, we must reach out to man's higher aspect and then filter down to his everyday life and the choices he makes. Only that way will change come about.*

At another session, Manu provided the group with food for thought about the changes which are happening on Earth at the moment and the part they as individuals may have to play in these developments. He talked about the fact that they were destined to be living at this time, bringing the energies from ancient times with them, and how this energy forms a perfect loop – energy coming to the Earth and energy returning back. Similarly, crystals were used to store energy ready to be awakened by initiates who would return in the fullness of time. That time was now.

At a subsequent session, Manu expanded on the subject of Earth sounds and vibrations:

> *The last time we spoke together, I told you about many underground places and it is good that you are aware, because certain people will take a great interest in sound vibrations from the Earth. Many will seek out these ancient sites and make recordings (as you do) with tape recorders. It is as if there is a song to the Earth's inhabitants, coming from deep within the Earth itself. It is these vibrations that will assist us all in our quest to lift mankind to a heightened awareness, a heightened unified consciousness that will lead him higher and higher in his own perspective of life.*
>
> *You see, at this time in man's evolution, it is the heart centre that is being worked upon. It is this age that you are in which is causing the heart centre to be activated. This happens to individuals whether they are working on this or not. Those who are consciously working on these spiritual matters, such as groups like yours, can help others who are not yet aware. You will yourselves help to bring about this awareness.*
>
> *We have spoken before about people who come here with a balance between heart and mind. The mind – the intellect – is not enough. The heart has to participate in unison with the mind. If people are working from the heart and are open to all the love that is pouring in, then, from their perspective, all is*

done with love, and they will find that they can harm no one. That is why this centre is so very important at this age of man.

At the end of your experimental sessions, when you start your healing exercise, you and other groups open yourselves to this inflowing power of love. As you think of the people of this Earth, and the very Earth itself, so you help to activate these ancient vibrations that are coming forward at the moment. The age is right for this to happen.

There was more to come on this subject from Mrs Bradshaw:

I thought it was rather interesting that Robin was talking about sound and about how, in Egyptian times, they had a great knowledge of sound. They used it in healing, but also they had the knowledge of how to connect the sound vibrations with the art of building. This is something that has been totally lost over the centuries, so much so that it has disappeared in the main from the human consciousness. Perhaps not completely, however – it must be registered there somewhere in the background, but it is not to the fore, as it should be at this time.

You yourselves recognise the connection with sound vibration and destruction. We all know what happens when an opera singer sings a note at a certain vibration. The glass shatters, doesn't it? Well, it was the same with the walls of Jericho, you know! Exactly the right sound vibration was given out and the destruction followed. But what has been lost even more is the art of construction using sound. People connect in with the destruction part and have a reasonable understanding of how that can happen. It is the knowledge of fusion with sound that has been lost, but I think that this is going to come round full circle again, like so many other things...

In fact, I do know of somebody working on it right now. Well, as you know, I do get about and like to see what's going on in the world today. Somebody is certainly working on this. A scientist. I don't know his name, and it isn't really important, but certainly this concept has entered his consciousness. From an outside influence, you see. It will come.

Manu reminded the group constantly of the vital importance of keeping an open mind. He explained that the group would not have been contacted if they had not been open to the experiences in the first place. Part of their purpose was to show people the importance of opening their hearts and minds to the possibility of all kinds of communication from many types of communicators, bringing the power of love with them, and then their lives would truly be enriched. The reason for these events happening now is because people were seeking answers beyond what has been offered to them within our world.

The group commented:

Our understanding of what Manu told us is that humanity has consciously or unconsciously been sending out a signal asking for help for our world for some time and that many loving beings have heard our plea. They are now coming in response to our request to aid us in any way they possibly can. It seems that the many dimensions are bound together with the common thread of love. This love transcends all other things. What a truly wonderful notion that is.

CHAPTER ELEVEN

THE FUTURE

**Absorb the energy into yourselves;
become shining ones, and then send out
the light to others.**

Manu

The SEG, via the New Spiritual Science Foundation, has been sharing its findings and experiences with groups around the world for some time. After the publication of the first issue of *Spiritual Scientist* in December 1994, there were soon subscribers from Australia, Belgium, Canada, Egypt, Finland, Germany, Hong Kong, Italy, Luxembourg, New Zealand, Switzerland, and the USA, as well, of course, as the UK. Today, *Spiritual Scientist* is also available in German and plans are underway for French translation.

The group's first experimental trip abroad took place back in October 1995, before the scientific investigation began. As already mentioned, Dr Hans Schaer, who had joined the group for an experimental session at Scole a few weeks previously, had invited them all out to Ibiza to spend a week with him at his holiday home, a remote farmhouse on the island. Just before the group went away, Manu instructed them to take a set of bells with them and said the team was working on the possibility of using another container instead of the dome in which to concentrate the creative energies, as this would alleviate the need to take the fragile glass dome on an aircraft:

> *We will gather together the creative energy and blend it in the Scole cellar first, even though the group will be physically abroad. We will then transfer the energy to the venue in Ibiza, where it will be used to achieve the desired phenomena...*

There are two options for your trip abroad. The first of these is for you to take the very small mini-dome with you. This, however, is not the alternative we favour. Second, it is possible that we might use a crystal cluster on the central table in Ibiza. We could concentrate the necessary energy for our operational needs in this cluster. This would be our preferred option. The energised cluster could then be used on every occasion in the future when you travel abroad. The spirit team will shortly bring a suitable quartz cluster to you. When this arrives, please place it on your central table so that we can energise it for future use.

Mrs Bradshaw also confirmed at this time that it would be acceptable for the group to include four guests (three from Australia and one from New Zealand) at a session planned for a few days later. Demonstrations of the work to foreign delegations were also being planned. The team had recently agreed that the group could hold a full-day seminar and experimental sitting for Dieter Wiergowski's German group during November. It is clear that there was already international interest in the Scole Experiment.

At the next session, Manu came through first as usual, then returned later with the promised quartz crystal cluster. This was to be known as the 'travelling crystal'. The apported crystal had arrived silently, which was very unusual, since most apports the group had received, even tiny ones, had landed with great crashes and thuds on the central table. Even the newspapers made a 'plop' sound. The travelling crystal, however, had been carefully placed on the table. Manu said that much of the available energy at that session had been used to 'energise' it for the future journeys. Its vibrations had been synchronised with the energy conditions at Scole and it should therefore provide the correct conditions at any given point in the world. The crystal cluster was beautiful, with 'a sort of small internal cave at one end. It had obviously been carefully chosen by Manu.'

The guest session of 22 September, at which the group was

joined by David and Patricia Hayes and Gordon Hewitt from Australia, together with Meg Simpson from New Zealand, was an excellent one. Manu expressed the spirit team's wish that they might be able to spread the word about the work when they returned home.

The group's first experiment away from Scole took place in Dr Hans Schaer's holiday home in Ibiza. Set in the higher reaches of a fertile wooded valley, the centuries-old house was graced by outer walls of solid stone over a foot thick, reminiscent of the walls one might find in a fortress. Dr Schaer was satisfied that the team could not have faked anything in his own home. Both experimental sessions took place in the main living room, an extremely large and lofty room, which, according to the group, had a lovely atmosphere. The spirit team explained that, due to its inherently rocky nature, the island had a number of columns of the special energy that was needed for the production of objective psychic phenomena in the new way. In fact one particularly large column, some twenty feet in diameter, was apparently in the immediate vicinity of the ancient farmhouse itself.

Whether for this or some other reason, both experimental sessions produced a variety of phenomena, including spirit lights, spirit touches and solid spirit forms. The string of bells, hanging from one of the very high beams in the room, rang several times and the team also demonstrated controlled levitation of both the table-tennis ball and a balsa-wood cube. At one point the two very solid outer doors of the room were banged upon by the spirit team. The group had experienced this particular phenomenon in the cellar at Scole, so they were not alarmed. Dr Schaer, on the other hand, immediately thought that someone was trying break in to the property!

At one point Mrs Bradshaw announced:

> There is a spirit lady who is present. She lived in the building herself around the year of 1883. She was a very religious person in her day and is still attached to the house. Her cat is also present. The lady is a little confused by the presence of the Scole spirit team in 'her' house so the team is being very careful to respect her wishes with regard to the property.

By the second session, however, this spirit lady was rather more confident. According to the team, she even began taking an active interest in the proceedings.

The spirit lady was not the only one intrigued by the work of the Scole Experiment. On their return from Ibiza the group had to prepare for the forthcoming seminar with twenty-two German delegates. This took place on Sunday 26 November 1995. The visiting party was led by Dieter Wiergowski. He and his wife, Conny, run a newspaper called *Die Andere Realität* (The Other Reality). Not many of the visitors spoke good English, but Karin Schnittger agreed to act as interpreter for the day.

In the morning, the group presented a series of lectures, which included a slide show of the photographs they had received. This aroused a great deal of interest. Then, after lunch and another lecture covering all the tangible phenomena that might be witnessed, the visitors went down to the Scole Hole for an experimental session.

This session was one of the largest that the group had ever given. There were twenty-eight people there in all, making conditions rather cramped. However, this did not stop the phenomena. In the event, the session proved to be far livelier than anyone had dared to hope. The visitors were treated to an array of phenomena: lights, touches, tugs, raps, taps, and evidential messages.

'But then again,' said Robin, 'we had to admit that the spirit team had never let us down on any previous "special experiment" occasion. It's almost as if they can pull the stops out when they need to.'

For several of the visitors, these were the very first tangible paranormal phenomena they had ever witnessed. Afterwards it was clear that the whole day had been a great success. It was then that the idea of publishing a regular German language version of *Spiritual Scientist* was born. Karin Schnittger volunteered to do the necessary translation.

In the summer of 1996, the group made more international progress, paying another visit to Ibiza as guests of Dr Hans Schaer, then March 1997 saw them setting out from Heathrow *en route* to

Los Angeles. Montague Keen travelled with them. He was hoping to arrange a Scole experimental session for scientists and researchers in the San Francisco area. He also wanted to compare the experiments in Scole with those abroad.

In America, the group was welcomed by their host, Brian Hurst, a very well-known medium in the USA. As they recalled:

> Brian had spent considerable time and money converting his spacious garage into a room suitable for our experimental sessions.
>
> We had all sorts of interesting people – Kathryn Grayson, of *Showboat* and *Desert Song* fame, and Jay North, former star of American TV's *Dennis the Menace*. We also had Dr Steven Ross, who heads an international research foundation to find alternative treatments for many health conditions. The people who attended were very interested and enthusiastic. Intervals between the different types of phenomena that were produced by the spirit team were filled with applause and spontaneous choruses of 'Wow' and 'Great' and 'Neat.'

Apart from the 'usual' phenomena, a highlight of the first session was the unannounced levitation of the central table. For the other sessions in America, the group made sure that the luminous tabs were put underneath the table as well as on the top, so that people could see its movements clearly.

The phenomena experienced at the first experimental session set the standard for the rest. A completely new phenomenon was when the central table levitated, then turned on its side and spun round like a cartwheel, without a single crystal falling off. More than once, participants had spirit lights actually enter them. People received spiritual healing in this way. Visitors had tapes playfully pushed down their socks. Spirit animals such as cats and dogs were present – a number of people felt the animals' feet, fur, and tails as they padded about the room.

Brian Hurst commented:

I can confirm that the light did indeed enter the bodies of several of the people present. Tricia Loar, who had been plagued by torn cartilage and other knee damage, experienced a light entering both her knee and her foot. She said that the foot entry was extremely ticklish and she could feel the light moving about inside. The pain in her knee had gone by the next day. Physicist Dr Ulf Israelsson also attended one session. He expressed a very positive opinion about his experience.

Considering the fact that these new energy-based phenomena had never before been demonstrated in the United States, they were received with remarkable intelligence, understanding and enthusiasm by everyone who experienced them. It is a credit to the group that they worked so hard, and with such good humour, in order that so many Americans could experience this proof of survival and the reality of a spiritual dimension. Here they are remembered with love and awe, and everyone is asking, 'When will they return?'

George Dalzell is a licensed clinical social worker who holds a Master's degree in social work. He lives in Hollywood. He is the author of *Messages: Evidence for Life After Death* (Hampton Roads, 2002), a book which explores the authenticity of mediumship.

PERSPECTIVES

GEORGE DALZELL

On April 7 1997, I attended a demonstration of the SEG in the darkened garage at the home of medium Brian Hurst in California. Hurst was a mentor to world-famous medium,

James Van Praagh, bestselling author of *Talking to Heaven* and *Reaching to Heaven*.

My interest in attending the Scole group's demonstration had its origin in researching the application of mediumship as an intervention for people suffering from bereavement resulting from loss. It stands to reason that proof of life after death may minimise the duration and intensity of the bereavement process.

In the darkened garage, twenty participants were treated to a series of extraordinary physical phenomena. A table at the centre of the room appeared to lift and stand on its side while crystals and various objects on the table mysteriously stayed in place, seeming to defy gravity. People began to report that invisible hands materialised and reached out and caressed their hands.

Suddenly, the room began to be filled with spirit lights that can be best described in size and appearance as resembling fireflies with constant illumination. At times, these bluish-white lights would hover in front of spectators, and at other times, they would travel across the floor and appear to climb up the table in the centre of the room and fly up through the rafters of the garage.

It occurred to me that if the light phenomenon was being facilitated by an invisible team of spirit scientists, as the group's Robin Foy alleged, then perhaps I could communicate with one of these scientists directly and silently with my thoughts. In this way, I could test the authenticity of the Scole phenomena without the awareness of the Scole group and the twenty participants. I held out both of my hands in the dark and thought silently, *Touch my right hand. Send a light to my right hand if you can indeed hear me just now.*

With that, a light flew from above the spectators' heads and across from the Scole team and touched the index finger of my right hand. I was incredulous. I could feel the light *physically* touch me and could plainly see that it was not a fibre-optic cord or light projection, but rather a self-contained sphere of bluish-white light of indeterminate source. I called this event to the attention of the group at the time and this is documented on tapes belonging both to Hurst and the Scole group.

Shortly after this event, Mrs Bradshaw asked if she could relay information from a male spirit endeavouring to speak to me. I asked her to proceed and the resulting astounding exchange was another evidential contact with the spirit of my friend, Michael Keller. Mrs Bradshaw relayed detailed information unknown to Brian Hurst or any other participant and I was left with no doubt as to the authenticity of the exchange.

Suffice it to say, my interaction with the Scole group transformed a life's worth of limited perceptions overnight. It isn't often that one's point of view can change in such a short time; the more observed fact is that change occurs gradually.

The group had spent three weeks working in California and demonstrated the experimental results to about 200 people at nine separate sessions. One particular feature of these sessions was the large amount of personal evidence of survival supplied, mainly through Emily and Edwin. Not only was a wealth of survival evidence given, but it proved to be extremely accurate. It should perhaps be noted that none of the Scole group knew any of the visitors apart from Brian Hurst, whom they had met once before when he attended a session in the Scole Hole.

As well as members of the public, participants at a 'scientists' session' included a number of scientists from the space agency NASA and others from the Institute of Noetic Sciences near San Francisco as well as representatives from Stanford University.

At the scientific experimental session, the NASA and other scientists came together as a group, about fifteen of them. Interestingly, some of the astrophysicists later started a group of their own. The Scole group did not know in advance who was going to attend the scientists' session, nor even where it was to be held. Montague Keen had deliberately not told them where they were going so that they could not be accused of preparing the venue. Twenty-four hours before the session, he phoned to give the address so the group could plan how to get there. They later learned that Montague himself did not know the venue until very late in the day, as it had been changed to ensure that the group had a room which could be completely blacked out. As the group explained:

> The place was up a blinking mountain! The road was unbelievable. We were driving a hire car and it was a very narrow road with a sheer drop on one side. It was a hair-raising journey.
>
> When we arrived for the session we weren't introduced to anyone by name. Although there were some smiles and 'Hi's, we hadn't a clue who the people there were. We were ushered downstairs to the gym below the house and told to set it up ready for the experiment. This large room was ideal, being cut out of the rock below the house. Then the scientists came down and searched it before we started.
>
> It was a good demonstration. We had a Native American materialise during it. He was doing a tribal dance and chanting. Then the drums began beating. These were on the wall, behind and high above a settee full of scientists, about ten feet from where we were sitting.

It was agreed by everyone present that the group members could not have reached the drums if they had wanted to. The whole room was full of people and the spirit team correctly called some by name, although the group had not been introduced to them. Mrs Bradshaw and Edwin came through and told the gathering that the area was an ancient Native American sacred site. The people who had lived there many years ago had had an understanding of spiritual and Earth energies, and were influencing the session.

Another of the US sessions was attended by the medium James Van Praagh, who had written the bestseller *Talking to Heaven*

(Piatkus, 1999). 'James came into the session quite sceptical,' reported the group, 'and he searched the room for devices, etc. He and the others who searched admitted afterwards that they expected to find something under our chairs. They were amazed, not only by the phenomena, but also by the love that was created in the room. James said he could "feel it".'

Soon after this trip, the group was invited to show their work at various venues around Europe, including Switzerland, Ireland, Holland and Germany. In early May 1997, they gave a lecture and slide show at the Zurich branch of the Swiss Parapsychological Society (SPS). Although this meeting had been advertised only to members, almost ninety people attended. This was followed by similar presentations at the St Gall branch of the SPS, where the group members were the guests of Dr Hans-Peter Stüder, and in Basle, where they met Dr Theo Locher, a psychical researcher since the 1950s. Dr Locher commented that he had never seen anything like it in all his forty years of research.

'We really did get the feeling that these overseas trips were to get the message across, to make people think,' said Alan.

Robin lectured at the PSI-Tage Congress in Switzerland in November 1997. He was told that maybe a 100 or 150 would attend, as the work was very new out there. Each morning he held a 'signpost session' which allowed speakers to give a short ten-minute 'taster' on their subject to the 2,000 delegates. After this, about 600 people wanted to come to hear about the Scole Experiment, and they had to find a bigger room.

At the PSI-Tage conference Robin met Dr Andreas Liptay-Wagner, a man involved in running Hungary's main psychical research society, which was founded in 1871. As a result, Robin was invited to address a congress in Budapest. On arrival there, he met Dr Pal Kurthy, secretary of the Hungarian Psychical Research Society, 'a gentleman nearer to ninety than eighty, who seemed much younger than his years, something he put down to his daily practice of yoga. His experience of psychical phenomena was vast and he was fascinating to listen to.' The next day, Robin lectured to 250 people at the modern congress centre booked for the event by the Hungarian society. As he recalled, the Scole Experiment was very well received:

> There was particular interest in our video experiments
> and what was starting to come through during them.
> The spirit team had predicted there would be pictures
> of interdimensional beings on television during 1998.
> We had no idea how this might come about, until it
> happened in Hungary. There was such interest that
> they showed Blue on national television.

The interest really did seem to be building. Back home, the group
kept in touch with its international following via the Internet,
Spiritual Scientist and *A Basic Guide* booklet. Other groups were
also helped by the booklet and, by mid-1998, many hundreds of
copies had been issued world-wide. The *Basic Guide* has been
published in both English and German. It has also been translated
into Dutch and French, although not yet published in those
languages. A Hungarian translation is expected in the near future.
Sandra said:

> We thought that, if just 10 per cent of the groups which
> acquired *A Basic Guide* went on to successfully
> develop phenomena, this would be a significant
> number of groups in many different countries, all
> providing evidence that this new phenomenon is real.
> Groups have already achieved success in the UK,
> USA, Ireland, Canada, Australia, New Zealand,
> Germany, Switzerland, Finland, Holland and Hungary.
> There has also been interest from Japan recently.

One group experimenting successfully is interesting, but if, say,
100 groups were all doing the same thing, this would really be a
step towards convincing the world that survival is a reality.

At this point, we thought it would be constructive to invite our
own set of investigators to meet the Scole group, for an independent
view. With this in mind, we arranged a meeting for Saturday 26
September 1998. The 'investigative team' included Harry Oldfield,

a biologist and physicist and inventor of energy-imaging systems and electronic treatment methods utilising crystals, Professor Michael Laughton, a specialist in electrical engineering from London University, Peter Williams, who trained as a chemist but became a publisher of very wide-ranging scientific journals and books, Joanne Sawicki, a former Head of Programme Development at Sky Television and now an independent film and television producer, and our literary agent, Roger Houghton of Lucas Alexander Whitley.

During a very interesting day at Street Farmhouse, we were shown a large number of the photographs, slides, and videos the group had amassed during the Scole Experiment. They also demonstrated the evidence of audio-communication collected with and without the germanium receptor, and showed us how they set up all their experiments with the microphones, thermometers, video cameras, still cameras, films, domes, compass crystals, mirrors, air flow meters and so on in the Scole Hole. At one point they demonstrated the total darkness that can be achieved in this subterranean laboratory.

Towards the end of the day, the group reminded us that the whole point of the work was to prove the reality of survival to the whole of humanity, once and for all. To this end they were continuing to present evidence to audiences around the world. The team had recently stated that evidence would soon be presented via the television and film media.

Joanne Sawicki found this interesting since she was due to travel to France for a film festival a few days after the meeting at Scole. A short while later, she told us that she had decided to present the Scole Experiment to a number of film companies. When she returned, she contacted Roger with details of all the television companies that had shown an interest in the Scole group. One American network had said that, of all the hundreds of projects they had seen, the Scole Experiment was the most exciting.

The wheels were thus set in motion for more publicity for the group's work.

Not only this, but more investigations were planned. Professor Laughton was interested in asking questions of the spirit team involving a circuit, now in the public domain, which had been developed by a German inventor in the 1930s and which had exhibited strange behaviour. Harry Oldfield and some colleagues meanwhile planned to start similar experiments. So it seemed that serious researchers were prepared to at least be open-minded to what was going on at Scole.

We considered this to be an indication that it was certainly worth further study. Then, late in the evening of Monday 23 November 1998, some five years after the Scole Experiment began, Robin phoned us:

> I have some troubling news. The team has told us we have to shut down operations with immediate effect. A personality from the future is interfering with the interdimensional doorway every time we open it. He is experimenting with a crystalline time-probe and his motives are not entirely benevolent. The team has made efforts to overcome this problem, even to the extent of consulting specialists in time and space in the other realms. They have not been successful and are therefore under pressure to close the doorway. All the work will cease for the time being.
>
> We're going to send you a fax. It's the statement we are going to make to our magazine subscribers and others who follow our work. We'll speak to you again when you've had a chance to read it.

A few seconds later, the familiar bleeping and flickering red lights on the computer confirmed the arrival of the fax:

STATEMENT FROM THE
SCOLE EXPERIMENTAL GROUP

As some of you may already know, we have been experiencing considerable interference during our experimental sessions over the past few months. The source of this interference was, until recently, unknown, and was for some time the subject of much concern and discussion amongst us.

We are now fully informed regarding the adverse situation that has arisen as a result of this interference, and since the outcome will affect many of you who have been involved in our work over a long period of time, we must now sadly pass this information on. We feel that we must be totally honest with our friends at this time, although it is extremely painful for us to report what has happened.

We have discovered that the result of our four energies coming together, added to nature of the pioneering work we were doing in spiritual science, has caused space-time problems relating to an interdimensional doorway that was created for our experiments.

One result of this doorway being created was that it enabled the work to move forward rapidly, thus allowing a number of spiritual energies to come to the Earth at this time in order to help raise man's spiritual consciousness.

However, the vortex of energies within this doorway also attracted experimenters, from the future, who were (are? or will be?) drawn to what we were doing. It was the interaction between their experiments and the doorway which caused serious interference with our work. As a result of this, the team found it increasingly more difficult to communicate with us during our experimental sessions.

During a final brief communication with us, members of our Scole spirit team suggested linking in with personalities from another dimension who, with their expert knowledge of time and space, were in a better position to assess the situation and to possibly help.

After several quite amazing combined visual and vocal communications, which came from a knowledgeable being from this other dimension, it became apparent that the difficulties could not be overcome at all.

We were told that since the interference was contrary to the strict laws of time and space, it must not be allowed to continue. We expected that the members of the team of beings from other dimensions who were working with us would find a solution, but we were to be disappointed in this belief. It then emerged that the only practical option was for them to ask us to co-operate: we were to cease all experimental sessions immediately and so avoid opening the doorway.

This, of course, was at first unthinkable. But after much debate and heart-searching, we realised that there was no other option but to comply. We have known our 'team' for a number of years and have worked with confidence under their loving guidance – therefore we knew that all other possibilities must have been tried and failed before this request was made of us.

Those of you more closely involved with our work at Scole will appreciate how devastating this news is to us. As individuals and as a group it is hard to put into words how we feel. Our friends from the team are sadly missed already and the loss seems irreplaceable at the present time.

However, the team said that it is only when our four energies are reaching out in spiritual communion that this interference from the future takes place, thus creating a situation that may have unknown consequences. Hence all experiments involving the four of us together have now ceased as requested.

Although the communication 'links' with our team no longer exist, we do feel that we must continue with our efforts to bring their 'message' to the attention of the world. We therefore regard these events here described as an opportunity to go forwards, even though our work cannot take the same form as it did before.

We have begun new experiments with computers and tape recorders as two couples rather than one group of four and we hope that in time this will yield results.

We have been told that, as this dreadful situation only affects the SEG, it is totally safe for other energy-based experimental groups to proceed with their work. We intend to continue our efforts in helping other groups to develop phenomena which is similar to our past results.

The New Spiritual Science Foundation was always separate from our group. This organisation will soldier on as was always intended, helping those interested in developing physical phenomena to achieve their aims.

This difficult decision we have had to make will, we know, have many repercussions, as we had a number of unfinished projects in process. Needless to say, as far as is humanly possible, we will try to help everyone in whatever way we can.

The Scole Experimental Group

This was indeed devastating news. We were totally taken aback – and not quite sure how to react. Somehow, even in the light of the other Scole evidence, this 'interference from the future' proposition seemed to be challenging to the rational mind. And what implications did it have for the dissemination of the spirit team's message and the planned investigations?

We soon learned that Montague Keen and Professor Fontana were due to present the Scole evidence at the Institut für Grenzgebiete der Psychologie und Psychohygiene in Freiburg, Germany, where much research into parapsychology is undertaken, and they were still going in spite of this new development. We had a conversation with Montague and he said, quite logically, that this latest turn of events did not change anything. What had happened, had happened. No-one could change the fact that the scientific investigation had taken place. The findings would stand. As he said:

> Although we would have greatly preferred to have had the opportunity to conduct a few more research sessions and were pretty devastated by the shutdown, the Scole experiments constitute, in my personal view, perhaps the most impressive evidence for survival of the human personality yet gathered. We have an obligation to present them for scrutiny.

We started to reflect on this and on what the spirit team had always said: that they were learning, too, that there were things outside their control and that the future is uncertain.

Uncertain it may be, but as the days passed, things seemed to be looking up. The scientific investigation team was going ahead with publication of *The Scole Report*. The TV projects were progressing. Meetings were being planned, research done, budgets considered. So, the Scole project was still forging full-steam ahead, apparently propelled by some unknown and unseen organisational process. At the time, given what had happened, this seemed to be against all the odds, but on reflection, we should not perhaps have been so surprised. If there is anything that many years of association with these phenomena should have taught us, it is that nothing is what it seems.

Throughout this period of uncertainty, we remained in regular contact with the Scole group. At first, they too had been devastated by the shocking news. Gradually though, they had begun to piece together the meaning behind some of the last communications from the spirit team. They had been told time and time again that they would one day be required to stop their own experiments in order to concentrate their efforts on helping others to establish experimental groups. This is why they had set up the New Spiritual Science Foundation. As they said, 'We knew the plan, we just hadn't anticipated that it would come about so dramatically.'

As if by way of some sort of confirmation for us, on Tuesday 1 December, Lin Brady, a friend who lives in Dorset, rang us with some news. It appears that friends of hers had been getting Morse code on tape recordings from a team of spirit communicators 'for ages', using a device 'a bit like the Scole germanium receptor but with five coils'. Now one of the group had started going into trance and they were getting all sorts of communicators coming through on audio-tape.

'Do you think it has anything to do with the Scole phenomena?' Lin asked.

We wondered about this. Certainly the Scole group had been told that many other groups were going to be doing similar work. In fact the Scole group themselves told us that other groups had already had amazing results. Images had even been received on television screens that were *turned off!* Robin said:

> Some of the researchers within the trans-communication network say they are regularly receiving messages from the spirit world via their telephones, computers, and fax machines. We have decided to see whether we are able to achieve such results ourselves. I am using my home computer. I had already mentioned my interest in this work to the team prior to the shutdown and was told that because of my request for co-operation on this new work, a young man in the spirit world had in fact already been assigned to me with the objective of achieving good results on the computer.
>
> We know there has even been speculation about the possibility of an Interdimensional Internet. This might sound a bit far-fetched to some people, but why not? After all, computers are based on semi-conductors and the spirit scientists often told us that these semi-conductors, like germanium and silicon, have important properties that allow the bridges between the dimensions to be crossed.

The idea of the Interdimensional Internet illustrated the possibility that contact with other dimensions may become a reality for all rather than the province of a few. As we have said, the first step appears to be the expansion of the work to other groups who are working with their own spirit teams.

NEW GROUPS

Reviewing some of the contributions to *Spiritual Scientist,* we found that new groups appear to be springing up all round the world. The 'Northern Energy Group', for example, in the UK, started getting phenomena during their very first experimental session – bright flashes of light, finger-tapping noises and 'extra' voices on tape recordings of the sitting.

This group stresses the importance of not expecting any particular phenomena to occur saying:

> You must trust your spirit team. Let them discover the easiest way to communicate with you at the start. Once communication has begun, they will be able to advise you about your group and perhaps suggest what items they would like you to bring into the sessions.

On the opposite side of the world to the Northern Energy Group, in Sandy Beach, Australia, David and Patricia Hayes are experiencing similar phenomena:

> We sit in our blacked-out room [with] sitters' chairs and a wooden circular table upon which we have placed the 'dome', which itself is set upon a stand similar to the one used at Scole.
>
> Since we started our group we have had much energy activity, swirling white clouds, pinpricks of white light all over the room, rather like the Milky Way, black shapes moving around the room, raps and cracking noises. Sometimes we 'push our luck' and ask Spirit to make that 'noise' say another three times more during the session. They do this exactly.
>
> Sitters have felt brushing up against their arms and legs and also prods into the body and neck. We have also experienced smells both scented and musty. Over the past fifteen months we have been getting regular communication from our spirit team through David, who is in light trance. They answer a variety of technical questions for us and also enter into some happy-go-lucky banter from time to time. We find these experiences very rewarding.

Other groups have also had some rewarding communication with the spirit world. A group based in Cheshire, UK, run by Anne and

Fred Child, has experienced 'unbelievably marvellous music coming both from our tambourine and from the string of bells and wind chimes which we have hanging from the ceiling' and has received several apports, including a penny and small screwed-up notes with messages such as 'Hello', 'Trust us' and 'I'm back' pencilled in a shaky hand.

Some groups have been busily experimenting. The 'E' group, run by Tom Sawyer and his wife, started their experiments on 3 February 1998. They used a glass sphere, with a Perspex base on legs, in the centre of the table and they put a Polaroid SX-70 photographic film in a light-proof envelope. They left this under the sphere on the table. A week after the sixth session, the film was removed from the envelope in the darkroom and developed by passing it through the rolling press of the camera. The result was a success: lavender and white colours on the film.

The 'E' group are not alone in this. What is the significance of such experiments? Can they really be considered proof of the survival of consciousness?

The matter is currently open to scientific debate. With regard to this, government scientist Piers Eggert states:

> It is my view that a big stumbling block in the minds of sceptical scientists is that of fear. They have been trained to believe that everything is measurable and understandable, to the extent that they think that anything that can't be tied down and understood by physics cannot possibly exist. This blinkered and arrogant way of thinking has led to a scientific community that is afraid of being shown up as not knowing all the answers. I can see nothing wrong in saying, "I don't know." After all, there is so much that we don't know and where is the shame in admitting it? The most sceptical people will not have their comfortable world turned upside-down and will deny the very best of proof. For them, it would mean having to re-write the science books and the laws of physics.

Some scientists, however, are willing to at least keep an open mind. One scientist who attended a session at Scole said he would like the light to go round his linked hands. Could it be repeated, he asked, to show the sceptics it was not someone swinging a rod around? The light passed through the table and out underneath. It then complied with the request, touching the scientist's hands in such a way as to satisfy the most cynical sceptics.

During a later session, Albert, the spirit scientist, began to converse with Professor Archie Roy, who had been invited by the scientific investigators. Albert explained that, in his lifetime, his work was not considered orthodox but he worked on various theories out of 'sheer intellectual curiosity'. Albert and Professor Roy (an astronomer) talked at length about binary stars, the demise of the dinosaurs and a theory known as 'Nemesis'. The conversation then turned to the 'triple star problem' and a lively and interesting dialogue followed. Albert showed he was aware of the latest measuring techniques with regard to gravity. Most of this conversation was baffling to everyone else present. Professor Roy later remarked that he felt he had been speaking to someone who was very knowledgeable indeed about such matters.

The Spring 1997 issue *of Spiritual Scientist* reported:

> Interestingly, whenever a new scientist comes... it seems the team has attuned the energy already and can demonstrate something that will totally capture the new visitor's interest in the work.

Capturing people's interest was, of course, one of the primary aims of the Scole spirit team during their five-year experiment. In this they have succeeded. But have they managed to provide proof of survival beyond physical death? Some say that it is not yet possible to conclude categorically that this is the case, even in the light of the Scole Experiment evidence. However, the fact that the experimental work is continuing around the world at least suggests the possibility that we will one day find out for certain one way or the other.

If we accept what has been said by the communicators, then in the future there will be much more co-operation between the dimensions, to the benefit of us all.

Whether you put this book down and never think about it again, or whether you have been inspired to start your own experimental group as soon as possible, we would like to leave you with a thought from the team of spiritual beings who participated in the Scole Experiment:

> *Have an open mind and an open heart. Changes in the thought and behaviour patterns of individuals create changes in the conditions of humanity as a whole. We often hear you say, 'I cannot do anything about this or that problem because it is too far away or nothing to do with me.' Well, know this, all things, whether tangible or intangible, and all events, whether of yesterday, today, or tomorrow, have everything to do with everyone. This is a fact of spiritual science that we are attempting to share with you. If enough individuals receive what we are now able to send and adopt a position of openness, harmony, and love in their interactions... untold wonders will then be available to all.*

AFTERWORD

Professor David Fontana is one of the three principal authors of *The Scole Report.* While its signatories were in broad agreement about much of what transpired during the investigations which led to the *Report,* there were, inevitably, differing views as to what might be deduced and concluded from the recorded events. Professor Ellison has commented in the Foreword, and Montague Keen specifically contributed to Chapter 9. Professor Fontana's perspective follows:

OUR THANKS TO THE SCOLE GROUP

I must begin by recording our great indebtedness as investigators to the Scole group. Without their co-operation and their unfailing kindness, our work could not have taken place. Many of those who spend time and energy attempting to develop psychic abilities are deeply suspicious of scientists, seeing them as concerned only to belittle their efforts and explain away any results as at best self-delusion and at worst as fraud. By contrast, the Scole group was only too ready to enlist the help of suitably objective scientists. Having satisfied themselves of our sincerity, they welcomed our interest and, as far as they were able, gave us every facility and encouragement to conduct our observations. They freely shared their experiences with us, they gave us generous hospitality and they asked nothing of us in return. And in case it be thought that their generosity was an attempt to buy our favour, let me emphasise that it was clear to us that this was not their intention. In fact, although the Scole group must speak for themselves, our impression was that we would have forfeited their respect if we had on the one hand so misread their kindness as to consider it an attempt at bribery and on the other been so weak in our scientific resolve as to allow hospitality to deprive us of scientific objectivity.

SCIENCE AND PSYCHICAL RESEARCH

The essence of science is good observation. Whether in the laboratory or in the field, the scientist has an obligation to observe the data under investigation with all the care at his command, to record his observations as fully and as accurately as possible and then to publish these observations for scrutiny by his colleagues. Subsequent to publication, he must attend to the criticisms others may make of his observations, and answer them if he can and assent to them if he cannot. Clearly observation in the laboratory, where scientists can apply stringent controls to ensure that the observable effects are not distorted by extraneous circumstances, and where methodologies can be progressively refined and developed in the light of results, is considerably more foolproof than observation in the field. For this reason among others, many scientists confine their work to the laboratory and take less account of the results obtained elsewhere.

Nevertheless, laboratory work and fieldwork should, wherever possible, proceed in conjunction with each other. Effects which are first noticed in the laboratory can then be looked for in the field, while effects first identified in the field can be studied under the stricter conditions of the laboratory. However, since the 1930s, when Professor J. B. Rhine and his colleagues first developed methods for studying psychic phenomena (under the new title 'parapsychology') in the laboratory, there has been a tendency to concentrate upon laboratory work at the expense of fieldwork. Without doubt laboratory work in parapsychology has stood us in excellent stead in that it has demonstrated to the satisfaction of many shrewd researchers that psychic phenomena do in fact take place and need to be accounted for within our scientific paradigms (see Radin's *The Conscious Universe* for an excellent recent summary of laboratory findings). But effects which are confined to the laboratory have limited relevance to our understanding of normal experience.

It is our recognition of this fact that prompted my colleagues and I to investigate the reports of what was happening at Scole. In carrying out this investigation we felt governed throughout by the

246

need – essential in all areas of scientific research – to retain open minds. If scientists decide in advance that the effects for which they are looking either exist or do not exist, their observations inevitably become seriously biased. Nowhere is this more true than in psychical research, and in that area of psychical research that enquires into possible human survival after death. For in spite of arguments to the contrary, science has not in any generally acceptable sense been able either to 'prove' or 'disprove' such survival.

One may observe the extinction of all vital physical signs at the moment of death and decide that there is no survival, or one may look at so-called post-mortem communications and decide that there is. Neither of these decisions can be regarded as fully scientific. Vital physical signs do indeed cease at the moment of death, but mental life may not depend entirely upon these signs and therefore may not be extinguished along with them. Post-mortem communications may indeed appear impressive, but are open to alternative explanations such as misinterpretation or the operation of super-PSI. Therefore in the strict terms of current scientific understanding, we just do not know. But what we do know is that, in the absence of conclusive evidence either way, science must continue the search for more and better data.

THE SCOLE REPORT

The Scole Report, which Grant and Jane Solomon quote in this book, is the result of our investigation. We observed as carefully and as closely as we could, drawing not only upon experience gained from our own previous investigations of phenomena of this kind, but upon our knowledge of the many investigations carried out by others and our familiarity with the various methods that fraudulent mediums have used over the years in order to deceive those who placed their trust in them. Our *Report* gives an account of these observations and examines in all the detail at our command the possibilities that the phenomena we witnessed could be the result of fraud. And make no mistake, fraud is the only alternative explanation that can be offered for these phenomena.

There is no question of our having been deceived by our own imagination or of our having exaggerated the things that we witnessed in order to support our own preconceptions.

It is not the job of science to make up people's minds for them, but to present evidence and allow others to draw their own conclusions. We have set out this evidence in detail in our *Report* and readers who are interested may wish to study it. However, as fraud is the only alternative to genuine phenomena in the Scole investigation, it is right to say that during the two years in which we attended the sittings we never saw any direct evidence that fraud was taking place or had grounds for suspicion that it might be. Nevertheless, we failed to achieve the watertight conditions under which fraud would have been rendered impossible. We got tantalisingly close on several occasions, but the final step eluded us.

We sought a four-step protocol which involved the use of our own film, the use of our own secure container to house the film during the sittings, our control of this container during the sittings, and our control of the subsequent development of the film. Such a protocol was necessary if the doubts of critics not present at the sittings were to be laid fully to rest. In the absence of such a protocol, such critics have drawn attention to aspects of the images found on the films which they consider suspicious, for example the facts that some of these images are taken from readily available books and that the reproduction is in some cases suggestive of the work of human hands. Suspicion has also been cast upon the Alan box, as it is contended that the hasp can be dislodged and the box opened without breaking the paint security seals.

No matter how unlikely it is that fraud was perpetrated given the conditions under which the sittings took place, the fact that it *could theoretically have been perpetrated* is enough for these critics to claim that it therefore might have been. And this in spite of the fact that similar claims are not made against the great majority of phenomena observed in other less contentious areas of scientific investigation, even though faking could conceivably (and sometimes quite easily) happen there as well. The very improbability of psychic and/or mediumistic abilities is sufficient to make many critics prefer the charge of fraud, no matter how difficult it may be to sustain. And it must be confessed that the presence of loopholes, however small, are unsatisfactory in any area of research. Within psychical research they leave us wondering why so-called communicators cannot present watertight evidence. Perhaps William James, one of the founding fathers of modern psychology and a man with a keen interest in psychical research, may have been right when he suggested that the Almighty may have decreed that the area of the paranormal should forever retain its element of mystery!

If readers decide that, on the balance of probabilities, the Scole phenomena were genuine, they may then wish to speculate on explanations. Do the phenomena support the notion that the personality survives bodily death and is able to communicate with those still on Earth or is it possible that they were the result of the Scole group's own psychic abilities, whether employed consciously or unconsciously?

Let us take the second of these possibilities first. If we go back to laboratory evidence for a moment, we would have to say that there is no evidence that the macro effects witnessed at Scole can be produced by the human mind. There is indeed laboratory evidence (Radin's *The Conscious Universe* gives the details) that the human mind can influence the behaviour of inanimate objects, but to date the effects concerned are very small and undramatic, and bear little direct comparison with the macro effects at Scole. If the members of the Scole group were indeed capable of consistently producing such effects by the action of their own minds, then they would have been far better advised to demonstrate the fact in the laboratory. In no time they would have become psychic superstars. In fact, judging by the track record of at least one well-known if controversial psychic, they could quickly have made their names as entertainers and have earned a great deal of money in the process.

In the absence of evidence that humans possess the ability reliably to demonstrate macro psychic effects of the kind seen at Scole, the first of the above possibilities, namely that they may have been due in some part to the action of individuals who have survived physical death and are able to interact with this world, demands consideration. We must make it clear that during our investigation we never received information through any of the supposed communicators that might convince hardened sceptics that they were indeed speaking to us from the next world (although others involved in work at Scole may have done so). I mean highly obscure information about their earthly lives which does not appear in books or newspapers and which is unknown to any of those present, but which turns out subsequently to be correct.

In fairness, it must be made clear that we never asked for such information, largely because we had hoped that the investigation would continue and yield opportunities to proceed to work of this kind once we had completed our research into the other phenomena. What we did receive (e.g. the two *Ruth* films and the various puzzles and clues that were given to us through the mediums), intriguing as it was in many ways, is unlikely to satisfy all critics in that with one or two exceptions it is already available in published works and could therefore readily be accessed by super-PSI or other means.

In the absence of such information, what other evidence was there that might have pointed towards survival? Grant and Jane Solomon build up a case on the strength of a range of relevant examples taken from the accounts given by the many investigators who have worked with the Scole group and I have no intention of casting doubt on this case. We also have to face the question that if the phenomena were genuine, and if it seems unlikely that they were produced by the direct action of the minds of the Scole group upon their environment, then what agent or agency was responsible? Could it have been people from beyond the grave? One way of trying to answer this question is to consider the personalities of the various supposed communicators. Did these seem to be separate in any significant sense from the personalities of the Scole group themselves?

Investigators in many past cases have speculated that communicators may be sub-personalities of the mediums rather than individuals in their own right. All that can be said with any certainty is that the communicators at Scole each showed marked consistencies of speech, mannerisms, preoccupations, interests, intellect, memories and personality characteristics (e.g. degrees of extroversion, of reserve, of humour, of social graces) throughout our investigation. Psychological research does not suggest that sub-personalities, on the few occasions where they have been observed as supplanting the individual's dominant personality, show this kind of consistency. They tend instead to be highly idiosyncratic and emotionally unstable, rarely capable of sustained rational discourse, with the result that they appear more like dramatised fragments of the individual's repressed inner life than whole human beings. None of the communicators at Scole fitted into this stereotype. Whether speaking through the mediums, or when apparently through what are usually referred to as 'direct' or 'independent voices', they were reminiscent of cultured, erudite, and self-restrained members of the middle-class. (Interestingly, with the exception of Emily Bradshaw – who held centre stage for much of the time and spoke exclusively through Diana – they were all male and spoke either through Alan or through the direct voice.)

Critics may of course propose that although the physical phenomena might be accepted as genuine, the voices may all have been fraudulent. Assuming the mediums were only simulating trance, they could (given a good measure of dramatic skill), have impersonated the various communicators. This remains a possibility, although an unlikely one. If the physical phenomena were genuine, why bother to supplement it with stagey voices particularly if, to sustain the fiction of being in trance, the mediums would then have had studiously to avoid letting slip during the lengthy discussions of the physical phenomena that followed our sittings any hint that they had witnessed these phenomena for themselves? More importantly, during the sittings the voices frequently commented accurately upon the phenomena *before* they actually took place. This could not have happened if the former were spurious and the latter were genuine. And if the voices were fraudulent but the phenomena were genuine, we are faced once again with the problem of how to account for the latter.

We are left with the conclusion that unless one rules out in advance the possibility of human survival, the simplest and most rational explanation is that if one assumes the physical phenomena were genuine then it is reasonable to assume that so were the voices, with the latter proving in some way responsible for the former. Whether, if genuine, the voices were owned by individuals or were representatives of some form of group soul is another issue that we had hoped to explore more fully had our investigation continued.

My fellow investigators and I would like to sign off by sending the Scole group our very best wishes for the future. The members of the group are distinguished by their dedication to their work, their desire to be of service to others, and their remarkable qualities as men and women. We felt it a privilege to be allowed to conduct our investigation into their work and we look forward to the day when we will be able to resume it. In spite of the current pause in the proceedings at Scole, we feel confident that that day will not be too long delayed.

POSTSCRIPT
1999 EDITION

The scientific investigation conducted during the five years of the Scole Experiment was unique. However, as the project progressed, it appeared that a number of other groups were beginning to get similar results to those achieved during the early days at Scole. This brings us on to perhaps the most convincing aspect of the Scole Experiment: transferability. Hundreds of groups throughout the world have begun to experiment along similar lines, all following the instructions set out in the Scole group's *A Basic Guide* booklet. As already mentioned, many of these new groups are reporting consistent results. If just a few of them get off the ground, then a significant number of people will be doing this work around the world in the next couple of years. We intend to invite those conducting these experiments to report on their experiences.

We have also started our own experiments and will be inviting the investigators from the Society for Psychical Research to attend sessions if positive results are achieved. Perhaps, with these new experiments and with investigation from serious researchers like those from the Society, we can all move a little further towards producing further solid scientific evidence in support of the survival hypothesis.

Stay tuned!

POSTSCRIPT
2006 EDITION
THE NORFOLK EXPERIMENT

Having been in regular contact with Alan and Diana, the Scole mediums, since the cessation of proceedings at Scole, we were very pleased to hear from them, in early 2006, with an invitation to visit. They had, we learned, been working 'in a different way to Scole', and results had started to come through.

We travelled to their home in Norfolk, wondering what might be in store. If the portal(s) had indeed been re-opened for communication with other dimensions, we speculated on what form that communication might take.

On arrival, Alan brought us up-to-date by showing us an article which had been published in the Scole Group magazine, the *Spiritual Scientist*, which read as follows:

> So many times people would say to us, 'Oh how disappointed you must be, not being able to carry on with the Scole Experiments'. Well yes, there is always some sadness when something like that comes to a premature end, but we were always told to try and be positive in our thoughts whenever possible. So sadness and disappointment should only really be short-lived, and not allowed to dominate our thoughts and lives.
>
> Although we (as a group) have not been carrying out experimental sessions at Scole over the last few years, we have as individuals been exploring our own particular interests in psychic phenomena and healing.

Having been very much involved (Diana and I were the two mediums at Scole) at the cutting edge of psychic research, we decided, after a long break, that we were not prepared to stop working altogether. We owed so much to those in the higher realms that we knew in our hearts we would continue to experiment in one way or another. I have always seen, in my mind's eye, a phoenix rising from the ashes with renewed vigour to live through another cycle.

Diana has always had that wonderful gift of 'far sight' and receiving guidance in her dreams, so it was no surprise when she told me that she had 'seen' the two of us working together again. She was told how we should take the first step, in the form of a shared spiritual experience.

We followed her vision of a simple experiment using a crystal, where the two of us linked together mentally and shared a journey of exploration.

This experience was incredible; we were both shown such wonders and places. We were guided by a sentient being through a wonderful 'magical mystery tour' where we met another being whom we conversed with.

Through several other forms of communication we were shown how to set up an experiment that would, they explained, enable us to glimpse into other worlds (dimensions). We found that it was necessary to continue to follow our intuition, and to be 'guided' by them, if we were to achieve satisfactory results. It has required total dedication and perseverance as well as an open but still discerning mind.

Before I continue, I would like to mention one very important factor, and that is that old chestnut 'total darkness'. We were 'guided' to do this new work in full light. After so much criticism in the past regarding the physical phenomena obtained at Scole being in total darkness, we decided that we would only continue to work as mediums, in full light. This has proved not to be prohibitive in anyway whatsoever, as we have already achieved very encouraging results.

These experiments are primarily attempts to see into, and capture a view into, other dimensions of existence. To be more precise, these views are more like frozen images or pictures, of different moments in time as we look into these dimensions.

Since that first experiment, Diana and I have conducted many more, progressing and building on what we have learnt. It seems that the possibilities are endless, as we modify and introduce other equipment into the experiments.

It involves the use of some leading edge technology and can be quite complicated to set up. It is based on the idea that there are dimensions not only beyond our own but within them also. By using a combination of electronic and photographic equipment coupled to image enhancement computer software (for magnification purposes only) we have been fortunate enough to obtain fleeting glimpses into these 'other' dimensions during our experimental sessions.

What lies at the very 'heart' of these experiments is the process we are using to access these dimensions. As I have already said, we were told just how to set up these experiments and how it would involve the use of light and colours. This is very important.

It also requires our joint input in the form of a powerful visualisation to create a central focal point for the experiment.

Refracted light is then focused onto this point through several lenses before the computer software captures the images.

Our current experiments mainly take the form of a joint meditative session, where we raise our consciousness and focus together on our objective for that experiment.

The equipment is pre-configured and ready to run, allowing us to concentrate on the 'higher' aspects of what we are doing. We usually have several 'takes' during a typical session, again leaving it to what feels right as we rarely know for sure if we have been successful in capturing any faces. Some of the best results we have obtained have been with ordinary photographic equipment.

We now find ourselves using our own intuition and not relying entirely on 'spirit' communication for direction. This, I have to say, has been very interesting, exploring the different possibilities and approaches to the experiments, by allowing our 'higher minds' to guide us.

Only guessing:

We can only guess as to what is actually happening when we receive a positive result, and by following the 'intuitive' suggestions offered we feel we are giving the experiment the best possible chance. We have felt for some time that the chances of a good result are greatly improved if we offer as many variables as possible within the experimental framework. By this I mean thinking of the experiments themselves as multi-dimensional and not just a singular attempt to get a singular result. I firmly believe that by supplying a randomized source of material for the 'other side' to use, we (and they) stand a far greater chance of success.

Although not exclusively, faces seem to be the most common results up to this time (see plate section). From the many images we have, around 90% are faces, or parts of faces. Some are literally half faces, which lend themselves to the use of a mirror to make a more complete face.

Mirror images:

By this we mean images (usually faces) that appear to be mirrored as well as captured using mirrors. We do not see any reason why the use of mirrors should be seen as reducing the value of a positive result. On the contrary, we believe that any equipment which aids the results is useful.

It was explained to us through 'communications' that experimenting with reflected and refracted light would give us a much wider field to explore. It was implied that water was also important and could help.

We have used various types of mirror during our experiments over the past few years. Coloured (polished metal) mirrors have given some of our best results, full of colour and definition. It would seem that colour and definition go hand in hand in our work, as the monochrome images, although still very interesting, seem to lack the quality that the coloured ones have.

We have used these mirrors to reflect a light source back into the point of focus (where we capture the images), to give the subject depth. Have you ever looked through a simple microscope and seen how adjusting the mirror (light source) gives the object greater depth and makes it stand out against its background? This is similar to what the camera sees during our experiments.

Refraction and Reflection:

With our light experiments, we generate a vast spectrum of colour and intensities by passing the light source through crystal. This source itself is variable, which, in turn, causes many different light patterns and colours to be formed. Some of the light frequencies generated are of course beyond our own visible spectrum, so the resulting light contains much more information than we realise.

We may include a mirror between the source and the crystal (focus) or beyond the focal point, allowing the light to flood back onto the subject. Apart from ordinary mirrors, we have used convex and concave mirrors to very good effect. We have also experimented with polished metallic disks such as brass (yellow) and copper (red), which have created some of the more striking images

History:

'Scry' and 'Discry' mean looking at things at a distance using your own inner vision. Mirrors and other reflective surfaces have been used for centuries for these purposes. 'Scrying' is also the term used to describe the technique of looking into a mirror or crystal to see (using your higher consciousness) into other dimensions. When a crystal is used, scrying is known as catoptromancy or crystallomancy, but historically anything reflective has been used.

One aspect that excites us in particular is that this new approach is only now possible with the advancement in electronics and the related computer technologies. Therefore, it is interesting to wonder where will we be, and what will we discover, in the years ahead?

Image examples:

Images were captured during an experiment we were conducting using a Herkimer quartz crystal (see plate section*). We were focusing a concentrated light source onto the side of this crystal and capturing from the image generated.*

We have to study the resulting images in the minutest detail; a task which has to be repeated over and over again to ensure we haven't overlooked a positive result.

Sometimes we resort to using magnification, as

some of the faces we see are very small. We cannot overemphasize the importance of studying every detail, and these particular results are a good example of what could be missed. We had put most of the originals aside, after looking at them in depth several times but, on a further study and using a mirror as an aid to recognition, the results were there for all to see.

Modern Means

Diana then continued, confirming that they were very interested in using 'modern means' in 'light conditions'. She explained:

'Technology is moving forward rapidly, and, even since *The Scole Experiment* finished, there have been advances in the equipment available to record the events that may occur during our sessions. This is the way we wanted to move forward, with "modern means".

'One particularly interesting piece of equipment we wanted to use was a "light-imaging" system called the "Intra-Spectral Imaging System" or "ISIS". This instrumentation enabled us to see "energies" not discernible with the naked eye, and also, because it used a video camera, there was a record in lighted conditions and in real-time of the "energy" present.

'We had seen and used ISIS in relation to the viewing of light patterns around the human body (see plate section and *Further Information*) for complementary medicine applications, but soon discovered it had other applications in relation to our experiments with crystals and other inanimate objects.'

The Norfolk Group

After we had heard about the exciting new developments, the conversation came around to 'what next?' To cut a long story short, the four of us decided to form a new experimental group and conduct research sessions, to which others may be invited in future.

We were excited at this new prospect. Unlike our research for *The Scole Experiment*, where we interviewed participants and specialists – and reported their experiences and comments – *after* the events, we would now be in a position to both participate in experimental sessions and report events as they occurred.

The First Session of The Norfolk Group – 19th February 2006

We followed Diana and Alan in to the experimental room, where the equipment comprised digital video and still cameras, tripods, crystals, bright spotlights and mirrors (see plate section). We each took one of the four comfortable chairs around the central table, on which sat a high resolution camera mounted on a tripod. The zoom lens of the still camera was extended and focused on a crystal lit by a bright beam from a small spotlight.

Diana opened the session with an invitation to those from other dimensions to join and work with us.

Fast-Forward?

We have no way of fast-forwarding to the future. We neither know what will happen in sessions of the Norfolk Group, nor who will be taking part as participant/observer (from whichever dimension of existence).

However, we do know what occurred during *The Scole Experiment*, and, on that basis alone, look forward to chronicling more about these events and all that happens at the sessions of the Norfolk Group in a forthcoming book…

The Norfolk Experiment

Meanwhile, for updates, you can visit:
www.thescoleexperiment.com

Aspects of

SPIRITUAL SCIENCE

THE SPIRIT TEAM

JOHN PAXTON

John Paxton was an evolved spirit entity who said he had lived in the thirteenth century. A commanding personality and a member of the ruling Council of Communion, Paxton helped to oversee the operations in the SEG. The council made the decisions about the progress and planning of experiments, not only for the work of the Scole group, but also for others like them.

MANU

Manu was a powerful and extremely spiritual guide, who always spoke first, and whose job it was to blend together the available energies for use by the spirit operators during a session. He was the 'gatekeeper' from the spirit world. He always started the sessions by putting in place the conditions under which communications from the other realms were possible. This involved creating a 'canopy of energy' over the group and a 'golden doorway' between the dimensions.

Manu said he had 'enjoyed many incarnations'. One of these was in 'what you now call South America'. In that life he was apparently from Peru and of the Inca race.

It was Manu and his Victorian child helpers who brought apports to the group on a regular basis.

PATRICK McKENNA

According to the group, Patrick was 'a delightful soul' of Irish origin who had been a priest, 'but not a very good one', during his

Earth life. He had a liking for pints of Guinness and fat cigars. He was the appointed 'spiritual co-ordinator' of the communicators and was ultimately responsible to the spirit world for the group's activities and progress.

Patrick was *in situ,* via Alan's trance, for the greater part of each session and was the second communicator to speak, his presence generally being announced by the physical ringing of a string of cowbells. He was also the last to bid farewell and told the group when it was time to close the session, usually after some two to two and a half hours.

Part of Patrick's job was to manoeuvre 'casual communicators' to the right position to make their communication, while at the same time helping them to get their messages across. He was especially good at putting visitors at their ease with his corny jokes and witticisms. As Robin says fondly: 'I don't think Patrick was satisfied with kissing the Blarney Stone – I think he swallowed it!'

RAJI

Raji was a lovable Indian character who was once in the military. While on Earth he was a 'Rajpoot', a type of prince who belonged to a caste of ancient Hindu warriors. He had served as a soldier on horseback during his lifetime, and continued to be very fond of marching music, which he requested when he came to speak to the group and visitors.

One of Raji's functions was to help people with their spiritual development. He often advised the group and their guests on how to get the most out of meditation. Although he was very serious at times, he had a great sense of humour and often had everyone in stitches. He was also involved with the group's healing work, which he enhanced by apporting small amounts of very special sacred ash which was said to have healing properties.

Raji was given the job of organising the early photographic experiments, as well as those experiments involving messages on sealed audiotape. For his work with the group, this kindly character often used the services of his assistant, 'Small Boy', who was later, for some reason, renamed 'Charlie No. 1'.

MRS EMILY BRADSHAW

Mrs Bradshaw was a pleasant and precise spirit helper. Her speciality was providing extremely accurate evidence of survival, which never ceased to amaze members of the group and their visitors. She spoke in an educated, matter-of-fact clipped Oxford accent, which was pleasing to hear and easily recognisable.

Mrs Bradshaw also had a wider function, performing a similar job to Patrick through her own medium, Diana, in helping spirit communicators to come forward and make themselves known. She either assisted them to speak directly through trance, or relayed messages from them to the appropriate recipient.

Mrs Bradshaw was clearly a lady when on Earth and she had been heavily involved in charity work. Her originally severe tones mellowed with time, and, like Patrick, 'Mrs B.', as she became known, spent most of the time *in situ* during sessions, occasionally interjecting an appropriate remark or playfully taking Patrick to task over his explanation of a particular point. Mrs Bradshaw and Patrick were quite a double act and both kept up with modern trends and humour.

The members of the spirit team said they kept up to date by listening in to conversations on Earth and by speaking to modern people when they passed to the spirit world. It was quite amusing to the group and their visitors to hear Mrs Bradshaw, a very prim and proper lady in her time, talking about 'surfing the net' and 'double-whammies'. Often, at the end of a session, she would leave with the words, 'Well, it's good night from me, and it's good night from him.'

EDWARD MATTHEWS

A wonderfully sensitive soul, Edward visited the Scole group on an intermittent basis and showed a strong desire to be a part of the communicating team. The group could sense the love and emotion in his voice when he spoke.

Edward was very knowledgeable on many subjects and could converse on several topics, including the business that was run by his father in south London in the early part of the twentieth century. He tried especially hard to brush up his stories and anecdotes for the entertainment of visitors. The one thing he was unable to bring himself to discuss with visitors was the subject of his passing during the First World War. The conditions around that time were unbearable, and the manner of his death was very traumatic. Since he found the subject too distressing, guests were asked not to raise it during sittings.

In addition to his conversational contributions, Edward was heavily involved in the organisation of several scientific experiments and often familiarised group members with the spirit team's plans.

THE SPIRIT SCIENTISTS

When it became clear that regular interaction with invited scientists was going to take place, the team decided that new personalities should come through to communicate on a more regular basis. This meant that some of the earlier communicators were no longer taking such an active part.

William, Albert, Joseph, and Edwin were four of the spirit scientists who communicated with the Scole group. William, a quietly spoken English scientist who lived at the end of the nineteenth century, had been interested in the paranormal during his lifetime. He was an expert on photography and glass and used to edit a photographic magazine.

Albert was not an orthodox scientist when on Earth, but apparently a bit of a maverick. He certainly got things moving in the sessions. As we know, physical apports appeared in the cellar. Things also *disappeared* from the cellar. These were known as 'asports'. Albert was always involved when asportation took place.

'Joseph' had been a noted scientist in his day, but he became very cautious when the scientific investigators arrived at Scole and questioned him about his real identity. He felt the work was of paramount importance and that focusing on personalities might detract from it.

Edwin was a medical doctor rather than a scientist. He had obtained his medical degree at Edinburgh. Edwin was to become a regular communicator, especially when investigators were present.

The team seems to have been made up of a very large number of such specialist individuals. Many of the names were probably pseudonyms. Changes in the communicators were made as required.

APPENDIX TWO

FIGURES

The following diagrams show the layouts of some of the experimental rooms and technical equipment used during the Scole Experiment.

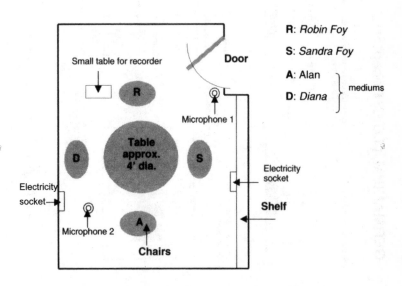

Figure 1: This shows the layout and seating arrangements of the cellar or 'Scole Hole'. It also shows where the recording equipment was placed.

GERMANIUM (T.D.C. Receptor)

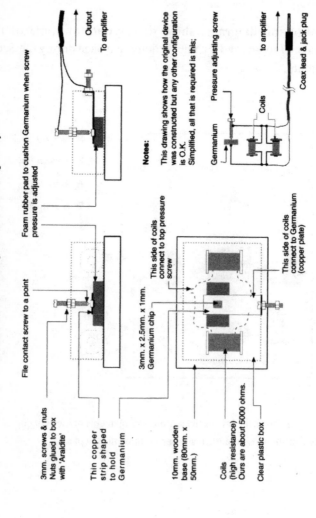

Figure 2: The germanium (TDC) receptor.

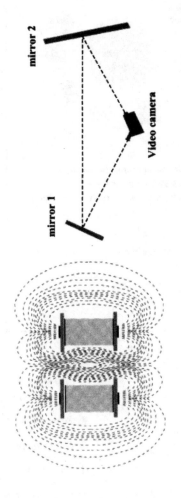

Figure 3: An electromagnetic field.

Figure 4: The set-up of the mirrors and video camera used during Project Alice.

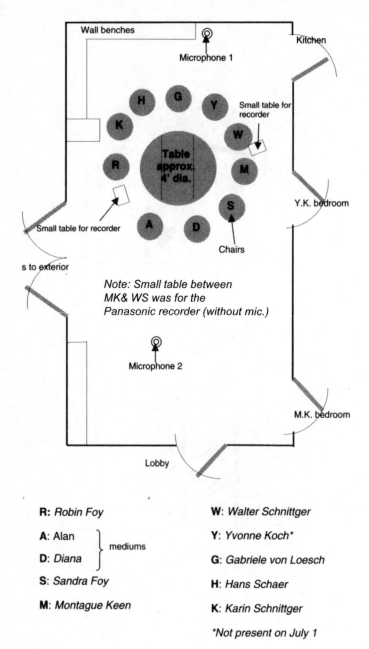

Figure 5: The seating plan for the Scole group experimental sessions in Ibiza, 29 June and 1 July 1997.

THE CODE OF CONDUCT FOR VISITORS

A major feature of the new energy-based work being carried out during the Scole Experiment was that it did not pose the same threat to the health of mediums and sitters as the traditional methods such as those which used ectoplasm.

However, this did not eliminate the need for strict security and a recognised Code of Conduct for visitors. The New Spiritual Science Foundation introduced this new Code of Conduct in its first issue of the *Spiritual Scientist* bulletin.

THE NEW SPIRITUAL SCIENCE FOUNDATION CODE OF CONDUCT FOR VISITORS

For best results at a physical sitting, it is important for all invited sitters to observe a recognised Code of Conduct designed to encourage communication, evidence and phenomena. We suggest, as a matter of course, that visitors dress casually, and warmly, to combat the psychic coldness which usually accompanies physical phenomena.

Men, for instance, should ideally wear an open-necked shirt, trousers and sweater to a sitting, whilst for ladies, perhaps a blouse, jumper, and slacks are more comfortable than a dress.

Sitters must not wear scent or aftershave, as the smell of these could later be confused with psychically created smells. Handbags and the contents of pockets should be left locked in a car or somewhere outside the room.

It is very important to attend any physical experimental sitting in the right frame of mind, as the thoughts and moods of sitters can positively or adversely affect the results, and to this end, a happy atmosphere is always best.

Guests should try to approach the session with a totally open mind as to what they might witness. Open scepticism is fine, but if visitors sit in at an experiment with the predetermined view that what they are about to witness is not genuine, then their thoughts can definitely block phenomena, thus spoiling the session for other sitters. There will be ample time to discuss individual views and impressions **after** the event.

Throughout the sitting, visitors must try to sit perfectly still but relaxed, keeping hands either in their laps or on their knees. **They must not stand up or move about during a sitting** and should a spirit light or any other levitated object come close to them or touch them at any time, **they must not make any attempt to grab at it – or to move their arms about in any way** – unless specifically requested by the spirit team to do so.

It is paramount for sitters to try and help keep the atmosphere happy and harmonious, as this will always produce better results.

It is also likely that, during the course of an experimental sitting, some visitors may receive personal messages and survival evidence from the spirit people. Sitters should listen carefully when communication of this nature is taking place and if any of the messages are for them, they must **answer audibly** if a spiritual entity asks for them or speaks to them personally. The sound of the recipient's voice is most important to the communicator for them to establish a strong link, and without it, the communication is likely to simply fade out.

Sitters should not, however, volunteer specific information gratuitously to any of the spirit communicators, but should nevertheless co-operate with them and encourage them to speak so that they can supply evidential information and messages of their own free will, the content of which could not possibly be known to the medium – only to the recipient.

When the session is over, prior to the proceedings being properly closed in prayer, all sitters should keep quiet until the medium or mediums are fully conscious. Afterwards, when the mediums have recovered sufficiently and are suitably refreshed, then they or other group members will be happy to chat about the experimental sitting and answer questions.

PERSONAL SENSATIONS

It is only natural that visitors at a group sitting, and particularly at their first physical sitting, should be a little apprehensive, but we can assure them that although they might witness some amazing things, with lights flying around the room at considerable speed and heavy objects levitating, etc., **they will not come to any personal harm in any way.** This fact is constantly emphasised by the spirit teams, who work with groups such as the Scole group to allay the fears of those with little experience to date of physical mediumship. All the phenomena are strictly controlled by the spirit helpers to prevent any accidents.

There are a few physical sensations, which visitors may or may not experience (as the case may be), during a sitting. The first of these is associated with all physical phenomena groups and takes the form of a definite coldness in the room. It is generally felt around and below the knees, and is the most common experience during such experiments. Sometimes this coldness can also be accompanied by a psychic breeze.

During sittings of the Scole Experimental Group in particular, there may be a feeling of slight nausea in some sitters. This could also be linked in some cases to a slight dizziness. There could possibly be some heaviness of the limbs and a gentle pulling sensation from various parts of the body. It is important to emphasise again at this point that these sensations are normal and only temporary during a sitting. **The health of visitors and guests at the experimental sitting is not at risk in any way and will not be adversely affected either in the short or long term.**

SCIENTIFIC INVESTIGATION SESSIONS [SPR]

The scientific investigation sessions which specifically involved the members of the Society for Psychical Research are set out below:

1995	2 October	**1997**	3 January
	16 December		11 January
			24 January
1996	3 January		8 February
	13 January		21 February
	17 February		28 February
	16 March		4 March
	13 April		7 March
	18 May		15 March
	15 June		27 March
	13 July		5 April
	10 August		29 June
	14 September		1 July
	9 November		16 August
	11 November		
	18 November	**1998**	28 March*
	22 November		
	14 December		

This was a special session at which Dr Hans Schaer was the sole investigator. It involved the video experiments; significant results were obtained.

APPENDIX FIVE

THE LIGHTS

From the many testimonies we have received and reviewed, it is clear that the lights that manifested in the cellar constituted a spectacular experience. *The Scole Report* referred to the light phenomena as follows:

> The most immediately striking feature of the series of sittings we attended... were the displays of light... Contemporary notes were supplemented by and cross-checked against transcripts of tapes on which the sounds and comments accompanying the phenomena were recorded.
>
> At every sitting, save those specifically dedicated either to a discussion... or to the production of films or messages on tape, light phenomena appeared. Invariably Manu came through first and we had discussions with spirit voices. We give below a fairly comprehensive summary of the various phenomena involving light which all or some of us have witnessed, often on several occasions.
>
> We cannot, however, ignore the several written testimonies we have also had from others, including several members of the Council of the Society, Professor Ivor Grattan-Guinness, Dr Rupert Sheldrake and Ingrid Slack, individuals who have attended Scole seminars either at Scole or elsewhere, and in particular from Walter and Karin Schnittger and Dr Hans Schaer...
>
> All of these have testified to many of the phenomena we describe.

The following is the reported experience of the investigators based on testimony contained in *The Scole Report* and has been checked by its authors:

The (normally single) light point would -

A. Dart around at great speed and perform elaborately patterned dances in front of us, including perfect, sustained circles executed at high velocity and with a precision which appeared inconsistent with manual manipulation;

B. Become visible to one of us but not his next-door neighbour, and then reverse this arrangement as a demonstration of occlusion capacity and intelligent motivation;

C. Settle on outstretched hands and jump from one to the other;

D. Respond to requests, such as alighting on and irradiating parts of our bodies;

E. Enter a crystal and remain as a small point of light moving around within the crystal, or permeating light throughout its structure;

F. While performing a perfect circle of light, switch on and off certain segments of the circle;

G. Diffuse light through a Pyrex bowl, upturned or otherwise;

H. Leave at the base of the Pyrex bowl a three-dimensional image of a glowing crystal which is found to be insubstantial when seized by the investigators, then converting the glowing essence of this crystal into a solid form which could be picked up and replaced – and repeat this procedure twice, to the satisfaction of three close observers, one of whom (AE) placed his head immediately above and close enough to the bowl to preclude the entry of a normal hand, his face being clearly visible to MK and DF in the light from the crystal;

I. Strike the top of the table with a sharp rap, or the glass of the dome or dish with an appropriate ping, and do this repeatedly while remaining visible as a sharp pinpoint of light;

J. Appear inside the ping-pong ball which was ejected from its position inside the Pyrex bowl on the table to the far side of the room, to be discovered on the floor after the session;

K. Create a diffused glow on the ceiling, on the floor, on the wall furthest from the table, about a metre and a half distant from the table, or around the hands and knees of sitters, sufficient to enable their hands and sometimes faces, as well as MK's notebook and pen, to be seen by the investigators; create the same glow in mid-air, unreflected from any surface;

L. Illuminate sitters' feet below the edge of the circular table despite the barrier formed under it by the solid quadrant compartments which effectively precluded contact with any of the members of the group;

M. Settle on and apparently enter the chests of investigators, who reported internal sensations immediately thereafter, then leaving from a different part of the body;

N. Enter a glass of water held by an investigator (DF), and agitate the water visibly and audibly without being extinguished, his face being immediately above the glass, precluding unobstructed entry of any physical device.

O. Illuminate simultaneously with a generalised glow six separate 5-cm high solid Perspex supports of the wooden plinth carrying the glass dome;

P. Settle on the open palms of a guest investigator (Prof. Grattan-Guinness) who then enfolded the light inside his hands, momentarily, to satisfy himself of the absence of any physical link;

Q. With the aid of a silhouette of the hand and fingers of an apparently discarnate entity, elevate a crystal illuminated from within by a spirit light and transport it to the other side of the table;

R. Illuminate from within a light bulb suspended well above the sitters' heads, with no light coming from the filament;

S. Produce a glow in different parts of the glass tank and move around there;

T. Appear in a form similar to a large glass marble which rolled across the table to one of the investigators, producing enough light to illuminate his hands;

U. Move in time to tape-recorded music;

V. Produce 'lightning flashes' in an area of a large room some three to three-and-a-half metres distant from the group sitting round a table (MK Ibiza report);

W. Appear as two separate lights simultaneously;

X. Undertake several aerial 'bombing raids' on the table top, hitting it very audibly and visibly, and appearing to emerge from an area immediately below the table (USA Los Angeles report and at Scole, where the light typically re-emerged between two of the quadrants supporting the table);

Y. Remain for a minute or more as a motionless, sharp, small, steady glow immediately above the table at head height;

Z. Change shape from a pinpoint of light to a generalised irradiation or glow;

AA. Charge with visible light a ping-pong ball which was levitated, dropped on the floor at the feet of a sitter and moved away from his grasp into a dead-end corner of a quadrant beneath the table, having previously been stationary;

BB. Markedly increase in brightness in apparent response to collective hand pressure on the knees of sitters;

CC. Move at very high speed describing at times perfect geometric shapes within a foot or two of visitors' faces, but without making any sound or creating any perceptible air movement;

DD. Illuminate the fingers of a full-size spirit hand which the percipient describes as soft and cool to the touch;

EE. Build up from a faintly diffused glow into materialised objects on or floating above the table, the objects variously taking the shape of small draped figurines, or a vague 'face' with apparent movement of lips, the various objects being subject to movement, some rising towards the ceiling before disappearing;

FF. Instantly vanish on occasions;

GG. Build up from nothing to a rock-like shape which rises in the air and passes in front of one investigator before halting in front of another, then returning to its place of origin and gradually disappearing.

The *Report* further states:

> It soon became apparent, and is evident from the preceding descriptions, that the phenomenon of light cannot be dissociated from many of the sounds and

touches, and other visual phenomena. Nor, for that matter, can it be entirely divorced from the anticipatory comments of the team and the contemporaneous remarks of the investigators. They offer further evidence of what is being observed or experienced. An apt illustration is the frequency with which luminous tabs on the table were momentarily shrouded or occluded, or when light phenomena were clearly apparent to and commented on by one sitter when his adjoining neighbour could see nothing.

A passage from MK's note on the ninth sitting of 15 June 1996 is worth quoting:

Perhaps the most remarkable phenomenon of the sitting arose after RF exclaimed repeatedly how he could see a bright light in front of him which neither AE nor I could see. Just as I was attributing this in my mind to RF's imagination, a very sharp, bright light performed figures-of-eight and minor gyrations just in front of me. It did this on three occasions, for very short periods, while I described what was happening, surprised that others failed to see it. Shortly thereafter, Sandra, on my left [DF could not attend this session], had the same experience: none of us could see what she was describing. Finally AE witnessed a similar light which, even though I bent towards him, I could not see. We concluded that the light in each case must have been occluded as though screens were placed in front of it and directed towards each of us in turn, with a fairly narrow arc of perhaps no more than 15° or 20°. The light was pinpoint, very sharp and bright, not rays or glows, and moved swiftly.

THE APPORTS

Below is a list of many of the apports received at Scole:

Churchill coin

Silver necklace - could be of African origin

Aconite shells

Wooden monkey

Marcasite necklace

Two pieces of metal

Obsidian bracelet

Silver necklace

Green-coloured chemicals

Small rose quartz crystal ball

Silver bracelet

Liquid - water

Small pebble-like piece of stone 'not from Earth'

Indian Military Campaign medal

Large amethyst crystal cluster

Silver sports medallion

Silver thimble

Sacred ash from funeral pyre of Indian holy man (on two separate occasions)

Large quartz 'travelling crystal' cluster

Three buttons from Indian Army tunic

Two silver lockets

1928 one franc piece 'token'

Comic seaside postcard with legend 'If living, please write - if dead, don't bother'

1940 British penny

Lady's handkerchief with motif 'H'

1936 British penny

St Christopher medallion

George V/Mary large Empire medallion 1911

Silver charm of 'Grim Reaper'

Tiny gold disc/medallion with hieroglyphics, source of which has not yet been identified

Silver St Christopher
medallion (hexagonal)
Small wooden, square incense
stick holder
Ornate silver and ceramic
brooch
Incense stick that was ignited
psychically
Two brass farm animals
(appear homemade)
Original copy of *Daily Mail*
1/4/44
Bone spoon
Original copy of *Daily
Express* 28/5/45
Ornate spoon with decorated
bowl, writing and twisted
handle

Teddy bear, given to visitor
from Polaroid
Penknife with mother-of-pearl
handle
Small figurine of elephant,
given to Bill Lyons
Silver charm with cross,
anchor and heart, engraved
'Faith, hope and charity'
Carved ivory cocktail stick
Pearl and mother-of pearl
leaf-shaped brooch
St Bernadette medallion
inscribed 'Kara'
Pearl tie pin
Burnt paper and ash
Mother-of-pearl necklace

SCIENTIFICALLY CONTROLLED FILM SESSIONS

A number of sessions with the scientific investigators produced positive results on films. We set them out below:

Date*	Film Type+	Present#	Transmission Received
13/1/96	Polaroid (1)	AE,MK,DF	Star-light images and cog wheel shape (2)
17/2/96	Polachrome (3)	AE,MK,DF	Greek lettering on green background
16/3/96	Polapan (4)	AE,MK,DF	Night star patterns (5)
16/3/96	Polagraph	AE,MK,DF	*Diotima* cryptic puzzles (6)
25/5/96	Polaroid	D.Fairburn + 9	Latin message in mirror image
31/5/96	Polaroid	W&K Schnittger	Blurred German Poem (7)
13/7/96	Polachrome	A.Roy,MK,AE	Latin Golden Chain (*Perfectio*) message
26/7/96	Polachrome	WS & KS	Clear German Poem (7)
9/11/96	Polachrome	AE,MK,DF	Wordsworth (*Ruth* 1) poem (8)
9/11/96	Kodachrome (9)	AE,MK,DF	Wordsworth (*Ruth* 2) poem
22/11/96	Polachrome	WS,KS,H.Schaer	*Wie der Staub* message (10)
6/12/96	Polachrome	WS,KS	X-rays of fingers and thumbs (10)
11/1/97	Kodachrome (9)	DF,I.Slack,MK	Electrical diagram, instructions and signatures (11)
17/1/97	Polachrome	WS,KS	Dragon and *Quadrans Muralis*, etc. (12)
24/1/97	Kodachrome (9)	A.Gauld, D.West & MK	Daguerre, Can You See Behind the Moon, etc.

General notes and security procedures adopted:

1. Polaroid = Instant, 600 Plus
2. Film placed in sealed safety bag. Poor quality. Team said bag created problems
3. ASA 40, very slow
4. Black-and-white film
5. Security bag used
6. Signed sticky label security label used
7. Film tub held by investigators
8. Film placed in padlocked wooden box and held by DF until developed on 11/11/96
9. Developed by Kodak at Wimbledon
10. Padlocked wooden box held by investigators throughout experiment
11. Drawing to help AE improve germanium gadget promised during sitting
12. Padlocked wooden box, keys in car, box on marked paper, film marked

* For simplicity, date refers to session when a particular experiment started. In some cases the films were not developed until subsequent sessions.

+ Film types used were as follows:

♦ Polaroid 600 Plus (flat instant films used in the Polaroid cameras)
♦ Polapan 35mm (slide films, black and white, ISO 125)
♦ Polagraph 35mm (slide films, blue and white, ISO 400)
♦ Polachrome 35mm (slide films, colour, ISO 40)
♦ Kodachrome 200 (slide transparencies)

\# Regular investigators were:

AE: Arthur Ellison
DF: David Fontana
MK: Montague Keen

PHOTOGRAPHIC
EXPERIMENTS

The New Spiritual Science Foundation, via the Scole Experimental Group, conducted many photographic experiments during the five years of the Scole Experiment. They mainly used Polaroid film under test conditions, followed by the immediate processing of all film. Whilst there were many failed attempts, the film was often 'successfully influenced'. These regular manifestations of physical phenomena greatly helped to enhance the 'scientific' and 'evidential' value of the work.

All the pictures received fell into one of four categories:

1. Images of existing photographs;
2. Images of 'creative' energy that has 'influenced' the film;
3. Images of other realms (called 'areas of existence' or 'areas of communication' by the team);
4. Images direct from communicators (signatures, portraits, cryptic puzzles, etc.) containing meaningful messages.

The group used four basic types of Polaroid instant film and received positive and successful results using the following materials:

1. Polaroid 600 Plus (flat films for Polaroid cameras)
2. Polapan 35mm (slide films, black and white, ISO 125)
3. Polagraph 35mm (slide films, blue and white, ISO 400)
4. Polachrome 35mm (slide films, colour, ISO 40)

Should any other groups decide to experiment along the same lines as the Scole Experimental Group, the New Spiritual Science

Foundation recommend all of the above films for their suitability; although the 35mm films did require a separate power processor for development purposes.

Consequently each 35mm film came complete with a disposable cartridge of chemicals so that, a few minutes after its use, the Polaroid processor could develop it. These films could then be made into individual slides for viewing in a projector.

The group later used Kodachrome (ISO 200 Colour) film transparencies from Kodak, which could only be developed in one laboratory in the country. This procedure formed part of the continuing scientific protocols being requested by the independent investigators.

Some of the images received in these experiments were very impressive. A number appeared as continuous images along the length of the films. In one instance the result measured around fifty inches (four feet), when a 36-exposure roll was used. It should be noted that many of these were unopened photographic films, just held or left in a box or bag on the table during experimental sessions and processed afterwards.

Throughout the book, we have mentioned some of the images that were received on photographic films. Some constituted puzzles for the group and the investigators to solve. In the plate section we have included a number of them in the hope that readers might be able to offer solutions to some of the puzzles.

APPENDIX NINE

THE CONCLUSION OF THE SCOLE REPORT

The following is from the Conclusion of *The Scole Report:*

Whatever our defence, the determined critic would ultimately offer a sad shake of the head and utter the words that have formed the epitaph of so many past investigations: If only you had thought (or been able) to control for... Field work in psychical research is so vulnerable to this kind of dismissive verdict that one may well question if in fact it is worth the major investment of time, energy and money which it involves. Our answer is that in any area of human behaviour, effects that are only observable under the tightly controlled conditions of a laboratory are not really of enduring use or interest. If psychic abilities exist, then they may reasonably be supposed to happen not just in the laboratory but in real life, whether in the séance room or in more familiar surroundings. If they do, it is equally reasonable to propose that they are worth looking into, that efforts be made to find the ways in which they are compatible with the rest of our known science: indeed, ways in which they may not only add to our scientific knowledge, but augment our understanding of what it is to be human and whether or not life carries meaning outside that attributed to it by reductionist philosophies.

It was with these considerations in mind that we conducted the Scole investigation, with these considerations that we have compiled this report and it is with these considerations that we would undertake further such investigations, should the opportunity arise. In the meantime, we will be more than happy to co-operate with any conjurors who wish to try and replicate in our presence, accurately and under comparable conditions, the effects we witnessed at Scole.

Our final word is that whatever is made of our investigation by others, now and in years to come, we feel privileged to have been allowed to undertake it.

A STATEMENT BY DR HANS SCHAER FROM THE SCOLE REPORT

THE BUGLE TESTIMONY

The experience and testimony of Dr Hans Schaer, a member of the SPR and one of the investigators, is important since he had considerable experience of *The Scole Experiment.* A Swiss lawyer and businessman residing in Kusnacht, near Zurich, and the owner of a holiday home on the Mediterranean island of Ibiza, Dr Schaer sat with the Scole Group on thirteen occasions. His sessions were in both his homes, on the premises of the Parapsychological Society of Zurich in Zurich, and at Scole itself. The Scole group members were his guests for sessions in Ibiza in October 1995. They were invited back the following summer, for sessions on 28 June and 1 July 1996.

The following account relates to the sitting held on 28 June 1996 and is based on an interview conducted by Robin Foy with Dr Schaer.

> The room in which the two sittings took place, the main living room of the house, had all doors and windows very carefully covered with either black plastic or plasticised black cloth. The main door was locked in three different ways (see Figure 5).
>
> None of the other doors leading into the room could have been opened without the removal of the attached material. I sat alone with the four members of the group. No-one else was in either the room or the house.

We sat round a table of about one metre diameter on which were placed five crystals, the largest in the centre and the others round the edge, pointing directly to north, south, east and west, as determined by Robin Foy's compass, which he had brought with him for the purpose of correct alignment.

Robin sat at the west end, I sat on his left, his wife Sandra next to me, and then Alan and Diana to complete the circle. All the group wore their luminous armband strips. No light could be seen anywhere in the room.

I have a collection of trumpets at my home in Kusnacht, one of which I had with me in Ibiza. Before the sitting I had asked Robin whether he thought it would be possible to establish a musical contact with the spirit side, since we had already experienced our regular oral contact, both through the mediums and via 'direct voice'.

My hope had been to get Louis Armstrong, or some other well-known jazz musician, to play a solo for me and make himself recognisable that way. Would the spirits be willing to go along with such an experiment?

He replied: 'You can always ask. I suggest you take the trumpet with you into the sitting room and place it beside your chair on the floor.' That is precisely what I did. The trumpet was the only musical instrument in the whole house.

When I was asked during the sitting whether I had any questions, therefore, I asked about the possibility of the musical communication. The answer from the spirit side was that they were completely unprepared for such an experiment, since they had concentrated on the film experiments throughout recent sittings.

Nevertheless they said they would see what they could do. The spirit voice told me to put the trumpet on the table. I lifted it up and laid it on the table in such a way that the mouthpiece was parallel with the edge of the table, lying directly in front of me.

A spirit light approached the trumpet and hovered over it, distributing enough light to enable everyone to see that the instrument was lying on the table. After a while, again in total darkness, a few light trumpet sounds were heard, indicating that someone was operating the valves of the trumpet.

At that stage I felt a breeze over my face and it was apparent that the trumpet was being blown into. A full note was produced, followed by three or four other notes. These were followed by a number of sequences of various sounds, which sounded like military bugle notes, but no melody was played. When we put the light on at the end of the session, the trumpet had moved about 10cm towards the centre of the table.

I must comment that the Scole group, to say nothing of the spirit team, could not have been prepared in advance for my request. Indeed, this was one of the reasons I wished to have a sitting in Ibiza, where there was no possibility that the group might install hidden microphones, loudspeakers, tape recorders, etc.

I also knew that none of the group could play a trumpet and that there would have been no opportunity to make prior recordings of the trumpet noises. Moreover, the fact that the mouthpiece was placed on the table in the manner described ensured that not even the most experienced trumpet player could blow into it, even if he had been able to kneel down in front of it where I was sitting against the table.

Even then, my right hand was placed next to the trumpet's mouthpiece. Thus it was surprising that they could not only get a few light sounds from it but later a real blast which almost threw us off our chairs.

As the tape recording of the sitting demonstrates, there were also drumbeats coming from the table, although there were no instruments or implements which could have produced these sounds normally.

The sounds made were more typical of metal than wooden sticks, such was the strength of the drumming. I had expected to see marks on the table, which would have been normal for such hard drumming, but there was nothing to be seen. I must emphasise that the security was good: I could see the armbands of the group and felt in control of the whole sitting.

Accounts such as this are hard for some who were not there to accept. We can perhaps get an indication of the reactions that such reports arouse by the following from *The Scole Report:*

Taken to its extreme, moral disapproval implies the sort of reasoning which led one critic, on hearing the tape recording at which a trumpet was played and drumming was heard during a sitting at which Hans Schaer was responsible for the controls, to dismiss the episode on the grounds that the trumpet was badly played. Such observations may be accurate, but they simply reflect disapproval of method, not a criticism of genuineness.

'WE DON'T BELIEVE IT UNLESS WE CAN SEE IT'

Many people ask, 'Why can't we go to the cellar? We will only believe it if we see it with our own eyes.'

The logical counter might be best explained using the analogy of the Apollo expeditions. Many of us would, perhaps, like to visit the moon. However, most of us understand that for various reasons, including scarcity of expertise and resources, there can only be very few of us who go and have the experience.

When astronauts travel to the moon, they bring back still pictures, videos and samples. In addition to scrutinising these physical records, we listen to and accept their testimony, and that of the scientists who sent them there, as to the reality of the whole experience. In this way, a small number of specialists contribute to the shared experience of the whole population. Human society is full of such examples of specialisation and much of our progress is made in this way.

However, the position of the arch sceptic would be that, since they did not *personally* go to the moon, it is still debatable whether such a thing is indeed possible. If you think this is far-fetched, there is still a large group of people who contend that the Apollo moon landings were all part of an elaborate hoax on the part of government.

In the case of this book, the astronauts are the investigators and members of the Scole group, and the moon is the spirit world.

Even though the Scole Experiment involved relatively few people, the spirit world is, said the team, attempting to provide evidence for a much wider range of people. They are expanding the phenomena to other groups all around the world. As more people have the experience, the concepts involved will become more believable to the general population. We will chronicle the progress that has been made with other groups in due course.

A HEALING PERSPECTIVE

This perspective is taken from an article in *Spiritual Scientist.*
    On Sunday 25 August 1996 Tina Laurent was one of nine people who had been invited to sit with the group.

It was not without some trepidation that I arrived at Scole. Not because I had any personal doubts about the phenomena witnessed there, but because a recent head cold had left me with an irritating, tickling cough and I was afraid that I might be excluded from the sitting because of the intrusive noise.

However, this was not to be the case and, with a comforting glass of water by the side of my chair, I settled in with my twelve companions to what, on my part, turned out to be the most memorable day in my life of fifty-nine years (and I've had one or two!) It far exceeded my initial expectations. Oh, if only personal proof of the world of Spirit could be passed on!

Two days later I am still reliving certain moments of that afternoon and I still feel enveloped by the love I was given there. I shall try to be as brief as possible. I am not a scientist or academician but an ordinary woman who happened to be involved with EVP (the electronic voice phenomenon) for over fifteen years and who has experienced many things which have led me to believe in survival of the human spirit.

I will not go into detail with the complete session, but shall tell you what made the strongest assault on my senses.

A spirit light, after impressing us with its movements and dancing ability, now approached me and hovered gently in front of my face.

We communicated and I said, 'Yes, you can enter.'

It immediately whooshed into my solar plexus area, making a small plop as it entered my body (felt, not heard). It moved around for a little while, giving me a tickling sensation (like a bee trapped inside my jumper) and then moved quickly down my arm and plopped back into the room through the back of my hand.

What do I make of all this? Well, I know that the love encountered in the cellar that afternoon was very real and tangible, and, surprise, surprise, I haven't coughed since then! There are no words really adequate to thank the Scole experimental group and the spirit team for their combined efforts in allowing us to visit them and participate in their work, the importance of which is incalculable for the human race.

THE PROFESSOR'S COUGH

At one experimental session, Professor Fontana had a tickly cough. A spirit light landed in his glass of water and, according to the Scole group, 'did a passable impression of drowning'. The professor was then asked to drink the water. The cough stopped.

HEALING REPORT

Following a request by a *Spiritual Scientist* subscriber in Australia, a little girl, Shannen Miller, was put on the Scole group's healing list in June 1996. She was facing an operation to remove scar tissue from her lung.

On 14 May 1997, Shannen's mum, Deborah Miller, wrote to

the group enclosing a photograph of the smiling little girl:

> Dear Scole group,
>
> Two years ago my daughter was diagnosed with TB. After treatment, she seemed to improve, but later, it recurred. After further medication and investigations, it was then decided to operate to remove the rest of the mass on the lung.
>
> My Nana asked you to put Shannen on your absent healing list. As I believe Nana has told you from X-ray, when they decided to operate, to a CAT scan on 14 April, the mass had reduced to a point. Consequently the medicos decided not to operate. A bronchoscopy of the lung field is clear.
>
> I would just like to thank you for the healing and thoughts you have sent that helped my daughter Shannen to get well again. May I ask that Shannen be kept on your healing list for a little while, to help her complete recovery.
>
> God bless your work.

Some time later, further information was received from the Australian subscriber that filled in a few of the gaps:

> The original problem had filled Shannen's left chest. She had been on medication for nine months and the doctors did not think that the 'mass' would go by treatment alone – they were pretty sure that it would have to be surgically removed. This was back in June 1996. At this point, as per my request, absent healing was started and I linked in to help with this.
>
> Shannen was unable to have this operation in early 1997 because she was in hospital again with pneumonia. In April, she had a CAT scan to determine how big the 'mass' was that they had to remove. No 'mass' could be seen on the scan, just minuscule scar tissue, and that was all. Everyone

was delighted, but very surprised. This also applied to the doctors specialising in infectious diseases and the respiratory field.

At this point, Deborah – Shannen's mum – told the doctors she had a 'confession' to make! She told them that Shannen had had a bit of help through spiritual healing.

The doctor gave a wry smile and said: 'I don't care what sort of help she's been having. The fact is that something has been working!'

Shannen surprised everyone. They never thought the problem would go away on its own, always assuming that surgical removal was the only option they had. This case has been written about in the *Paediatric Journal,* and has been presented in different countries, as well as Australia.

The Scole experimental group was very proud to have been involved in this case and to have done its own small bit to try and help this lovely little girl.

Healing appears to be a very important part of spiritual science. Its expansion could help lots of people. There are many more Shannens out there.

THE CURRENTLY UNCONVINCED

The cause of truth is not served by omission or evasion. It would constitute neglect on our part if we did not make the reader aware that there are those who are currently unconvinced about a number of aspects of the Scole Experiment.

The Society for Psychical Research, for example, as an organisation composed of individuals who have a wide range of specialist knowledge, has no collective view and its members are free to express their opinions. The members all have their own perspective and, in the main, they have historically adopted an extremely cautious approach when assessing psychic phenomena.

Consequently, there is some disagreement about certain aspects of the scientific protocol employed during the investigation. There are also varying interpretations of the data collected amongst those who have reviewed *The Scole Report* at the time of writing (i.e. before its publication). Given the pioneering nature of the work, it is inevitable that other criticism will follow.

As we mention elsewhere, this is the nature of scientific progress and is to be welcomed if criticism is fair and reasonable. There is little that can be done, however, about unreasonable challenges and readers will have to take their own view as to which criticisms have some basis in reason and which do not.

A very important characteristic of the Scole Experiment is that it appears to be transferable and repeatable. Other experimental groups will be able to establish themselves by following the advice set out in the Scole group's *A Basic Guide* booklet. These groups should then be able to invite the investigators in. The Society for Psychical Research has been established for well over a century and its collective knowledge and experience may prove invaluable to future investigations. The Society seems ideally placed to adopt such a role.

It is possible that these further experiments will satisfy the concerns of the currently unconvinced. It is possible that they will not. We look forward to chronicling the developments.

DISCUSSION: PAST, PRESENT, AND FUTURE

There was much talk of the future in the final sessions of the Scole Experiment. One evening, Manu spoke for one of the longest periods the group could recall:

> *Each of you in the Scole group undertakes special work at night during your sleep state. You are helping to build new columns of energy for other groups to use. This is a very important part of the changes that will occur soon.*
>
> *Along with the energy work being done by human groups, there are many new energies being transmitted to Earth from the spirit realms at this time. The effects of this will be dramatic. You will see a change in everything connected with the Earth in the very near future, even in the plant life of the planet.*
>
> *Electrical things will become inefficient. You will be especially interested, Walter [Schnittger] that there will be better ways of working with car engines than the use of electrical ignition systems.*

At another session, the group was informed by one of the spirit communicators: *'Your bodies will be very different in the future, your nervous systems are already changing.'*

'A number of other comments gave rise to speculation that beings like Blue might be the shape of things to come for our species,' said the group. This was certainly an interesting comment. We were thus led to wonder about the relevance of the clue on the *Diotima* film: It is not yet apparent what we will become.

In this regard, we were fascinated to watch a science programme on television in early 1999, which showed what might happen to human beings when we become space travellers. In zero gravity, our bones may become brittle and our muscles may atrophy. Our limbs could become elongated and our bodies shorter. We may have a different diet. Basically we would evolve and adapt to our new space environment. This might sound far-fetched but what do we really know about who and what we *have been,* let alone what we *will be*? So, we could add another thought to the one on the *Diotima* film: It is not yet apparent what we have been.

In mid-April 1999, there were newspaper reports of a skeleton found in Ethiopia which might provide the 'missing link' in human evolution. This skeleton was thought to be two and a half million years old, perhaps three to five times as old as previous estimates of the date of our early ancestors. Anyone suggesting this time-scale the day before the discovery would quite possibly have experienced ridicule from the 'experts'.

New planets have been discovered around a star similar to our own sun. Might these support life as we know it? Might we one day go there? It is certainly possible that we will become space travellers. Searching the heavens with telescopes has led on to exploration with craft that can carry us to the planets in our solar system. In the future, other craft may well carry us to the stars.

Current theories about the laws governing the operation of the universe are based on relativity and a constant speed of light. This gives rise to the familiar story of the inter-stellar twins. One thirty-year-old twin travels to the nearest star at the speed of light whilst the other stays at home on Earth. After, say, ten years, the traveller returns... to find his twin has died of old age. In current thinking about the nature of the universe, time passes differently, relative to the conditions each observer experiences. So, according to the theory, time is not an absolute, it is related to the speed of light and the speed of travel through space. Current theories therefore leave a number of unanswered questions to which the emerging field of spiritual science may provide solutions. What would happen if we were to discover how to propel our space exploration craft at *beyond* the speed of light? If time does not exist in the spiritual dimensions, might we be able to relay messages to our own past or future via these dimensions? Could we ever travel to our past or future?

On the basis of ideas such as these, allowed for within current scientific theory, perhaps we should keep our minds open to past, present, and future possibilities. Otherwise, we might miss something important.

When discussing what we have become it is clear that we have progressed somewhat when compared to our primitive ancestors. But how do we compare ourselves to what we may become? Relative to our potential – as demonstrated by the lives of Krishna, Buddha, Jesus, Mohammed, Nanak, Sai Baba, and the other 'Shining Ones', as Manu puts it – are we not somewhat Neanderthal by comparison? Many of our interactions suggest the operation of a concrete-jungle law of 'ape kill ape with clothes on'. We are perhaps not as advanced as we think. Surely there is scope for change, evolution, development into something better.

We will leave you with another thought. Our ancestors were hairy and muscular when compared to our present form. Could it be that Blue represents our future in two and a half million years' time? Are we Blue's 'apes'?

THE SCOLE REPORT FIVE YEARS LATER

by Montague Keen and David Fontana

Follow-up papers are often published after accounts of investigations into psychic phenomena have been in the public domain for some time. An article, 'The Scole Report Five Years Later', was published in the SPR's *Paranormal Review* in January 2006.

In this article (written with Montague Keen before his death in 2004), Professor David Fontana notes that 'fresh criticisms have been conspicous by their absence', magicians have not come forward in response to invitations to replicate phenomena, and the phenomena observed were so variable and so numerous as to make trickery 'inconceivable'.

Rather than criticism, there has in fact been further evidence 'in favour' of the Scole phenomena being genuine. This evidence includes subsequent identification of an anomaly in the Rachmaninov 2nd Piano Concerto, the testimony of George Dalzell at the Scole Debate, and more evidence in favour of the genuineness of the *Daily Mail* apport.

Professor Fontana concludes: '... if we accept that the communicators at Scole really were the deceased, not only may this throw light on which aspects of the mind may survive physical death, it may suggest that even during our lifetime these aspects are not due solely to physical processes. At Scole we found that the communicators showed humour and other emotions, intelligence of a high order, significant powers of memory, and what seemed a genuine and continuing compassion towards others. In addition they manifested consistent signs of individual identity throughout the two years of our investigation, and never varied in terms of accent, use of words, mannerisms and interests. Five years after the end of the Scole investigation, the need for a philosophy of parapsychology is as evident as ever.'

FURTHER INFORMATION

THE SCOLE EXPERIMENT

Information about some of the people who took part in, and some of the subjects covered by, *The Scole Experiment*, can be obtained from the addresses below.

The Society for Psychical Research:
www.spr.ac.uk

For copies of *The Scole Report* by Montague Keen, Arthur Ellison, and David Fontana, apply to:
The Society for Psychical Research, 49 Marloes Road, London W8 6LA

For comments, criticisms, and replies, since the publication of *The Scole Report* and *The Scole Experiment*:
www.thescoleexperiment.com

George Dalzell, the clinical social worker who contributed a Perspective:
www.georgedalzell.com

For information on Electronic Voice Phenomena:
www.aaevp.com

To contact Robin and Sandra Foy of the Scole Group, write to:
Street Farmhouse, Scole, Nr Diss, Norfolk IP21 4DR

THE NORFOLK EXPERIMENT

For updates on *The Norfolk Experiment*:
www.thescoleexperiment.com

For more about ISIS, the light imaging system being used by the
Norfolk Group in *The Norfolk Experiment*:
www.resolutions.org.uk
info@resolutions.org.uk

For authors, Grant and Jane Solomon:
www.campionpublishing.com
info@campionpublishing.com

INDEX

Index

Index

Index

Index

Index

Index